JUDGING FOR DEMOCRACY

This book examines how constitutional courts can sustainably contribute to advancing democratic norms in hybrid regimes, i.e. regimes that are neither fully democratic nor fully authoritarian. Using a comparative approach analysing cases from across the globe, particularly from Hong Kong, Pakistan, and Uganda, Julius Yam makes the case that courts can assume a democracy-enhancing role in hybrid regimes. The book reveals the challenges faced by courts in performing such a role. It also proposes an adjudicative framework that systematically integrates principled judging with judicial strategy, and suggests nonadjudicative techniques that judges can adopt to reinforce democracy. While theoretical in substance, this book is informed by empirical studies and draws on a wide range of disciplines, including law, political science, sociology, and psychology. The book will be a key resource to judges, academics, and practitioners who are interested in the study of democracy and courts. Its insights are particularly pertinent in an age of democratic backsliding and resurgence of authoritarianism. This title is also available as open access on Cambridge Core.

DR JULIUS YAM (1992–2024) was Assistant Professor of Law at the University of Hong Kong. He was posthumously awarded the Wedderburn Prize for his article 'Judging Under Authoritarianism' (2024) 87(4) *Modern Law Review* 894. He obtained his LLB from the University of Hong Kong, LLM from the University of Chicago, and DPhil in Law from Trinity College, University of Oxford.

CAMBRIDGE STUDIES IN CONSTITUTIONAL LAW

The aim of this series is to produce leading monographs in constitutional law. All areas of constitutional law and public law fall within the ambit of the series, including human rights and civil liberties law, administrative law, as well as constitutional theory and the history of constitutional law. A wide variety of scholarly approaches is encouraged, with the governing criterion being simply that the work is of interest to an international audience. Thus, works concerned with only one jurisdiction will be included in the series as appropriate, while, at the same time, the series will include works which are explicitly comparative or theoretical - or both. The series editors likewise welcome proposals that work at the intersection of constitutional and international law, or that seek to bridge the gaps between civil law systems, the US, and the common law jurisdictions of the Commonwealth.

Books in the series

The Anti-Nazi Origins of Militant Democracy: Germany's Constitutional Tribunes Samuel Miner

Courts in the Age of Polarization: Supreme and Constitutional Courts in Politically Divided Societies Iddo Porat and Moshe Cohen-Eliya

Militant Rule of Law: Legal Imperfection and What To Do About It András Sajó

Judging for Democracy: Principles and Strategies in Hybrid Regimes Julius Yam

Hans Kelsen on Constitutional Democracy: Genesis, Theory, Legacies Sandrine Baume and David Ragazzoni

Alter-Native Constitutionalism: Common-ing 'Common' Law, Transforming Property in South Africa Sindiso Mnisi

The Failures of Others: Justifying Institutional Expansion in Comparative Public and International Law Michaela Hailbronner

Constitutionalizing the Private Sphere: A Comparative Inquiry Christina R. Bambrick

Beyond Expropriation Without Compensation: Law, Land Reform and Redistributive Justice in South Africa Edited by Olaf Zenker, Cherryl Walker and Zsa-Zsa Boggenpoel

Trust, Courts and Social Rights: A Trust-Based Framework for Social Rights Enforcement David Vitale

The Collaborative Constitution Aileen Kavanagh

Non-Statutory Executive Powers and Judicial Review Jason Grant Allen

The Law as a Conversation among Equals Roberto Gargarella

Micronations and the Search for Sovereignty Harry Hobbs and George Williams

Fundamental Rights and the Legal Obligations of Business David Bilchitz

Courting Constitutionalism: The Politics of Public Law and Judicial Review in Pakistan Moeen Cheema

Ruling by Cheating: Governance in Illiberal Democracy András Sajó

Local Meanings of Proportionality Afroditi Marketou

Property Rights and Social Justice: Progressive Property in Action Rachael Walsh

Carl Schmitt's Early Legal-Theoretical Writings: Statute and Judgment and the Value of the State and the Significance of the Individual Lars Vinx and Samuel Garrett Zeitlin

Remedies for Human Rights Violations: A Two-Track Approach to Supra-national and National Law Kent Roach

Europe's Second Constitution: Crisis, Courts and Community Markus W. Gehring

A.V. Dicey and the Common Law Constitutional Tradition: A Legal Turn of Mind Mark D. Walters

Administrative Competence: Reimagining Administrative Law Elizabeth Fisher and Sidney A. Shapiro

Legal Sabotage: Ernst Fraenkel in Hitler's Germany Douglas Morris

Proportionality in Action: Comparative and Empirical Perspectives on the Judicial Practice Edited by Mordechai Kremnitzer, Tayla Steiner and Andrej Lang

Constitutional Dialogue: Democracy, Rights, Institutions Edited by Geoffrey Sigalet, Grégoire Webber and Rosalind Dixon

The Veiled Sceptre: Reserve Powers of Heads of State in Westminster Systems Anne Twomey

Vigilance and Restraint in the Common Law of Judicial Review Dean Knight

The Alchemists: Questioning Our Faith in Courts as Democracy-Builders Tom Gerald Daly

Australia's Constitution after Whitlam Brendan Lim

Building the Constitution: The Practice of Constitutional Interpretation in Post-Apartheid South Africa James Fowkes

Dimensions of Dignity: The Theory and Practice of Modern Constitutional Law Jacob Weinrib

Reason of State: Law, Prerogative, Empire Thomas Poole

Bills of Rights in the Common Law Robert Leckey

The Guardian of the Constitution: Hans Kelsen and Carl Schmitt on the Limits of Constitutional Law Translated by Lars Vinx, with an introduction and notes by Lars Vinx

Parliamentary Bills of Rights: The Experiences of New Zealand and the United Kingdom Janet L. Hiebert and James B. Kelly

Lawyering for the Rule of Law: Government Lawyers and the Rise of Judicial Power in Israel Yoav Dotan

Balancing Constitutional Rights: The Origins and Meanings of Postwar Legal Discourse Jacco Bomhoff

Judges on Trial: The Independence and Accountability of the English Judiciary Shimon Shetreet and Sophie Turenne

Proportionality and Constitutional Culture Moshe Cohen-Eliya and Iddo Porat

The Politics of Principle: The First South African Constitutional Court, 1995–2005 Theunis Roux

The New Commonwealth Model of Constitutionalism: Theory and Practice Stephen Gardbaum

Searching for the State in British Legal Thought: Competing Conceptions of the Public Sphere Janet McLean

Judging Social Rights Jeff King

Proportionality: Constitutional Rights and their Limitations Aharon Barak

Parliamentary Sovereignty: Contemporary Debates Jeffrey Goldsworthy

JUDGING FOR DEMOCRACY

Principles and Strategies in Hybrid Regimes

JULIUS YAM
The University of Hong Kong

CAMBRIDGE
UNIVERSITY PRESS

CAMBRIDGE
UNIVERSITY PRESS

Shaftesbury Road, Cambridge CB2 8EA, United Kingdom

One Liberty Plaza, 20th Floor, New York, NY 10006, USA

477 Williamstown Road, Port Melbourne, VIC 3207, Australia

314–321, 3rd Floor, Plot 3, Splendor Forum, Jasola District Centre,
New Delhi – 110025, India

Cambridge University Press is part of Cambridge University Press & Assessment,
a department of the University of Cambridge.

We share the University's mission to contribute to society through the pursuit of
education, learning and research at the highest international levels of excellence.

www.cambridge.org
Information on this title: www.cambridge.org/9781009734998

DOI: 10.1017/9781009734981

First published 2026

Cover image: James Leung

A catalogue record for this publication is available from the British Library

A Cataloging-in-Publication data record for this book is available from the Library of Congress

ISBN 978-1-009-73499-8 Hardback
ISBN 978-1-009-73497-4 Paperback

CONTENTS

Preface *page* ix

1 Hybrid Regimes, Constitutional Courts, and Democratic Principles 1

2 The Hybrid Regime and the Constitution 26

3 Constitutional Courts in Hybrid Regimes 51

4 Five Democratic Roles 79

5 The Legitimacy Paradox 134

6 Democratic Judging under Authoritarianism 157

7 "Mingling in the World" 191

8 Conclusion: Of Judicial Choices 243

Appendix: Applying the Framework – Socializing a Way Out of Hong Kong's National Security Law? 246

Index 258

PREFACE

The book you are about to read is based on Julius Yam's doctoral thesis, which he completed in 2022. Julius was in the process of revising the thesis for publication when he died in 2024, at the age of thirty-two. In the months before his death we had many conversations with Julius about the book, and agreed that if he died before completing the project, we would guide it through its final stages. After his death, the time came for us to review his manuscript, and it was with mixed emotions. Mixed, because we were glad to find that the book needed only limited intervention, and that Julius' voice would speak clearly through the pages, but we were also saddened to realize just how close Julius had come to seeing the fruits of his hard work.

The two chapters that required most intervention were Chapters 6 and 7, each of which Julius had modified and published as articles. A version of Chapter 6 appeared as "Judging Under Authoritarianism" in *Modern Law Review* 87(4) (2024), 894–925, and a version of Chapter 7 appeared as "When Judges Are Not Judging" in *University of Toronto Law Journal* 75(1) (2024), https://doi.org/10.3138/utlj-2024-000. We knew, through our conversations with Julius, that these articles embodied his most recent thinking on the topics, and that he intended to use the articles as the basis for the revised chapters in his book. A certain amount of modification was needed to adapt these articles back into chapter form, particularly with Chapter 7, where, it seemed to us, Julius had omitted some valuable elements included in the original thesis to satisfy the space constraints of the journal. We are grateful to the editors for allowing us to use material from these articles. We also decided to include Julius' discussion of Hong Kong as an Appendix to Chapter 7. This discussion provides a sustained case study of the arguments in the book, and evinces Julius' deep love of, and concern for, his home.

In the preface to his thesis, Julius wrote:

> My doctoral journey would not have been possible without a number of wonderful souls. My most sincere thanks go to my supervisor, Nick Barber, for his outstanding guidance,

incisive comments and always being so generous with his time and support. I am indebted to Anna Dziedzic, the best office-mate that I could ever ask for, who also read every chapter of my thesis (and is basically my unofficial second supervisor). I am also grateful to Ran Hirschl for taking me in as a visiting scholar at the Max Planck Fellow Group in Comparative Constitutionalism and Alexander von Humboldt Chair of Comparative Constitutionalism, University of Göttingen. The three months in Germany were not only intellectually stimulating, but also some of my fondest memories of the DPhil. I must also thank: Cora Chan for being a great personal and intellectual friend; Hualing Fu for supporting my academic career over the years; Lisa Bernstein and Gerald Rosenberg, who played important parts in my intellectual formative years at Chicago Law School; Richard Ekins, Jeff King and Paul Yowell for their most helpful suggestions during the transfer, confirmation and viva stages; and Charlotte, Bart, Ben, Laura, Mark, Mary and Michael for making Oxford a once-in-a-lifetime experience. I have benefited from discussions with and comments from Benjamin Boudou, Lisa Harms, Michael Hein, Alex Hudson, Eugénie Mérieau, Wei Tian and Martijn van den Brink. I acknowledge with gratitude the generous financial support of the RC Lee Centenary Scholarship. Finally, I must thank my father Bryan, my fountain of knowledge, my mother Agnes for her unconditional love and support, my brother Felix for being my rock and most of all J, my partner in crime and life.

We would also like to thank Tom Daly, Rosalind Dixon, David Dyzenhaus, Anna Dziedzic, Hualing Fu, Tom Ginsburg, Ran Hirschl, Eric Ip, James Leung, Tom Poole, Yvonne Tew, Jacqueline Tsang, Po Jen Yap, and Mei Ling Young. Our special thanks to Alice Lai for her excellent research assistance. We are particularly grateful to the Faculty of Law at the University of Hong Kong and Trinity College, Oxford, for providing the funding that has made this book open-access. We are mindful that there are many others unknown to us who, if he were writing this preface, Julius would wish to thank. The best we can do is convey our gratitude to all those whose scholarship, support, and love have made this monograph possible.

Nick Barber
Cora Chan

1

Hybrid Regimes, Constitutional Courts, and Democratic Principles

1.1 Introduction

The book examines the role of constitutional courts in hybrid regimes. Specifically, it argues that constitutional courts have a democratic role to play in regimes that are neither fully authoritarian nor democratic. By "democratic role," I do not mean that a constitutional court is itself a democratic institution, or that it is capable of substituting for the political process. Instead, the central argument of the book is that constitutional courts can and should shore up democratic norms and resist authoritarianism in hybrid regimes. I explore the ways in which this role can be performed sustainably. Throughout this book, the terms "democratic role" and "democracy-enhancing role" are used interchangeably.

This chapter first situates my argument in the context of two global phenomena: the proliferation of hybrid regimes and the diffusion of court-centric constitutionalism. I then show why a normative look at constitutional courts in hybrid regimes is an important but overlooked topic in the literature. Next, the operating assumptions of the book are specified, and two basic terms are defined, including constitutional courts and democracy. The chapter concludes by offering a roadmap of the book.

1.2 Proliferation of Hybrid Regimes

The book is set against the backdrop of two intersecting developments. The first is the increased prevalence of hybrid regimes. A hybrid regime is a type of nondemocratic regime that exhibits both democratic and authoritarian characteristics.[1] A hybrid regime aims to create the impression of a functioning democracy, but, with unfair elections and the

[1] A more thorough definition of a hybrid regime will be provided in Chapter 2.

undermining of democratic institutions, its core remains authoritarian. In contrast with citizens in pure authoritarian regimes, those in hybrid regimes are able to participate in political processes, such as elections, to a limited extent.

Hybrid regimes are one of the main regime-types in today's world, complicating the traditional democracy-versus-pure-authoritarian-regime dichotomy. Freedom House's report in 2023 lists close to a third of the countries as "partly free."[2] According to *The Economist*'s 2022 Democracy Index, 21.6 percent of countries are "Hybrid Regimes"; another 28.7 percent are "Flawed Democracies."[3] One study also finds that "three-quarters of authoritarian states [during the 2000s] permitted more than one party to participate in these elections."[4] However one defines a hybrid regime, it is undeniable that a substantial portion of the global population lives under this ambiguous regime-type.

Hybrid regimes are not new, but their growth is unprecedented.[5] Several factors contribute to this phenomenon. The world's march toward democracy largely stopped after entering the twenty-first century. The third wave of democratization, which began in the late 1970s, has been overtaken by a new wave of autocratization.[6] Over the past decade or so, democratic backsliding has affected states around the world.[7] The optimism over third-wave democracies in the late twentieth century has been shown to be largely misplaced. New democracies at the time, such as Venezuela, Hungary, and Poland, have shown significant signs of decay, and those that were classified as semi-democracies or semi-authoritarian regimes, such as Uganda and Singapore, still struggle with authoritarianism. The rise of authoritarian powers like China and Russia is challenging and displacing global norms of democratic governance, further catalyzing autocratization. Even mature democracies like the United States have

[2] *Freedom in the World* (Freedom House 2023).

[3] *The Economist*, 'Democracy Index 2022: Frontline Democracy and the Battle for Ukraine' (2023).

[4] Dawn Brancati, 'Democratic Authoritarianism: Origins and Effects' (2014) 17 *Annual Review of Political Science* 313, 314.

[5] Steven Levitsky and Lucan A. Way, *Competitive Authoritarianism: Hybrid Regimes after the Cold War* (CUP 2010) 14.

[6] Anna Lührmann and Staffan I. Lindberg, 'A Third Wave of Autocratization Is Here: What Is New about It?' (2019) 26 *Democratization* 1095.

[7] Tom G. Daly, 'Democratic Decay: Conceptualising an Emerging Research Field' (2019) 11 *Hague Journal on the Rule of Law* 9; Larry Diamond, 'Breaking Out of the Democratic Slump' (2020) 31 *Journal of Democracy* 36.

not been immune to corrosion.[8] Unlike regime changes in the past, which were usually triggered by sudden events, like coups, this new wave of autocratization is gradual and insidious.[9] As a result, we have seen an increasing number of regimes stuck in between democracy and pure authoritarianism. And, refuting past assumptions, hybridization is not a transitional stage: hybrid regimes have proven to be very durable.[10]

A particularly interesting feature of this new wave of autocratization is that it tends to have a "legal façade."[11] Scholarship on "autocratic legalism"[12] and "abusive constitutionalism"[13] shows how authoritarians today have discovered ways to consolidate political power and undermine accountability through seemingly lawful means and by hollowing out democratic institutions. By adapting the language and form of constitutional democracy in their favor,[14] authoritarians have made contemporary degradation of the democratic process subtle. Detecting and defending against institutional corrosion that takes place behind a legal façade is a challenge for those who lack the necessary expertise. These circumstances heighten the need for judicial institutions to protect and nurture the democratic aspects of a hybrid regime.

1.3 Court-Centric Constitutionalism in Hybrid Regimes

This leads us to the other phenomenon – the diffusion of court-centric constitutionalism. More than a decade ago, Ran Hirschl observed a trend toward "juristocracy," by which he meant the "transfer [of] an unprecedented amount of power from representative institutions to judiciaries."[15] Juristocracy remains highly relevant today. Constitutional review is included in around 80 percent of the

[8] Tom Ginsburg and Aziz Z. Huq, *How to Save a Constitutional Democracy* (University of Chicago Press 2018).

[9] Nancy Bermeo, 'On Democratic Backsliding' (2016) 27 *Journal of Democracy* 5.

[10] Leonardo Morlino, 'Are There Hybrid Regimes? Or Are They Just an Optical Illusion?' (2009) 1 *European Political Science Review* 273, 283–5.

[11] Lührmann and Lindberg (n 6) 1104.

[12] Kim Lane Scheppele, 'Autocratic Legalism' (2018) 85 *The University of Chicago Law Review* 545.

[13] David Landau, 'Abusive Constitutionalism' (2013) 47 *University of California Davis Law Review* 189.

[14] See William J. Dobson, *The Dictator's Learning Curve: Inside the Global Battle for Democracy* (Random House 2012).

[15] Ran Hirschl, *Towards Juristocracy: The Origins and Consequences of the New Constitutionalism* (HUP 2004) 1.

world's constitutions.[16] Hardly a day passes without a constitutional court somewhere in the world deciding on issues traditionally thought to be outside the legal realm. These issues are far from trivial, and are often "mega-political" in nature,[17] or of fundamental importance to the very fabric of a polity. Indeed, there appears to be a tendency for constitutional scholars today to equate constitutionalism with constitutional review.

What defies conventional understanding, however, is that court-centric constitutionalism is not limited to democracies. The consensus used to be that courts in nondemocracies were mere puppets, and that judicialization of politics was impossible outside democracies.[18] The empirical evidence today reveals a more nuanced picture: While constitutional courts in hybrid regimes are weaker and less autonomous than their democratic counterparts, case studies and large-N research both show that "judicializing authoritarian politics"[19] happens all the time. More importantly, constitutional courts in nondemocratic regimes, especially in hybrid regimes, have decided on *and* resisted authoritarianism in important cases.[20] Just as hybrid regimes fall in the middle of the political spectrum, studies find that constitutional courts in hybrid regimes enjoy a measure of judicial independence if one allows that judicial independence is a matter of degree.[21] Judicial powers can be developed outside democracies and constitutional courts in hybrid regimes can be moderately independent institutions.[22]

[16] Tom Ginsburg and Mila Versteeg, 'Why Do Countries Adopt Constitutional Review?' (2014) 30 *The Journal of Law, Economics, & Organization* 587, 587.

[17] Ran Hirschl, 'The Judicialization of Mega-politics and the Rise of Political Courts' (2008) 11 *Annual Review of Political Science* 93.

[18] Tamir Moustafa, 'Law and Courts in Authoritarian Regimes' (2014) 10 *Annual Review of Law and Social Science* 281, 282. Even today, some still argue that it is basically impossible for a meaningful constitutional system to exist in an authoritarian regime. See e.g. Francesco Biagi, *European Constitutional Courts in Transition to Democracy* (CUP 2020) 25–6.

[19] Moustafa *ibid.*

[20] See e.g. Tom Ginsburg and Tamir Moustafa (eds), *Rule by Law: The Politics of Courts in Authoritarian Regimes* (CUP 2008); Yasser Kureshi, 'When Judges Defy Dictators: An Audience-Based Framework to Explain the Emergence of Judicial Assertiveness against Authoritarian Regimes' (2021) 53 *Comparative Politics* 233; Eric C. Ip, *Hybrid Constitutionalism: The Politics of Constitutional Review in the Chinese Special Administrative Regions* (CUP 2019); Tamir Moustafa, *The Struggle for Constitutional Power: Law, Politics, and Economic Development in Egypt* (CUP 2007).

[21] Brad Epperly, *The Political Foundations of Judicial Independence in Dictatorship and Democracy* (OUP 2019).

[22] *ibid* 12.

1.4 The Normative Turn (Informed by Empirical Analysis)

This book brings these two phenomena together and offers a first attempt at a normative-theoretical approach to constitutional courts in hybrid regimes. Specifically, it seeks to articulate the democratic role of a constitutional court and highlights the practical challenges to realizing this role. It also prescribes normative guidelines for constitutional courts in hybrid regimes to advance liberal democratic norms in a sustainable manner while also maintaining judicial independence in an authoritarian climate.

Normative constitutional theory has largely been preoccupied with constitutional systems and the constitutional courts of democratic systems. Despite the resurgence of authoritarian regimes, normative debates about the role of constitutional courts are largely centered around consolidated democracies,[23] new democracies undergoing consolidation,[24] and democracies that are resisting backsliding.[25] Normative constitutional scholars pay scant attention to authoritarian regimes.[26] On the other hand, political scientists and those who conduct empirical studies have begun to uncover the intricacies of constitutional courts operating under hybrid regimes and pure authoritarian regimes. Their research sheds light on the behavioral patterns and functions of these courts.[27]

[23] See e.g. Jeremy Waldron, 'The Core of the Case Against Judicial Review' (2006) 115 *Yale Law Journal* 1346; Aileen Kavanagh, 'Participation and Judicial Review: A Reply to Jeremy Waldron' (2003) 22 *Law and Philosophy* 451; Richard Bellamy, *Political Constitutionalism: A Republican Defence of the Constitutionality of Democracy* (CUP 2007); Jeff King, *Judging Social Rights* (CUP 2012); Rosalind Dixon, 'The Core Case for Weak-form Judicial Review' (2016) 38 *Cardozo Law Review* 2193; Rosalind Dixon, *Responsive Judicial Review: Democracy and Dysfunction in the Modern Age* (OUP 2023).

[24] See e.g. Theunis Roux, *The Politics of Principle: The First South African Constitutional Court, 1995–2005* (CUP 2013); Samuel Issacharoff, *Fragile Democracies: Contested Power in the Era of Constitutional Courts* (CUP 2015); David Landau, 'A Dynamic Theory of Judicial Role' (2014) 55 *Boston College Law Review* 1501.

[25] See e.g. Sujit Choudhry, 'Transnational Constitutionalism and a Limited Doctrine of Unconstitutional Constitutional Amendment: A Reply to Rosalind Dixon and David Landau' (2017) 15 *International Journal of Constitutional Law* 826; Aziz Z. Huq, 'Democratic Erosion and the Courts: Comparative Perspectives' (2018) 93 *New York University Law Review Online* 21; Tom Ginsburg, 'The Jurisprudence of Anti-Erosion' (2018) 66 *Drake Law Review* 823.

[26] Possible reasons for this gap will be suggested in Chapter 3.

[27] See e.g. Moustafa (n 20); Ip (n 20); Lisa Hilbink, *Judges Beyond Politics in Democracy and Dictatorship: Lessons from Chile* (CUP 2007); Gretchen Helmke, *Courts under Constraints: Judges, Generals, and Presidents in Argentina* (CUP 2005); Alexei Trochev, *Judging Russia: The Role of the Constitutional Court in Russian Politics 1990–2006* (CUP 2008).

These studies tend to be devoid of normative content as their goals are descriptive and explanatory, or are only focused on institutional survival.[28] Nonetheless, they provide an important foundation for normative theorizing. This book sits at the intersection of normative constitutional theory and comparative judicial political studies, with a greater emphasis on the normative half of the discussion.

Two operating assumptions underpin this book. As previously mentioned, the first is the fact that a moderately independent constitutional court is a realistic possibility for a hybrid regime. More will be said about the sociopolitical foundation of this phenomenon in Chapter 3. The very fact that there is room for constitutional courts to challenge the incumbent regime motivates this research. It would be meaningless to talk about how judges should play a democratic role in pure authoritarian regimes when (semi-)independent judicial institutions do not exist, or struggle to even survive. Equally, judicial autonomy and judicial power[29] means little if it is unclear how judges should assert their authority. For example, judges of an autonomous court can use their powers for personal gain, or such powers can be wielded recklessly and cause the court to self-destruct. The possibility of judicial autonomy opens the space for much-needed normative discussion of the role of courts in a hybrid regime.

Another operating assumption relates to the constitutions of hybrid regimes. Given the illiberal and antidemocratic practices observed in nondemocratic regimes, it is tempting to conclude that constitutions there are "shams."[30] It is perhaps no surprise that most authoritarian constitutions typically promise more than they can actually deliver.[31] However, the formal elements of a constitution are not the only determinants of a state's constitutional performance:[32] whether effective

[28] For example, it is assumed under Helmke's strategic defection model that judges in Argentina are seeking survival under institutionally unstable environments. Helmke *ibid* 144–5, 170. There are also works that are not necessarily regime-type-specific but explore generally the techniques of institutional survival under harsher political climates. See e.g. Erin F. Delaney, 'Analyzing Avoidance: Judicial Strategy in Comparative Perspective' (2016) 66 *Duke Law Journal* 1; Rosalind Dixon and Samuel Issacharoff, 'Living to Fight Another Day: Judicial Deferral in Defense of Democracy' (2016) *Wisconsin Law Review* 4, 683.

[29] The idea of judicial power will be further elaborated in Chapter 5.

[30] David S. Law and Mila Versteeg, 'Sham Constitutions' (2013) 101 *California Law Review* 863.

[31] *ibid* 919.

[32] State is used in a sociological instead of legal sense. State, as a legal concept, is a system recognized under international law. Here, state is understood as a complex social group –

constitutional enforcement mechanisms exist or not is also crucial.[33] The effectiveness of a constitutional court – one of the most important constitutional actors within a constitutional order – also shapes a state's constitutional health. Importantly, a constitutional court's effectiveness partially stems from the formal design of a constitution. To some extent, the constitution determines the latitude possessed by courts. A constitutional court derives its legitimacy from the constitution; provisions relating to constitutional jurisdiction and human rights, for example, offer crucial ammunition for asserting its authority. A constitution that eliminates any meaningful space for constitutional review would render any normative discussion in this area futile.

Fortunately, constitutions in hybrid regimes do tend to offer the raw materials for constitutional courts to potentially play a meaningful role. As noted, the vast majority of constitutions in the world explicitly provide for constitutional courts. Most constitutional courts are expressly endowed with the constitutional authority to decide on constitutional matters. Large-N research also finds that constitutions in non-democratic regimes formally resemble those in democracies.[34] For example, constitutions in hybrid regimes contain similar numbers and kinds of rights to those of democracies, provisions that define the state as a democracy, and safeguards that give effect to judicial independence. The reason for this partial resemblance stems from hybrid regimes' attempts to capture the reputational gains of adopting democratic constitutional features. Adopting them can be a double-edged sword for authoritarians, who may be tempted to incorporate them to attract

with citizens, bound together by rules (i.e. the constitution) within a territory, interacting with the state, institutions, and one another; a state must be capable of claiming authority over its citizens. For instance, Hong Kong, as a Chinese Special Administrative Region, is not a state under international law, but it is a state sociologically as the Hong Kong government exerts control and asserts legitimacy over its citizens within the territory of Hong Kong. See N. W. Barber, *The Constitutional State* (OUP 2010) chapter 2.

33 See James Melton, 'Do Constitutional Rights Matter? The Relationship between De Jure and De Facto Human Rights Protection' (2013), available at http://citeseerx.ist.psu.edu/viewdoc/download?doi=10.1.1.375.9784&rep=rep1&type=pdf, last visited April 28, 2023.

34 David S. Law and Mila Versteeg, 'Constitutional Variation among Strains of Authoritarianism' in Tom Ginsburg and Alberto Simpser (eds), *Constitutions in Authoritarian Regimes* (CUP 2013) 165; Tom Ginsburg, Zachary Elkins, and James Melton, 'The Content of Authoritarian Constitutions' in Tom Ginsburg and Alberto Simpser (eds), *Constitutions in Authoritarian Regimes* (CUP 2013) 141; James Melton and Tom Ginsburg, 'Does De Jure Judicial Independence Really Matter? A Reevaluation of Explanations for Judicial Independence' (2014) 2 *Journal of Law and Courts* 187.

foreign investors and stimulate the economy, or to shore up popular support for the regime.[35] However, the incorporation of democratic constitutional features brings along constitutional norms that can (and should) be used against the authoritarian when the regime falls short of what the constitution demands. In other words, the constitutional elements borrowed from democracies are standards waiting to be held against the authoritarian. The democratic side of a hybrid regime constitution furnishes a constitutional court with options and grants it leeway to wrestle with a hybrid regime.

At this stage, some readers may feel that this book is overly confident about the democratic potential of constitutional courts in hybrid regimes. While the assumptions set out so far give us good reasons to think normatively about how constitutional courts can further the liberal democratic causes in hybrid regimes, one might point out that constitutional courts in real-life hybrid regimes are inevitably subject to authoritarian pressures. Case studies have shown that many courts are captured by the incumbent and are complicit in authoritarian oppression.[36] Some large-N studies also question the general effectiveness of constitutional courts. Adam Chilton and Mila Versteeg, for example, argue that "constitutional rights do not appear to be better protected in countries with independent courts equipped with the power of judicial review."[37] Instead, their findings suggest that "rights enforcement ultimately falls on citizens themselves."[38]

The book acknowledges the vulnerabilities and weaknesses of constitutional courts in hybrid regimes. Its tone is perhaps best described as cautiously optimistic. A constitutional court alone probably cannot bring about regime change, and political transitions rarely occur inside the courtroom. However, courts are positioned to create more favorable conditions for regime change to occur. Legal constitutionalism and political constitutionalism are not necessarily binary choices, and constitutional courts are able to empower the people and other constitutional

[35] See e.g. Daniel A. Farber, 'Rights as Signals' (2002) 31 *The Journal of Legal Studies* 83; Moustafa (n 20); Rosalind Dixon, 'Constitutional Rights as Bribes' (2018) 50 *Connecticut Law Review* 767.

[36] David Landau and Rosalind Dixon, 'Abusive Judicial Review: Courts against Democracy' (2020) 53 *UC Davis Law Review* 1313.

[37] Adam S. Chilton and Mila Versteeg, 'Courts' Limited Ability to Protect Constitutional Rights' (2018) 85 *The University of Chicago Law Review* 293, 297.

[38] *ibid.*

actors.[39] There are also secondary but meaningful effects produced by the legal decisions of a constitutional court. For example, constitutional courts can cultivate citizens' general understanding of their rights, enable their voices to be heard through the legal process in politically repressed environments, or even trigger mass mobilization by highlighting constitutional violations by the government. These effects are practically and morally significant even though the causal mechanisms behind them are hard to empirically verify. These contributions by constitutional courts may look modest, but can have wide-ranging consequences for hybrid regimes and the lives of citizens under them, especially when these contributions are aggregated over time.

While empirical research downplays the independent influence of constitutional courts in protecting rights and promoting democracy in a general sense,[40] it does not foreclose discussion over how constitutional courts in hybrid regimes should exercise their authority. It may well be the case that many constitutional courts exercise their constitutional authority and powers in ways that fail to maximize their democratic potential in a sustainable manner. Still, some have successfully brought about meaningful change, as we shall see later in this chapter. The paths taken by these examples offer much-needed direction and insights.

Many of the claims made in the book are supported by comparative examples from around the world. These comparative examples mainly come from, but are not limited to, hybrid regimes. There is a growing focus on how comparative constitutional research should be conducted, and the methodologies some constitutional scholars apply in their research have been accused of being inadequate. There is no one-size-fits-all method for comparative constitutional research because the methodology required depends on the research aim. Those seeking to establish causation should adhere to more rigorous standards of social scientific inquiry. My intention here is normative, and my comparative insights play a secondary (but still important) role. As Hirschl points out, "the legal philosopher is interested in formulating moral justifications or principles for best practices at the ought (rather than the is) level, and may thus be forgiven for supporting her insights with a small number of

[39] Some political constitutionalists accept at least a limited role for constitutional courts to play in democracies. See Adam Tomkins, 'The Role of the Courts in the Political Constitution' (2010) 60 *University of Toronto Law Journal* 1.

[40] Ran Hirschl, 'Epilogue: Courts and Democracy between Ideals and Realities' (2013) 49 *Representation* 361, 363.

possibly unrepresentative cases."[41] This is not to say that the illustrations I draw upon are particularly odd or exceptional, but that my selectiveness is perhaps forgivable and justified. The comparative evidence is used to strengthen the plausibility of my claims and to showcase the techniques that can be adopted by courts and judges in hybrid regimes.

Three jurisdictions are frequently referenced in the book: Hong Kong, Pakistan, and Uganda. More precisely, there will be a relatively large number of illustrations coming from the courts of post-handover Hong Kong from 1997 to 2019, Pakistan under General Pervez Musharraf from 1999 to 2008, and Uganda after its first national election in 1996. These jurisdictions and periods are singled out for two reasons.

First, although their democratic trajectories turned out to be quite different, these jurisdictions during the aforementioned time periods are widely considered by experts to have been hybrid regimes.[42] A more thorough account of a hybrid regime will be offered in the next chapter, but what these polities had in common was semi-competitive electoral systems, and their intention and efforts to mimic a constitutional democracy. They are full of contradictions, and their diverging impulses of democracy and authoritarianism have led to their ambiguous outlook. I now briefly describe the relevant periods of these jurisdictions.

While Hong Kong is a Chinese city, it operates under the "One Country, Two Systems" principle. Under this constitutional principle, Hong Kong retains its own political, economic, and legal systems. The Basic Law, Hong Kong's de facto constitution, simultaneously expresses China's assertion of its sovereignty over Hong Kong and its tolerance of the city's autonomy. Hong Kong aspires (or pretends) to be democratic, as the Basic Law specifies universal suffrage to be the ultimate method of

41 Ran Hirschl, *Comparative Matters: The Renaissance of Comparative Constitutional Law* (OUP 2014) 225.

42 For Hong Kong as a hybrid regime, see Brian C. H. Fong, 'State–Society Conflicts under Hong Kong's Hybrid Regime: Governing Coalition Building and Civil Society Challenges' (2013) 53 *Asian Survey* 854; Ngok Ma, 'Hong Kong's Democrats Divide' (2011) 22 *Journal of Democracy* 54; Julius Yam, 'Approaching the Legitimacy Paradox in Hong Kong: Lessons for Hybrid Regime Courts' (2021) 46 *Law & Social Inquiry* 153. For Pakistan as a hybrid regime, see Aqil Shah, 'Pakistan's "Armored" Democracy' (2003) 14 *Journal of Democracy* 26; Larry Diamond, 'Elections without Democracy: Thinking about Hybrid Regimes' (2002) 13 *Journal of Democracy* 21, 31. For Uganda as a hybrid regime, see Aili Mari Tripp, *Museveni's Uganda: Paradoxes of Power in a Hybrid Regime* (Lynne Rienner Publishers 2010); Valérie Arnould, 'Transitional Justice and Democracy in Uganda: between Impetus and Instrumentalisation' (2015) 9 *Journal of Eastern African Studies* 354; Sandrine Perrot and others (eds), *Elections in a Hybrid Regime: Revisiting the 2011 Ugandan Polls* (Fountain Publishers 2014).

electing the city's leader and lawmakers. Like other hybrid regimes, elections exist in Hong Kong, but are far from free and fair. The electoral system is plagued with institutionalized biases that favor pro-Beijing parties. Nevertheless, at least prior to the passage of the National Security Law in 2020 and the overhaul of the political system in 2021, Hong Kong civil society was reasonably active and the prodemocratic opposition had won a considerable number of seats in previous parliamentary and local elections. There were modest democratic reforms over the years, but these required Beijing's consent. It should be noted that Hong Kong is arguably no longer a hybrid regime, for it took a sharp, authoritarian turn in 2020. In response to the anti-extradition bill protest – the largest protest movement in post-handover Hong Kong's history – China launched a series of crackdowns, jeopardizing the city's reputation as an international financial center. With the enactment of the National Security Law, electoral reforms, rampant disqualifications and arrests of opposition lawmakers and candidates, and state-instigated attacks on civil society, political space for opposition is close to being completely eliminated.

Pakistan has a troubled history of military dictatorships, and Musharraf's Pakistan is one such example. In 1999, Pervez Musharraf overthrew then-Prime Minister Nawaz Sharif via a military takeover. After the bloodless coup, Musharraf proclaimed to be the president and formally took office in 2001. Local and national elections were held under his tenure. Freedom of press and information improved during this time as well,[43] but elections were far from free and fair. Describing Pakistan as a hybrid regime under Musharraf, Aqil Shah writes, "[Pakistan's] elections are not completely without meaning, but the principles of civilian rule and constitutionalism are honored far more in the breach than in the observance."[44] Election monitors documented the many irregularities of those elections, for example the misuse of state resources to support the incumbent's campaign, and the incarceration and intimidation of opposition figures.[45] Musharraf's presidency was extended for another five years after a controversial referendum staged in 2002, and the constitution was

[43] Marta Bolognani, 'Virtual Protest with Tangible Effects? Some Observations on the Media Strategies of the 2007 Pakistani Anti-emergency Movement' (2010) 18 *Contemporary South Asia* 401, 403.

[44] See Shah (n 42) 27.

[45] See Human Rights Watch, 'Elections since General Pervez Musharraf Took Power in 1999' (2008), available at www.hrw.org/legacy/pub/2008/asia/Elections_Under_Musharraf_1999-2007.pdf, last visited April 28, 2023.

amended to empower himself and the military.[46] As Musharraf approached the end of his presidency, he attempted to extend his tenure further by declaring a state of emergency and suspending national elections. These moves, together with the removal and arrest of judges, triggered a public uproar. His party was eventually defeated in the 2008 elections. With impeachment looming, he resigned, went into exile, and passed away in Dubai in 2023. His electoral defeat is a testament to the distinctiveness of a hybrid regime: Although elections are often rigged to favor the incumbent, opposition success remains possible.

Finally, another country with a checkered history of military dictatorship is Uganda. Taking power after a coup in 1986, Yoweri Museveni is the longest-serving president of postindependence Uganda, as well as one of the world's longest-serving leaders. He held his first national elections in 1996. Before the 2006 elections, Uganda operated as a "no-party democracy." Coined by Museveni himself, this system did not allow multiparty competition, and any opponents could only run as independent candidates. The system was packaged as a way to promote political inclusiveness and reduce party-political conflicts. Multiparty politics was eventually introduced in 2005 after a referendum. Once described as a "beacon of hope" by then-US Secretary of State Madeleine Albright,[47] Uganda made tremendous improvements economically and democratically under Museveni's leadership, especially in comparison with his predecessors. Like elections in Pakistan and Hong Kong, however, Uganda's electoral system is rife with irregularities. Corruption is widespread and electoral regulation is ineffective.[48] The incumbent party is routinely accused of using public funds to finance electoral campaigns.[49] Opposition candidates have been charged and kept in pretrial remand so as to limit their ability to campaign. Most controversially, Museveni amended the constitution a number of times to lift the age of retirement and presidential term limit. With an internet blackout before voting day,

[46] Husain Haqqani, 'History Repeats Itself in Pakistan' (2006) 17 *Journal of Democracy* 110, 111.

[47] Madeleine K. Albright and Yoweri Museveni, 'Joint Press Availability' (Kampala, Uganda, December 10, 1997), available at https://1997-2001.state.gov/statements/971210b.html, last visited April 28, 2023.

[48] The Inspectorate of Government, The Republic of Uganda, *The Third Annual Report on Tracking Corruption Trends in Uganda: Using the Data Tracking Mechanism* (December 2012) 33.

[49] See Julie K. Faller, 'The System Matters: Corruption and Vote Choice in Uganda' (2015) 53 *Commonwealth & Comparative Politics* 428.

the imprisonment of the main opposition presidential candidate and a large-scale crackdown on opposition protests, the most recent election in 2021 saw the lowest voter turnout rate in Uganda's history, and was described by a commentator as "one of the most violent in recent memory."[50] Through tactics of patronage and violence (both real and the threat thereof), Museveni remains undefeated in the ballot box.

Aside from all being hybrid regimes, the second reason for picking these jurisdictions is that they have courts with prolonged spells of successfully challenging the regime. The track records of these courts are not spotless, and they have suffered varying degrees of attacks from the incumbents. But, all things considered, the general consensus is that they are success stories despite the harsh political climates they operate in. The Hong Kong judiciary, as Eric Ip puts it, is "the only political organ that has ever succeeded in continually resisting Beijing in the constitutional history of the People's Republic of China."[51] Pakistan's Supreme Court "remained an active and organized democratic enclave under the military rule of Pervez Musharraf from 1999 to 2008."[52] The High Courts of Uganda are similarly described as a "vocal, assertive judiciary valiantly attempting to maintain its power and independence,"[53] which "consistently resisted government meddling in verdicts, efforts to ban the right to bail, and countless other attempts to limit its authority."[54]

One might observe that Pakistan is the only of the three that has arguably democratized (or headed down a more democratic route).[55] The fact that Hong Kong and Uganda went the other way or remain hybrid regimes, however, does not detract from the accomplishments of their respective courts. After all, transitioning to democracy, and regime change more broadly, is a complex process involving many actors within and beyond the polity. There is a tendency to reduce democratization to

[50] Sophie Neiman, 'Will the U.S. Still Back Uganda's Museveni Despite Another Sham Election?' *World Politics Review*, January 25, 2021, available at www.worldpoliticsreview.com/articles/29376/after-uganda-elections-will-the-u-s-still-back-museveni-s-brutal-regime, last visited April 28, 2023.

[51] Eric C. Ip, 'Constitutional Competition between the Hong Kong Court of Final Appeal and the Chinese National People's Congress Standing Committee: A Game Theory Perspective' (2014) 39 *Law & Social Inquiry* 824, 825.

[52] Bruce Gilley, 'Democratic Enclaves in Authoritarian Regimes' (2010) 17 *Democratization* 389, 393.

[53] Rachel L. Ellett, 'Emerging Judicial Power in Transitional Democracies: Malawi, Tanzania and Uganda' (PhD thesis, Northeastern University 2008) 408.

[54] Mari Tripp (n 42) 87.

[55] Other recent examples of hybrid regime incumbents losing in elections include Yahya Jammeh in The Gambia and Barisan Nasional in the 2018 Malaysian general election.

discrete events, and glorify those who play a prominent role in them. The reality, though, is that democratization is the logical outgrowth of a long, arduous struggle between the incumbent, the people, and other political actors, including the courts. Understanding democratization as a process as opposed to a single event helps us better appreciate what can be offered by constitutional courts. As the book later shows, the decisions and actions of judges may not always lead to a democratic transition, but they can certainly support democratic practices and structures, as well as forestall the erosion of democratic norms.

Courts from these three jurisdictions have made lasting contributions to advancing democratic causes. Courts in Hong Kong, for instance, time and again ensured fair and proper trials for dissidents, and promoted the development of civil rights. Regarded by the local community as the "guardian of the people's interests,"[56] the Pakistani Supreme Court "challenged the foundations of General Musharraf's regime in a series of landmark decisions"[57] and subsequently triggered the democratization movement in Pakistan. Notable feats of Ugandan judges include ruling unconstitutional a referendum that was allegedly rigged and going on strike to protest against attacks on the rule of law. Resisting a military dictator or one of the most powerful political parties in the world is no easy task. The successes of these judges can, to a large extent, be attributed to their vision of cultivating judicial independence and judicial power, their acumen in choosing the right battles to fight and their dedication to the values of constitutional democracy. These stories illustrate the normative claims I develop in subsequent chapters and demonstrate the potential for courts to play a modest democratic role in hybrid regimes. The techniques these judges have used may also inspire their peers in similarly repressed political environments.

1.5 Constitutional Court

This section and the next define two core concepts used in this book: constitutional court and democracy. The aim is twofold: to clarify what I mean when deploying these concepts, and to highlight some of their salient features, which will help develop arguments later in the book.

[56] Ayaz Amiz, 'My Lord the Chief Justice Takes Notice,' *Dawn*, May 5, 2010, as quoted in Asher A. Qazi, '*Suo Motu*: Choosing Not to Legislate Chief Justice Chaudhry's Strategic Agenda' in Moeen H. Cheema and Ijaz Shafi Gilani (eds), *The Politics and Jurisprudence of the Chaudhry Court 2005–2013* (OUP 2015) 305.

[57] Kureshi (n 20).

The account of a constitutional court proposed here is what I call "the standard account." It is uncontroversial and should accord with a common understanding of a constitutional court. Nevertheless, there are other ways of defining a constitutional court, and the standard account does not pretend to be a complete account. Under the standard account, there are three dimensions to a constitutional court: constitutional, political, and legal.[58] I discuss the crucial features of each dimension. In the following chapters, we will look at the salience of each dimension in a hybrid regime.

Beginning with the constitutional dimension, a constitutional court is a court that enjoys constitutional jurisdiction. These courts enjoy constitutional adjudicative powers to enforce the constitution, with access to a range of unique tools.[59] Of course, a constitutional court is not the only constitutional actor, as the people, political representatives, and political parties also have roles to play in defining, interpreting, and applying the constitution. Unlike these other actors, a constitutional court has more direct access to the constitution. Its authority over the constitution is especially strong because it derives a legal mandate from the constitution to interpret and enforce it. It is a powerful constitutional actor as well, because constitutional amendment requirements tend to be stringent. The harder it is to amend the constitution, the more constitutionally durable a constitutional court's decision becomes.

It should be emphasized that the term "constitutional court" as used in this book encompasses all models of constitutional court, including the centralized constitutional court (also known as the Kelsenian or European model) *and* the decentralized constitutional court (also known as the American model). Constitutional courts under these two models display important differences in terms of, inter alia, breadth of jurisdiction, form of constitutional review, length of judicial tenure, position within the judicial hierarchy and docket load.[60] Many suggestions proposed later in the book regarding how judges should advance democratic norms in hybrid regimes are contingent upon the institutional features of a constitutional court, and the specific *kind* of constitutional court at stake naturally affects how and the extent to which some of

[58] The standard account is inspired by Dieter Grimm's account of a constitutional court. Dieter Grimm, *Constitutionalism: Past, Present and Future* (OUP 2016) chapter 9.

[59] Some of the tools will be discussed in Chapter 4.

[60] For a comparison of the two models of constitutional review, see Alex Stone Sweet, 'Constitutions and Judicial Power' in Daniele Caramani (ed), *Comparative Politics* (OUP 2008).

the suggestions play out. For instance, centralized constitutional courts under the Kelsenian model and apex courts under the American model tend to have greater access to resources and support than the lower courts; accordingly, centralized constitutional courts and apex courts will have relatively more latitude when it comes to judicial strategizing. The arguments made in this book are relevant to all kinds of courts with constitutional jurisdiction. Issues common to constitutional courts are highlighted and addressed throughout the book, even though the extent to which they apply may vary depending on how a constitutional court is institutionally structured.

Because of a constitutional court's jurisdiction over constitutional issues, a constitutional court also has a political dimension. It has become fashionable for constitutional scholars, especially political scientists, to describe constitutional courts as political actors or political institutions. While one should apply this label carefully, as it may give an overly simplistic impression of how constitutional courts actually work, there is some truth in this characterization. A constitutional court is necessarily political because of its origin and impact. Constitutional courts are instituted by the constitution, and constitutional judges are appointed by political representatives. Both processes are political in nature because they involve political actors and depend on the distribution of political powers. More importantly, a constitutional court deals with constitutional issues, which often involve fundamental norms of a polity. A constitutional court regulates how political powers are exercised and checks to see if laws and policies are constitutionally valid. In addition to constitutional review powers, many constitutional courts possess ancillary powers, such as the power to issue advisory opinions, the power to correct legislative omissions, and the power to adjudicate electoral disputes.[61] Some would argue that these powers are beyond a constitutional court's role of a "negative legislator." Nevertheless, these functions are commonly found in today's constitutional courts and further enhance their political impact. A constitutional court is political in nature because its targets are political and the issues they face have strong political overtones.

What differentiates a constitutional court from the political branches of government is its legal dimension. It is legal in several senses. Unlike elected representatives, a constitutional court is not *directly* accountable

[61] Tom Ginsburg and Zachary Elkins, 'Ancillary Powers of Constitutional Courts' (2009) 87 *Texas Law Review* 1431.

to the people. Instead, judicial independence is the hallmark of a constitutional court. It is not a constitutional court's duty to track the preferences of the people; rather, its purpose is to give life to the constitution according to constitutional legal principles. The independent exercise of the constitutional court's functions is fundamentally important to the court's identity, because the demands of constitutional justice may run contrary to the views of the people and its representatives. The court's institutional isolation, especially compared to other political institutions, helps promote the values of impartiality and fairness. Despite the political significance of a constitutional court, what differentiates it from a statesperson is the fact that it *must* apply a legal methodology when executing its functions.[62] Constitutional judges must express their judgments in the language of the law. They must rely on constitutional-legal principles such as *stare decisis*[63] or canons of interpretation to decide cases. Judicial discretion still exists within the boundaries of the law, but the legal methodology considerably constrains judicial decision-making. Constitutional judges cannot reach an outcome simply because of pressure from an interest group, for instance. The legal methodology defines how a constitutional court should perform its duties. The principled nature of a constitutional court completes the standard account of a constitutional court.

While the book focuses on constitutional courts, the insights offered are potentially relevant to ordinary courts in hybrid regimes. Constitutional courts are singled out because their very nature brings them into close proximity with the constitutional politics of hybrid regimes. However, ordinary courts dealing with criminal trials of dissidents or adjudicating a private dispute between competing political factions, for instance, can also be constitutionally relevant and/or politically significant. Ordinary judges can be similarly committed to democratic principles *and* impacted by authoritarian pressures as well. Therefore, the normative and sociological discussions later in the book do, to some degree, apply to courts generally in hybrid regimes. The practical guidelines to be offered may also be helpful to ordinary judges.

[62] There are lawmakers who adopt the language of the law in legislative debates, such as resorting to proportionality tests in deciding the desirability of a bill or using burden-of-proof concepts to deflect responsibilities. The normativity of these practices aside, unlike constitutional judges, these lawmakers are not duty-bound to resort to legal principles or use legalese in these settings.

[63] Some constitutional courts are not bound by precedents but referring to precedents is often treated as a legitimate mode of argumentation.

The relevance of the book extends beyond constitutional courts or courts generally in hybrid regimes. Democracies, hybrid regimes, and pure authoritarian regimes are not hard categories, and a degree of fluidity exists among them. This is especially true today. As mentioned already, democratic backsliding has been a striking global development over the past decade or so, and authoritarianism is creeping into all types of regimes.[64] Contemporary processes of degradation of democratic institutions are usually gradual and subtle. Courts under other types of regimes may face similar challenges to hybrid regimes as a result. It is hoped that lessons imparted in the book will inspire not only courts in hybrid regimes but also those in democracies resisting erosion, as well as in post-authoritarian states struggling to institutionalize democratic ideals.

1.6 Democracy

Given the book is about the democratic role of a hybrid-regime constitutional court, it is necessary to define democracy. I conceptualize it in normative and not descriptive terms. We need to know what democracy means in order to evaluate whether a court is enhancing democratic norms. A normative account of democracy articulates the principles that are relevant to a constitutional court playing a democratic role. Like the definition of constitutional court put forward in this chapter, the account of democracy offered does not aspire to be a complete account, but aims to be enough for this book.

The theoretical framework I offer can accommodate robust accounts of democracy, but the book adopts a relatively minimalist conception of democracy. This is sufficient to animate the discussion and facilitate critical evaluation in the later chapters. The account of democracy adopted here is borrowed and adapted from Aziz Huq and Tom Ginsburg. In *How to Save a Constitutional Democracy*,[65] the authors identify three requirements for a democracy: periodic free and fair elections; the protection of first-generation or liberal rights such as freedom of speech, assembly, and association; and the rule of law. These "system-level properties … intertwine and interact closely"[66] to form a particular conception of democracy: liberal constitutional

64 Daly (n 7); Diamond (n 7).
65 Huq and Ginsburg (n 8).
66 Aziz Z. Huq and Tom Ginsburg, 'How to Lose a Constitutional Democracy' (2018) 65 *UCLA Law Review* 78, 87.

democracy. Accordingly, democracy is defined as pluralistic political competition within constitutional boundaries. Their account is well suited to the aims of this book, because the legal and institutional focus of the three components orients discussion about the moral qualities that inform how judicial power should be exercised. Next, I elaborate upon the three requirements, making some adjustments for the purposes of this book.

Free and fair elections are central to a democracy. Huq and Ginsburg follow Joseph Schumpeter by defining free and fair elections in relation to regularity in the transfer of power. That is, a free and fair election allows for "a genuine possibility of alteration in power."[67] The topic of how to determine whether elections are free and fair will be revisited in the next chapter. What I emphasize here is the guiding principle behind this element. Political equality is the foundational value of a democracy. There are many ways to justify this value, from equal respect[68] to nondomination.[69] Regardless of its many justifications, political equality is based on the idea that individuals are of equal moral worth, and a system of government should be designed to protect and promote people's equal political liberty. Disagreement among reasonable persons occurs in every social group, and the challenges polities face is finding a method to resolve disagreements without undermining the equality principle. Meaningful elections not only enable the peaceful transfer of power, but allow political equality to be realized amid disagreement. As a set of procedures for selecting political representatives, a free and fair electoral process instantiates people's equal right to participate in the political process. In institutional terms, the system must confer on every person an equal right to vote and to run for election, and establish fair rules for the conduct of elections and the transfer of power.

A democracy is not only about the moment of voting, however. Equal and universal suffrage would mean little if, for example, people were barred from exchanging or expressing their views freely. In addition to free and fair elections, the enforcement of liberal rights, or what might be called first-generation rights, is another important condition of democracy. These rights – including, but not limited to, freedom of speech, association, and assembly – guard against state interference with individual liberties and give people the power to influence politics. They

[67] Huq and Ginsburg (n 8) 10.
[68] Jeremy Waldron, *Law and Disagreement* (OUP 1999).
[69] Bellamy (n 23).

guarantee the communicative context necessary for the realization of political equality and the proper functioning of a democracy.[70] Huq and Ginsburg rightly acknowledge that the three rights specified do not exhaust the list of rights necessary for a democracy. The right to freedom of the press and the right to information are clearly extensions of the right to freedom of expression. People need to be sufficiently informed to have a meaningful exchange of ideas. Press freedom and freedom of information enable the realization of freedom of expression and ensure that people can make informed political decisions. Parliamentary immunity – that is, lawmakers' legal immunity for what they say during parliamentary proceedings – and the right to form political parties derive from the freedom of expression and the freedom of association respectively.[71] The authors also suggest a more novel example: the right against unreasonable search and seizure in the United States. This may not initially appear to be a liberal right, but it can and has been exercised in defense against state efforts to stifle political speech and association.[72] This second component of democracy (i.e. liberal rights) can encompass a wider range of rights and entitlements that serve to maintain the integrity of and conditions necessary for a democratic political process.

The final component is the rule of law. Its distinctive contribution is to define how powers should be structured and exercised in a democracy. Huq and Ginsburg argue that rule of law is "functionally necessary to allow democratic engagement without fear or coercion."[73] The authors follow Lon Fuller's famous institutional requirements, which state that the legal regime of a democracy must be public, transparent, predictable, and stable, among other things. Constitutionalism, as a form of institutionalized constraint, is commonly regarded to be the manifestation of rule of law. "A measure of institutionalization and legalized routines"[74] create "even-handedness and apolitical administration."[75]

Democratic politics can only take place in an environment that respects the formal demands of the law, and the institutional requirements of rule of law seek to minimize the chances and space for arbitrary power. Accordingly, the rule of law is, as Martin Krygier constantly reminds us,

[70] Robert Post, 'Democracy and Equality' (2006) 603 *The Annals of the American Academy of Political and Social Science* 24, 28–9.

[71] Huq and Ginsburg (n 8) 12–13.

[72] *ibid* 12.

[73] Huq and Ginsburg (n 66) 87.

[74] Huq and Ginsburg (n 8) 13.

[75] *ibid.*

a "response to a problem, often described as arbitrary power."[76] Power is commonly viewed as arbitrary when it is uncontrolled and unpredictable, and when it is exercised in a way that lacks due respect for its subjects.[77] Arbitrariness is a particular problem that characterizes authoritarian regimes. Aside from limited or nonexistent political pluralism, authoritarian regimes, including hybrid regimes, are said to have "ill-defined limits,"[78] a "pretense of accountability,"[79] and "arbitrary governmental authority."[80] Indeed, contemporary usage of the term "authoritarianism" tends to reference illiberal and oppressive political practices.[81] This is, of course, not incidental: that authoritarian regimes are prone to arbitrariness is a consequence of their unchecked powers.

While democracy depends on rule of law, as a democratic principle, rule of law cannot be fully satisfied without competitive elections. Aside from minimizing arbitrariness and creating a favorable environment for democratic interactions, rule of law seeks to ensure the law's purpose as *intended by a democratic legislature.* "The rule of law," as Nick Barber writes, "requires that law make the differences it purports to make."[82] Under a democracy, the difference the law purports to make is decided by the people. It is the consent of the people that gives law its legitimate authority. The spirit of a democracy is self-governance. Democracy seeks to create a system that is made for the people and by the people. Rule of law connects this democratic aspiration with reality by ensuring that democratically made laws are taken seriously. Without competitive elections, the contents of the law and the political system more broadly are easily manipulated by an unchecked power.[83] Rule of law would be significantly less valuable if it simply inscribed the will of the authoritarian in the law. Rule of law's relationship with democracy is, consequently, a mutually dependent one: rule of law is necessary to

76 Martin Krygier, 'What's the Point of the Rule of Law' (2019) 67 *Buffalo Law Review* 743, 746.

77 See Martin Krygier, 'The Rule of Law and State Legitimacy' in Wojciech Sadurski, Michael Sevel, and Kevin Walton (eds), *Legitimacy: The State and Beyond* (OUP 2019).

78 Juan J. Linz, 'An Authoritarian Regime: The Case of Spain' in Erik Allardt and Yrjö Littunen (eds), *Cleavages, Ideologies and Party System* (Westermarck Society 1964) 255.

79 Lee Morgenbesser, 'The Menu of Autocratic Innovation' (2020) 27 *Democratization* 1053.

80 Gábor Attila Tóth, 'Constitutional Markers of Authoritarianism' (2019) 11 *Hague Journal on the Rule of Law* 37, 47.

81 Marlies Glasius, 'What Authoritarianism Is . . . and Is Not: A Practice Perspective' (2018) 94 *International Affairs* 515.

82 N. W. Barber, *The Principles of Constitutionalism* (OUP 2018) 85.

83 See *ibid* 107–12.

protect the people's choices in a democracy, but a lack of meaningful elections would also undermine the efficacy of rule of law.

Together, the three components – free and fair elections, the protection of liberal rights, and the rule of law – form the concept of democracy that is used throughout this book. This is by no means the only way of conceptualizing a democracy (and rule of law). But, under this conception, a constitutional court emerges as a crucial actor in safeguarding democratic principles. Constitutional courts are needed to adjudicate on the propriety of an election, safeguard liberal rights, and to ensure that the incumbent administration is governing according to rule-of-law principles. The book later explores the democracy-enhancing functions of a constitutional court in a hybrid regime, and the analysis will be informed by this conception of a democracy.

1.7 Roadmap

The rest of the book is organized as follows. Chapter 2 presents an account of a hybrid regime and sets out its constitutional features. The chapter offers neither a thorough survey nor a critique of the debates within the field of regime classification. Rather, taking its cue from existing definitions, a hybrid regime is defined according to its efforts to create the impression of a democracy and its semi-competitive political system. This definition is broad enough to accommodate different institutional contexts and legal traditions, but specific enough to meaningfully distinguish a hybrid regime from a democracy, as well as from other kinds of authoritarian regimes. The constitution is shaped by the features of a hybrid regime, resulting in incoherent political legitimacy, an ambiguous institutional outlook, and a two-level constitutional dynamic that is constantly in flux. How these constitutional aspects of a hybrid regime are related to a constitutional court will also be highlighted throughout the chapter to set up the discussions later in the book.

Chapter 3 situates a constitutional court in a hybrid regime context by evaluating two common ways of understanding a constitutional court in an authoritarian context: the Pessimistic Model and the Optimistic Model. They are not categories of real-world courts, but different ideal types of a hybrid regime constitutional court, grounded in two different bodies of literature. A constitutional court is a very weak constitutional actor under the Pessimistic Model. That model sees a constitutional court as an instrument of the regime. In contrast, the Optimistic Model depicts a constitutional court as a democracy-builder, capable of, and tasked with, transforming a hybrid regime into a democracy. The two models reveal important insights: the prior calls attention to the empirical realities of authoritarian judicial politics, while the latter emphasizes the moral responsibility of judges in hybrid regimes. Nevertheless, I argue that both are incomplete. Reconciling the two models, I advance a more attractive account of a constitutional court under a hybrid regime – the Realistic Model – which recognizes what a constitutional court can realistically achieve. The Realistic Model informs the discussions of the subsequent chapters.

Chapter 4 examines the democratic role of a constitutional court in a hybrid regime. I begin by considering the counter-majoritarian difficulty or democratic objections against judicial review in the context of a hybrid regime. It has been argued by many that courts with constitutional review powers are democratically illegitimate because their exercise of such powers involves unelected judges exercising policymaking powers and deciding against the democratic will. These objections, I argue, are severely blunted as a result of the democratic deficit of a hybrid regime, which allows us to consider more closely how a constitutional court can uphold democratic ideals in a hybrid regime. Specifically, five different kinds of democracy-enhancing roles are proposed: (1) the referee role, (2) the interpretative role, (3) the participatory role, (4) the quasi-representative role, and (5) the educative role. As emphasized before, these roles do not substitute for the political process, but instead rely on familiar aspects of a constitutional court, and are responses to various kinds of democratic failures in a hybrid regime. These roles are limited, and one such limitation relates to constitutional courts' lack of competence to realize these roles. I argue that some of these concerns are answerable, and that a certain degree of departure from the normative boundaries imposed by competency considerations is also justified given the potential to advance democratic causes by these roles.

Chapter 5 looks at a practical problem a hybrid regime constitutional court faces: the legitimacy paradox. A hybrid regime constitutional court must be sensitive to the views of two different constituencies: the democratic constituency and the authoritarian constituency. The two constituencies are natural extensions of a hybrid regime. The problem, however, is that the two constituencies subscribe to fundamentally opposing ideologies and tell incompatible stories of judicial legitimacy. The different ways in which the two constituencies shape judicial power in a hybrid regime are then illustrated. Failure to accommodate either or both constituencies destabilizes a court's constitutional position and renders the normative discussion of its democratic roles redundant. The chapter draws on a sociological conception of judicial legitimacy and an audience-based framework to better understand the nature of the dilemma and its practical implications for a constitutional court.

Chapters 6 and 7 address the tensions arising from the application of the democracy-enhancing roles (Chapter 4) in the face of the legitimacy paradox (Chapter 5). More specifically, Chapter 6 proposes an adjudicative theoretical framework that systematically integrates democratically informed judging with judicial strategy. The framework involves two steps: identifying the "ideal position" with an institutional blindfold on (or, forming an initial view of what the law requires under the democracy-orienting approach proposed in Chapter 4) and lifting the blindfold to check whether – and, if so, how – the ideal position should be supplemented by judicial strategy. The framework helps judges determine when it is permissible to allow prudential considerations to impact judicial decision-making. The chapter also documents a wide range of adjudicative judicial strategies and describes how they can and should be deployed to accommodate authoritarian pressures and/or improve the judiciary's institutional strength. The goal of the adjudicative framework is a meaningful and sustainable realization of the judges' democracy-enhancing roles in hybrid regimes.

Chapter 7 discusses the non-adjudicative techniques judges can and should use to protect the judiciary and reinforce its democracy-enhancing roles. The chapter extends the audience-based framework proposed in Chapter 5 and draws attention to what judges can and should do outside the courtroom to create allies and defuse enemies. It highlights the institutions capable of protecting the court, and the techniques that judges can apply to build relations with these institutions. It also discusses the ways in which judges can address hostile parties, as well as more drastic measures they can resort to when the court or the polity faces an existential crisis. The tools discussed in this chapter may seem at odds with the traditional conception of the judicial role. Nevertheless, the fact that constitutional protection of the court tends to be relatively weak in a hybrid regime offers a justification for judges taking on a more socially prominent role. Focusing on the relations between judges and other political actors underscores the socially constructed nature of judicial power, especially in a hybrid regime. The Appendix illustrates how the techniques introduced in Chapter 7 can be applied using the case of Hong Kong.[84]

[84] This Appendix was not in the original manuscript. It was, however, part of the article, Julius Yam, 'Judging Under Authoritarianism' (2024) 87 *Modern Law Review* 4, 894–925, which was published subsequent to the completion of the monograph and was partly based on Chapter 7 of this book.

2

The Hybrid Regime and the Constitution

2.1 Introduction

This chapter has two objectives. The first is to answer the question of what a hybrid regime is. Hybrid regimes are an ambiguous regime-type. The concept was first introduced around the end of the Cold War,[1] and, at the time, was understood as capturing systems that "combine elements of both authoritarianism and democracy."[2] Many offshoot terms have subsequently been developed, including "illiberal democracy,"[3] "competitive authoritarianism,"[4] "partial democracy,"[5] "electoral authoritarianism,"[6] "semi-democracy,"[7] "semi-authoritarianism,"[8] "quasi-democracy,"[9] and "pseudo-democracy."[10] The "excessive proliferation"[11] of terms associated

[1] The existence of hybrid regimes was not a new phenomenon, but their proliferation after the third wave of democratization necessitated the delineation of a new concept. See Steven Levitsky and Lucan A. Way, *Competitive Authoritarianism: Hybrid Regimes after the Cold War* (CUP 2010) 60. Robert Dahl's model of polyarchy introduced in 1971 provided a rough model for conceptualizing middle-ground regime-types. See Robert Dahl, *Polyarchy: Participation and Opposition* (YUP 1971).

[2] Terry Lynn Karl, 'The Hybrid Regimes of Central America' (1995) 6 *Journal of Democracy* 72, 73.

[3] Fareed Zakaria, 'The Rise of Illiberal Democracy' (1997) 76 *Foreign Affairs* 22.

[4] Levitsky and Way (n 1).

[5] Lee Epstein, Jack Knight, and Olga Shvetsova, 'The Role of Constitutional Courts in the Establishment and Maintenance of Democratic Systems of Government' (2001) 35 *Law & Society Review* 117.

[6] Andreas Schedler, *The Politics of Uncertainty: Sustaining and Subverting Electoral Authoritarianism* (OUP 2013).

[7] Larry Diamond, *Developing Democracy: Toward Consolidation* (JHUP 1999).

[8] Marina Ottaway, *Democracy Challenged: The Rise of Semi-authoritarianism* (Carnegie Endowment for International Peace 2003).

[9] Diamond (n 7).

[10] Nic Cheeseman and Brian Klaas, *How to Rig an Election* (YUP 2018).

[11] David Collier and Steven Levitsky, 'Democracy with Adjectives: Conceptual Innovation in Comparative Research' (1997) 49 *World Politics* 430, 451.

with hybrid regimes has caused confusion in the field.[12] This book draws on some of these concepts, but retains the use of "hybrid regime" as it best captures their mix of democratic and authoritarian elements.

A hybrid regime presents itself as a functioning democracy, but the incumbent has disproportionate control over the rules of the game. Hybrid regime elections are therefore semi-competitive: although opposition success is possible, incumbent success is the more probable outcome.[13] Elections in a hybrid regime are also disingenuous: they pretend to be democratic but are actually unfair. Section 2.2 will explore this account of a hybrid regime in more detail.

The account presented is an ideal type, and, as such, it does not aspire to faithfully represent reality. Rather, by abstracting from real-world instances, it emphasizes certain characteristic features of a hybrid regime in order to illuminate subsequent discussion. It is not the only way of looking at a hybrid regime, but the features discussed here are shared among many hybrid regimes and are of significance to the book.

The second objective of the chapter is to identify points of tension between a hybrid regime's constitution and the constitution of a good state. This allows us to better understand the implications a hybrid regime has for a constitution. By constitution, I do not mean the written constitution, or large-C constitution, but rather the elements that build up and constitute a state. The chapter shows that three constitutional features tend to be found in a hybrid regime as defined here: rivaling constitutional ideologies of democracy and guardianship (Section 2.3); a trifurcated dual state legal order (Section 2.4); and two levels of constitutional battle (Section 2.5). Along the way, and to preface the next chapters, I suggest how these features might impact a constitutional court in a hybrid regime.

2.2 Defining a Hybrid Regime

Much of the literature in the field of comparative constitutional studies relies on the democracy-versus-authoritarian-regime dichotomy.[14] Democracy and authoritarian regimes are depicted as binary categories, with an

[12] See Lee Morgenbesser, 'Elections in Hybrid Regimes: Conceptual Stretching Revived' (2014) 62 *Political Studies* 21; Andrea Cassani, 'Hybrid What? Partial Consensus and Persistent Divergences in the Analysis of Hybrid Regimes' (2014) 35 *International Political Science Review* 542.

[13] See Schedler (n 6) 141.

[14] See Tamir Moustafa, 'Law and Courts in Authoritarian Regimes' (2014) 10 *Annual Review of Law and Social Science* 281, 294.

authoritarian regime defined negatively in relation to a democracy. That is, a state is classified as an authoritarian regime when it lacks any one of the necessary elements constituting a democracy, such as free and fair elections and civil-political rights protection.

The dichotomous approach has its methodological advantages. It makes it convenient and more feasible to conduct certain kinds of large-N empirical studies. It excels when the comparators exhibit sharp empirical differences. Nonetheless, the fact that a regime is not a democracy does not necessarily mean that it is authoritarian. Failed states, for instance, are neither democratic nor authoritarian. More importantly, this approach performs poorly when the subjects of the study sit somewhere along the spectrum between democracy and pure authoritarian regime. Under the dichotomous approach, a hybrid regime would be classified as an authoritarian regime because it falls short of a democracy. However, it is evident that the political structure of hybrid regimes like Pakistan or Turkey have little in common with regimes that are close to the authoritarian end of the spectrum like Mainland China or Saudi Arabia. The dichotomous approach obscures the distinct political patterns generated by a hybrid regime. Critiquing the current body of literature, Tamir Moustafa writes, "The once hard-and-fast distinction between democratic and authoritarian polities is increasingly blurred, as is clear from the proliferation of new adjectives and categories to describe hybrid regimes. A sharp dichotomy between democratic versus authoritarian political systems is less helpful than ever for understanding the way that power is organized, institutionalized, and contested in any given polity."[15] The emergence of regimes that are neither classically democratic nor authoritarian engenders a need to further differentiate between a hybrid regime and a pure authoritarian regime. In addition, introducing the concept of a hybrid regime also helps us recognize the normative superiority of a hybrid regime over a pure authoritarian regime, given that it embodies at least some democratic norms and institutions. Put differently, adopting the concept of a hybrid regime has both descriptive and normative implications for how we understand constitutionalism in these ambiguous states.

2.2.1 *Semi-competitive Elections*

There are two defining features (and several subfeatures) of a hybrid regime. The first relates to the regime's level of electoral competitiveness,

[15] *ibid.*

which is the most common way of defining a hybrid regime, especially among political scientists. A hybrid regime's level of electoral competitiveness is semi-competitive.[16] Semi-competitiveness is a relative quality and measured in degree: it lies in between free and fair, and noncompetitive. A free and fair electoral system defines a democracy, while elections in a pure authoritarian regime are noncompetitive or nonexistent.

To understand what semi-competitiveness is, it is helpful to first clarify what "free and fair" and "noncompetitive" mean respectively. As suggested in Chapter 1, a democratic system is understood to be the best means of giving substance to the idea of political equality. Democracy, then, is not only about universal suffrage or majoritarianism. To be counted as a democracy, formal features of a state's electoral system must be guided by the normative value of political equality. A free and fair electoral system treats citizens as political equals. It guarantees that all citizens can formulate and signal their preferences freely. Restrictions on the public's ability to participate and contest in elections should also be minimal.

How do we know if an electoral system is free and fair? Several kinds of analytical tools help answer this question. They also permit a diagnosis of electoral systems in the other regime-types. Samuel Huntington famously suggested the two-turnover test – that is, a state must survive two electoral turnovers of power – to check whether a democracy has truly been consolidated.[17] While looking at peaceful turnover rates can be indicative, this test is inconclusive. Applying it to postwar Japan, for instance, would lead to the conclusion that the country only became a democracy in 2009, even though democratic institutions and norms were entrenched well before this. The test fails to account for the fact that dominant parties can legitimately exist in democracies.

One way to address this gap is to examine the institutional guarantees of the state. A free and fair election requires certain institutional guarantees, including universal and equal suffrage, the right to run for office,

[16] It should be noted that some scholars make a distinction between hegemonic electoral authoritarian regime and competitive authoritarian regime: the incumbent almost always wins in the former, whereas the opposition enjoys a better chance in the latter. The difference is in the degree of electoral uncertainty. While the two terms offer a finer typology by establishing an additional cut-point, my account is sufficient for current purposes to highlight the distinctiveness of a hybrid regime, as compared to a democracy and a pure authoritarian regime. The current account covers competitive authoritarianism and, to a large extent, hegemonic electoral authoritarianism. See Schedler (n 6); Levitsky and Way (n 1).

[17] Samuel Huntington, *The Third Wave: Democratization in the Late Twentieth Century* (University of Oklahoma Press 1991).

freedom of expression and assembly, and alternative sources of information.[18] An electoral system is counted as free and fair when *all* these institutional conditions are present. In other words, democracy is treated as a "bounded whole" concept, whereby all institutional features constituting a democracy must be present in order for a given political entity to qualify as one.[19]

Besides looking at turnover rates and institutional conditions, the question can also be approached from the angle of the citizens. Andreas Schedler argues that a democratic system must guarantee the citizens' effective realization of "democratic choice."[20] This choice consists of seven interconnected dimensions and is conceived of as a logical sequence: (1) empowerment: citizens must be authorized to access state power; (2) freedom of supply: citizens must be free to select from a range of choices; (3) freedom of demand: citizens must be free to form preferences; (4) inclusion: all citizens are entitled equal opportunities to participate in the political process; (5) insulation: citizens must be free to express preferences; (6) integrity: citizens' preferences are weighed with equal consideration; and (7) decisiveness: elections must have consequences and these consequences must follow directly from the electoral results. The list, I reiterate, is interconnected. A fair electoral system must guarantee the complete fulfilment of all seven dimensions. Universal suffrage is meaningless, for instance, if choices are restricted. Suboptimal outcomes produced at one stage are carried forward and thus affect the entire chain of democratic choice. "Partial compliance with democratic norms does not add up to partial democracy," as Schedler warns, "[and] [g]ross violation of any one condition invalidates fulfilment of all others."[21]

Free and fair elections require maximizing the substantive value of political equality in the electoral process. At the other end of the spectrum, a noncompetitive electoral system is devoid of this normative value. Voting is meaningless and electoral results are effectively predetermined. Electoral results are expected with certainty because of ex ante and/or ex post repression and manipulation.[22] If an electoral system

18 See Dahl (n 1).

19 Giovanni Sartori, *The Theory of Democracy Revisited* (Chatham House Publishers 1987) 184.

20 Schedler (n 6) 83.

21 *ibid* 86.

22 For the relationship between certainty of outcome and democracy, see Adam Przeworski, *Democracy and the Market: Political and Economic Reforms in Eastern Europe and Latin America* (CUP 1991) 10.

exists at all, there is no expectation of electoral turnover. Marred by institutional deficiencies, the electoral system is designed to deliberately obliterate the democratic choice of the people. A noncompetitive electoral system is a sham and should be treated as distinct from elections in democracies and hybrid regimes.

A semi-competitive electoral system occupies the middle ground between a free and fair system, and a noncompetitive one. A semi-competitive system is characterized by an uneven playing field. Crucially, one party – the incumbent – can and does establish asymmetry. The incumbent has disproportionate control over the rules of the game, and it abuses its position to manipulate the playing field in its favor. A semi-competitive system is, however, neither merely decorative nor a tool to strengthen authoritarian rule. In this asymmetric arena for political competition, there is meaningful space for the opposition to compete, albeit from a disadvantaged position.

A semi-competitive electoral system may look similar to that of a democracy, but closer examination reveals substantive flaws. With self-evident titles, Schedler's article 'The Menu of Manipulation' and Nic Cheeseman and Brian Klass' book *How to Rig an Election* document the many strategies authoritarians can use to manipulate and rig elections.[23] Party bans, threats, bribery, divide-and-conquer strategies, and abusing emergency powers are some of the many familiar techniques that authoritarians have relied on to defeat their opposition. More creative ways to hack an election also exist. For instance, Musharraf introduced a requirement in 2002 that parliamentary candidates must hold a bachelor degree, a policy that denied 96 percent of all voters the right to run for office.[24] In Hong Kong, those who are not regarded as patriots cannot run for elections.[25] This rule, broadly interpreted by the incumbent regime, effectively bars a vast number of opposition members from competing in elections. While election-rigging is often quite public in nature, authoritarians also adopt clandestine strategies. For example, Turkey and the Philippines have used online troll armies to spread propaganda and counter critics, while a substantial number of

[23] Andreas Schedler, 'Elections Without Democracy: The Menu of Manipulation' (2002) 13 *Journal of Democracy* 36; Cheesman and Klass (n 10).

[24] Aqil Shah, 'Pakistan's "Armored" Democracy' (2003) 14 *Journal of Democracy* 26, 28. The policy was subsequently struck down by the Supreme Court.

[25] Decision of the National People's Congress on Improving the Electoral System of the Hong Kong Special Administrative Region (Adopted at the Fourth Session of the Thirteenth National People's Congress on March 11, 2021).

nondemocratic regimes have hired public relations firms to help diffuse or bury negative publicity.[26]

Because of the countless ways to weaken the democratic core of an electoral system, there is "extraordinary political diversity"[27] across electoral systems of hybrid regimes. In general, though, these violations of democratic norms are not as egregious as those in pure authoritarian regimes; the chain of democratic choice, though severely impaired, is not entirely severed. There is some resemblance between electoral results and voters' choice. Voting in a semi-competitive electoral system is not meaningless because reasonable opportunities and political space exist for the opposition to make electoral gains.[28] To win the same number of seats as the ruling faction, the opposition has to incur significantly higher costs compared to the incumbent. As Diamond puts it, "[opposition success] requires a level of opposition mobilization, unity, skill, and heroism far beyond what would normally be required for victory in a democracy."[29]

The silver lining, though, is that authoritarian success is not guaranteed, and the incumbent faces genuine electoral uncertainty, albeit to a more limited degree than in a democracy. Or, as Steven Levitsky and Lucan Way put it, "incumbents are forced to sweat."[30] Transfer of power through the ballot box unfortunately has never occurred in Museveni's Uganda or post-handover Hong Kong, but in both states the incumbents have had to invest tremendous resources in electoral campaigning and other strategies. Unlike elections in pure authoritarian regimes, those in hybrid regimes are nontrivial. The 2008 parliamentary election in Pakistan exemplifies how an election can unseat a hybrid regime incumbent, with Musharraf finally resigning to avoid impeachment after his party's electoral defeat. The electoral defeat of Yahya Jammeh in the Gambia in 2016 and Malaysia's 2018 general election are other examples of hybrid regime incumbents being unseated. Hybrid regime elections matter because they are sufficiently autonomous to affect the political trajectory of the regime.[31]

[26] Lee Morgenbesser, 'The Menu of Autocratic Innovation' (2020) 27 *Democratization* 1053.

[27] Milan W. Svolik, *The Politics of Authoritarian Rule* (CUP 2012) 19.

[28] Levitsky and Way (n 1) 8–12.

[29] Larry Diamond, 'Elections Without Democracy: Thinking about Hybrid Regimes' (2002) 13 *Journal of Democracy* 21, 24.

[30] Levitsky and Way (n 1) 12.

[31] Schedler (n 6) 375.

Schedler has an excellent way of describing elections in hybrid regimes: "at each election, authoritarian success is the rule (the probable outcome), opposition success the exception (the possible outcome)."[32] That is, as a result of the incumbent abusing its positional advantage, opposition success is only a possible outcome in this asymmetrical arena. However, the estimative words "probable" and "possible" also reflect the state of mind of political actors in an election. The opposition must *believe* that there is this possibility; else, their investment of time and resources in competing in an unfair election would be unjustified. The opposition's choices contribute to the definition of a semi-competitive election. The fact that they *choose* to compete and invest time and resources in campaigning creates the uncertainty that characterizes a semi-competitive election. The subjective belief of the opposition is formed in response to their institutional environment. It would be irrational for the opposition to maintain their campaign efforts if they perceived they had absolutely no chance of election victory. Since 2020, the Hong Kong and Mainland Chinese governments have implemented a series of measures that restrict the space for opposition in Hong Kong, including by enacting the National Security Law and by disqualifying a number of democratically elected opposition lawmakers.[33] The decision of virtually all remaining opposition lawmakers to resign together was a leading indicator of Hong Kong's authoritarian turn. This move was interpreted as a sign of protest against the regime, but, more importantly, it showed that the electoral system was no longer regarded as semi-competitive. The opposition's actions in this instance indicated that the system had entered a noncompetitive phase.

[32] *ibid* 141.

[33] The Law of the People's Republic of China on Safeguarding National Security in the Hong Kong Special Administrative Region (passed by the NPCSC and gazetted in Hong Kong in the schedule to L.N. 136 of 2020 on June 30, 2020); Decision of the Standing Committee of the National People's Congress on Issue Relating to the Qualification of the Members of the Legislative Council of the Hong Kong Special Administrative Region (L.N. 213 of 2020) and Announcement pursuant to the Decision of the Standing Committee of the National People's Congress on Issues Relating to the Qualification of the Members of the Legislative Council of the Hong Kong Special Administrative Region (L.N. 214 of 2020); Announcement pursuant to the Decision of the Standing Committee of the National People's Congress on Issues Relating to the Qualification of the Members of the Legislative Council of the Hong Kong Special Administrative Region (G.N. [E.] 607 of 2021).

2.2.2 "We Are a Democracy"

The second defining feature of a hybrid regime is its pretense to democracy. "Virtually all hybrid regimes in the world today are quite deliberately *pseudodemocratic*,"[34] Larry Diamond writes. Frequently described as the main game in town, democracy is "the most common . . . [claim to political legitimacy] to be found in the modern world."[35] Authoritarians today have accordingly felt an "unprecedented pressure" to adopt "the democratic form."[36] Wearing the democratic cloak not only legitimizes the regime to an extent, but it also comes with instrumental benefits, such as improving diplomatic relations, gaining access to international trade agreements, avoiding economic sanctions, reinforcing its soft power, and receiving international donor aid.

One way of pretending to be a democracy is to speak its language.[37] Uganda's "no-party democracy" before 2006 was packaged as a kind of democracy more suited to Africa. Even foreign donors were convinced by this system, with Western donors commenting at the time that "what is happening in Uganda is . . . your own type of democracy that is trying to fit into the Ugandan context."[38] Shortly after taking power through a military coup, Pakistan's Musharraf promised to restore the state to what he called a "real democracy."[39] Reforms, however, mostly occurred only on a local level,[40] and elections were routinely rigged.[41] Leaders from Singapore,[42] Hungary,[43] and Russia[44] have all consistently

[34] Diamond (n 29) 24.

[35] Craig Matheson, 'Weber and the Classification of Forms of Legitimacy' (1987) 38 *The British Journal of Sociology* 199, 203.

[36] Diamond (n 29) 24.

[37] Ottaway (n 8).

[38] As quoted in Nelson Kasfir, 'African Ambiguities: "No-party Democracy" in Uganda' (1998) 9 *Journal of Democracy* 49, 50.

[39] CNN, 'Pakistan Enters "Era of Real Democracy"' (March 23, 2008).

[40] Sumita Kumar, 'Sharif vs. Musharraf: The Future of Democracy in Pakistan' (2001) 24 *Strategic Analysis* 1861.

[41] Shah (n 24) 27.

[42] Lee Hsien Loong, 'Transcript of PM Lee Hsien Loong's Speech at the Debate on the Motion of Thanks to the President on 2 September 2020,' September 2, 2020, available at www.pmo.gov.sg/Newsroom/PM-Lee-Speech-at-the-debate-on-the-motion-of-thanks-to-the-president-Sep-2020, last visited April 28, 2023.

[43] The Economist, 'How Viktor Orban Hollowed Out Hungary's Democracy,' August 29, 2019, available at www.economist.com/briefing/2019/08/29/how-viktor-orban-hollowed-out-hungarys-democracy, last visited April 28, 2023.

[44] Radio Free Europe/Radio Liberty, 'Russia: Excerpts from Putin's State-of-the-Nation Speech,' April 25, 2005, available at www.rferl.org/a/1058630.html, last visited April 28, 2023.

described their states as democracies and cited democratic principles in support of their policies despite their clear violations of democratic norms.

In addition, a hybrid regime reminds people that it is a democracy by describing itself as such in a written constitution. "Democracy is achieved by the unremitting struggle of the people against oppression and tyranny," writes the Constitution of Pakistan in its preamble. The aspiration for universal suffrage is codified in Hong Kong's Basic Law, the city's mini-constitution.[45] The Constitution of Uganda stipulates a list of "democratic principles" that encompasses values like civic participation, representation, and political organization.[46] These constitutional promises are not entirely shams, as hybrid regimes do make some effort to give substance to those guarantees, and, as we shall see shortly, the claims made by hybrid regime incumbents are made believable by the existence of democratic institutions.

Another rhetorical technique is to manipulate concepts that are closely associated with a liberal democracy, most notably the rule of law. As a global financial hub that claims to be democratic, Hong Kong has cited the rule of law and "international practice" to justify controversial decisions and policies on numerous occasions, including the proposal of the controversial anti-extradition bill in 2019 and the subsequent crackdown on the opposition movement.[47] A similarly thin and narrow conception of the rule of law is routinely observed in Singapore.[48] Prime Minister Lee Hsien-loong calls "upholding rule of law key to Singapore's survival."[49] The rule of law, which seems to be equated with law and order, is used to justify dissent suppression and corporal punishment. By paying lip service to and manipulating liberal democratic ideals, a hybrid regime

[45] Basic Law of the HKSAR, Articles 45 and 68.

[46] Constitution of the Republic of Uganda, Objective II.

[47] Jennifer Creery, 'Hong Kong Leader Carrie Lam Says Gov't Cannot "Breach" City's Constitution in Conceding to Protester Demands,' *Hong Kong Free Press*, October 16, 2019, available at https://hongkongfp.com/2019/10/16/hong-kong-leader-carrie-lam-says-govt-cannot-breach-citys-constitution-conceding-protester-demands, last visited April 28, 2023; The Standard, 'National Security Legislation is International Practice: Chris Tang,' May 18, 2022, available at www.thestandard.com.hk/breaking-news/section/4/190277/National-security-legislation-is-international-practice:-Chris-Tang, last visited April 28, 2023.

[48] Yvonne Tew, *Constitutional Statecraft in Asian Courts* (OUP 2020) 109–12.

[49] Channel News Asia, 'Upholding Rule of Law Key to Singapore's Survival: PM Lee,' April 1, 2017, available at www.channelnewsasia.com/news/singapore/upholdingrule-of-law-key-to-singapore-s-survival-pm-lee-8709316, last visited November 5, 2020.

can "distract audiences from anti-democratic practices"[50] and deflect domestic and international criticism.

More importantly than rhetorical devices, a hybrid regime institutionalizes aspects of democracy. Hybrid regimes adopt the "trappings of democracy"[51] while simultaneously subverting them. This paradox stems from the regime's survival needs: to maintain political legitimacy while managing challenges arising from the adoption of democratic institutions. The more notable "democratic" institutions adopted by a hybrid regime include multiparty elections, a constitution with human rights protection, courts with de jure judicial independence, and a civil society with a plurality of voices. Indeed, elections in Musharraf's Pakistan, Museveni's Uganda, and post-handover Hong Kong were significant political events; constitutional challenges against these regimes were sometimes successful; and the civil societies in these states were reasonably vibrant.

The fact that democratic institutions exist in a hybrid regime does not mean their democratic substance is adopted wholesale, however. As discussed, elections in a hybrid regime are characterized by an uneven playing field that benefits the incumbent. A bill of rights may be selectively enforced in favor of the incumbent and its allies. De jure judicial independence, that is the formal guarantee of judicial independence, and de facto judicial independence, that is whether the courts actually enjoy autonomy, are related but separate matters. Courts in hybrid regimes, as I noted in Chapter 1, at best enjoy moderate levels of judicial independence. And, while there is political space for the opposition and dissidents to operate and organize in civil society, this space is constrained and controlled by the incumbent. The result is what Daniel Brumberg calls "dissonant institutionalization," whereby "competing images of political community and the symbolic systems legitimating them are reproduced in the formal and informal institutions of state and society."[52]

The key theme here is the paradoxical nature of a hybrid regime's institutionalization of aspects of democracy. This paradox dissolves, however, if the regime strays too close to authoritarianism. Its claim to democracy must be *credible* in order for it to exploit the benefits of making such claims. Even contemporary China and Zimbabwe self-

[50] Ozan O. Varol, 'Stealth Authoritarianism' (2015) 100 *Iowa Law Review* 4, 1673, 1716–17.

[51] Aili Mari Tripp, *Museveni's Uganda: Paradoxes of Power in a Hybrid Regime* (Lynne Rienner Publishers 2010) 1.

[52] Daniel Brumberg, *Reinventing Khomeini: The Struggle for Reform in Iran* (University of Chicago Press 2001) 33–4.

describe as democracies, but most external actors do not see them that way. Of course, this is not to say that pure authoritarian regimes are completely devoid of political legitimacy. They can still thrive on performance legitimacy or justify themselves using other political theories.[53] The point is that there are certain benefits associated with presenting a state as a democracy, and the claim must be sufficiently believable in order for the gains to be realized. This means that a hybrid regime's authoritarian impulses are tempered by its need to appear democratic. Hollowing out democratic institutions is against the spirit of hybridity, and a hybrid regime must retain at least a minimal level of normative substance in its democratic institutions.

In sum, elections in hybrid regimes are unfair but semi-competitive. Elections can be won by the opposition, but the incumbent makes this very unlikely by creating an uneven playing field. A hybrid regime purports to be a functioning democracy by adopting democratic institutions and deploying rhetorical devices, but at the same time subverts democratic institutions to limit opposition challenge.

2.3 Democracy and Guardianship: The Two Constitutional Ideologies

The sections that follow explore three implications of a hybrid regime for constitutions. At the end of each section, I briefly highlight those implications that are relevant to a constitutional court in a hybrid regime, in order to foreshadow the discussion in later chapters.

This first feature is two conflicting ideologies being encompassed by a single constitutional order, which creates a dissonance at the heart of a hybrid regime's constitution.[54] Constitutions are normally disharmonic, allowing room to accommodate different views in society.[55] The problem here is that the disharmony is foundational: the two ideologies of a hybrid regime represent two irreconcilable visions of a legitimate state: democracy, and guardianship, which as will be explained shortly is a political theory that most charitably explains authoritarian regimes. This is reflected in the way a hybrid regime institutionalizes aspects of democracy while stripping away its substance. As I later explain, the legal

[53] See Dingxin Zhao, 'The Mandate of Heaven and Performance Legitimation in Historical and Contemporary China' (2009) 53 *American Behavioral Scientist* 416.

[54] See also Feyzi Karabekir Akkoyunlu, 'The Rise and Fall of the Hybrid Regime: Guardianship and Democracy in Iran and Turkey' (PhD thesis, LSE 2014).

[55] Gary Jacobsohn, *Constitutional Identity* (HUP 2010).

order of a hybrid regime is structured in a way that no single form of political ideology is capable of legitimation. Democratic ideals can justify a hybrid regime's democratic institutions and practices, but clearly not its authoritarian ones, as they are against the very spirit of democracy.

The best normative reading of the authoritarian institutions and practices of a hybrid regime is that they exemplify guardianship. Guardianship is a theory of legitimate political authority that is, in many ways, the antithesis to democracy. As Robert Dahl puts it, guardianship is the "perennial alternative"[56] to democracy. Guardianship represents the idea that society should be governed only by elites. Guardianship is justified on instrumental grounds: that it is better at producing political decisions of a higher quality. The idea of guardianship can be traced back to Plato's *Republic*, where he argued that society should be ruled by a few with "the expert knowledge of kingship."[57] Political power under guardianship is distributed according to competence and virtue, as opposed to equally under democracy. The right to rule is reserved for those who can understand the interests of others and identify the best solution for realizing the common good, and who are capable of governing virtuously. Classically, guardians are likened to philosopher-kings. There are many contemporary versions of guardianship, including epistocracy[58] and meritocracy.[59] Newer models of guardianship do not rely solely on idealized guardians, but also on the institutional designs that structure the constitution according to guardianship standards. For instance, supporters have proposed restricted franchise (i.e. franchise restricted to those who pass a competence test) and weighted voting based on political knowledge (i.e. the weight of one's vote is determined by one's demonstrated knowledge of politics) to realize guardianship ideals.[60]

The intuitive appeal of guardianship should not be ignored. Over the past decade, this idea has regained traction among certain politicians and academia. The rise of populism and democratic backsliding have fueled skepticism toward democracy. As people turn against democracy, they look to guardianship-esque solutions. Singapore and China, with their lack of democracy but perceived stability and economic success, are seen

[56] Dahl (n 1) 52.
[57] Plato, *Republic* 426d, 477d–e.
[58] Jason Brennan, *Against Democracy* (Princeton University Press 2016).
[59] Daniel Bell, *The China Model: Political Meritocracy and the Limits of Democracy* (Princeton University Press 2015).
[60] Brennan (n 58) 15.

as the posterchildren of guardianship. Inspired by them, some elected leaders have begun exploring how guardianship can be incorporated into democracies.[61] Voters in democracies are blamed for making poor political decisions. Frustration with the "ignorant" has led to calls to exclude the irrational, the uninformed, or the unintelligent. These critics argue that incompetent voters need to be protected from their own ineptitude, and guardianship limits the harms caused by political ignorance.

It should be clear why guardianship and democracy are regarded as rival concepts of political authority. Political equality is a tenet of democracy, and guardianship clearly violates this principle. Guardianship trades political equality in exchange for improved political outcomes. Under guardianship, the political process is only a tool for reaching good collective decisions, and the attractiveness of a given political process depends on its ability to effectively fulfill this function.[62] As Jason Brennan argues, "democracy is a hammer . . . [as] it is a means to an end, but not an end it itself . . . [D]emocracy is not intrinsically just."[63] Supporters of guardianship suggest that it is not necessarily arbitrary: disenfranchisement is arguably just if it can foster a more competent electorate and yield better political outcomes.[64]

Authoritarianism is not the same as guardianship, and not all supporters of guardianship defend dictators. Authoritarianism, as commonly used today, refers to arbitrary and illiberal practices.[65] Like democracy, guardianship is an ideal: a normative political theory about state legitimacy. Many authoritarian regimes we see in reality are, to borrow from Aristotle, "deviant" versions of guardianship. Just like tyranny is the perverse version of kingship under Aristotle's classification of constitutions, real-life authoritarian regimes are often mistaken applications of guardianship. While democracy can also degenerate into populism or a tyrannical majority, guardianship is particularly susceptible to becoming an excuse for authoritarianism.

Under the political context of reasonable disagreement, it is immensely challenging to establish standards to determine the correctness of

[61] Joshua Kurlantzick, 'Why the "China Model" Isn't Going Away,' *The Atlantic* March 21, 2013, available at www.theatlantic.com/china/archive/2013/03/why-the-china-model-isnt-going-away/274237, last visited April 28, 2023.

[62] Brennan (n 58) 11–14.

[63] *ibid* 14.

[64] *ibid* 17–18.

[65] Marlies Glasius, 'What Authoritarianism Is . . . and Is Not: A Practice Perspective' (2018) 94 *International Affairs* 515.

political outcomes and the definition of political competence. Theories of guardianship fail to convincingly address these issues. The arbitrarily imposed will of the dictator would, as a result, fail to give due respect to its people. Guardianship is also vulnerable to abuse by leaders due to the absence of checks. Under a democracy, powers are dispersed and elections are periodic. These institutional guarantees drastically reduce the chances of elite entrenchment.[66] Conversely, guardianship breeds elite entrenchment, with the "elite" being arbitrarily defined. As competent as the guardians might be, the guardianship model incentivizes the abuse of power for personal gain. The success of guardianship relies on the self-restraint of the ruler, but people with this level of virtue are rare. Quoting Aziz Huq and Tom Ginsburg, "a healthy skepticism about political actors is a powerful force for keeping those leaders honest and faithful to the moral and legal obligations of office."[67] Despite its flaws, democracy is better at resisting authoritarian capture. In addition, as elections elicit the consent of people to be ruled, democracy must have greater respect for political equality and individual autonomy.

A hybrid regime is its own regime type because of its distinct institutional structure and the unique political dynamics this creates. Unlike democracy and guardianship however, a hybrid regime does not represent a political ideal. Instead, the two rival theories of legitimacy – democracy and guardianship – come together to supply the normative basis for a hybrid regime, despite their fundamental incompatibility. The clash between these two ideals creates a dissonance at the heart of the constitution of a hybrid regime. This creates a constantly shifting evaluative basis, as subscribing to both theories of political authority is impossible. For example, disenfranchisement is regarded as a flaw under democracy, but may be consistent with guardianship if its justification is to limit voter ignorance or promote state stability. This constitutional dissonance can be intensely destabilizing as the regime struggles to find a coherent theory to justify itself. It also creates polarization within society as different social groups embrace opposing ideologies. That is not to say that a hybrid regime is self-defeating. Empirical evidence shows that hybrid regimes can achieve stability by deploying microlevel political strategies to mitigate the practical effects

[66] Samuel Bagg, 'The Power of the Multitude: Answering Epistemic Challenges to Democracy' (2018) 112 *American Political Science Review* 891.

[67] Tom Ginsburg and Aziz Z. Huq, *How to Save a Constitutional Democracy* (University of Chicago Press 2018) 245.

of this dissonance.[68] Nevertheless, this dissonance cannot be fully resolved.

Two conflicting conceptions of a constitutional court emerge as a result of the constitutional dissonance of a hybrid regime: one based on liberal democratic principles, and another based on guardianship or the authoritarian's ideology. In a democracy, the constitutional court ideally acts as a check on arbitrary public power and applies the constitution in accordance with liberal constitutional principles. In contrast, guardianship creates an expectation that the constitutional court should obey and implement the will of the authoritarian, thereby reducing it to an instrument of the incumbent regime. The constitutional court in a hybrid regime faces what I call a legitimacy paradox, and this paradox will be taken up in Chapter 5.

Conflicting ideologies can be a valuable asset for a constitutional court, granting it the authority to push or nudge the hybrid regime toward a more democratic constitution. Ideological clashes only occur when the norms underlying the two political ideologies are being enforced and put into practice by constitutional actors. The constitutional court has a role to play in this ideological tug of war. Its role may be limited, in the sense that it is not a positive legislator and cannot initiate democratic reforms, but, through its decisions, and perhaps in an incremental fashion, the court can shore up democratic norms by holding the regime accountable to the constitutional democratic norms that the regime purports to abide by. The destabilizing effect of this dissonance may also weaken the regime's ability to rein in a court that can mobilize support from prodemocracy segments of the population. If exploited in the right way by the constitutional court, the inherent dissonance of a hybrid regime can become its Achilles' heel.

2.4 Trifurcated Dual State

A state's constitutional ideology shapes its legal order, and the principles that structure a legal order give flesh to a state's constitutional ideology. This section argues that the legal order of most hybrid regimes is best characterized as a "trifurcated" version of a dual state, to use Cora Chan's terminology.[69] Before offering my account of a trifurcated dual state, I will first explain what a dual state is.

[68] Honorata Mazepus and others, 'A Comparative Study of Legitimation Strategies in Hybrid Regimes' (2016) 37 *Policy Studies* 350.

[69] Cora Chan, 'Pluralizing Constitutionalism' in Vicki C. Jackson and Madhav Khosla (eds), *Redefining Comparative Constitutional Law: Essays for Mark Tushnet* (OUP 2025) 363.

Writing during the earlier years of the Third Reich, Ernst Fraenkel argued that the Nazi regime was far from lawless. It instead consisted of two "states": the normative state and the prerogative state. The two states are legal in character, but are not separate legal systems, and belong to the same legal order. The normative state is, according to Fraenkel, "an administrative body endowed with elaborate powers for safeguarding the legal order as expressed in statutes, decisions of the courts, and activities of the administrative agencies,"[70] whereas the prerogative state is the "governmental system which exercises unlimited arbitrariness and violence unchecked by any legal guarantees."[71] The normative state represents law-based governance, while the prerogative state represents arbitrary governance, which is sometimes law-like. More importantly, the normative state is subordinate to the prerogative state. The prerogative state has the jurisdiction to decide jurisdiction, or "kompetenz-kompetenz." It is hence misleading to describe the two states as two halves of a legal order, as they are not on equal footing.

While the dual-state concept was first developed to characterize Nazi Germany, it is now used as an analytical tool to study legal systems in authoritarian regimes.[72] Considering how central law is to how authoritarians today rule, it is not surprising that legal orders in many authoritarian regimes fit the dual-state model. The two states entail two different visions and principles of governance. The prerogative state enables the authoritarian to exert control over matters of fundamental importance. Curiously though, the normative state reflects the authoritarian's (weak) commitment to constitutional-legal norms. Typically, the normative state is sustained by the authoritarian for instrumental reasons, such as creating the stability and predictability necessary for the economy to flourish, and providing a democratic façade for a hybrid regime.

Under the traditional model of a dual state, the normative state is not a liberal and democratic system.[73] The authoritarian's political dominance affects the law-making process and the substance of the resulting

[70] Ernst Fraenkel and Jens Meierhenrich, *The Dual State: A Contribution to the Theory of Dictatorship* (OUP 2017) xiii.

[71] *ibid.*

[72] Jens Meierhenrich, *The Remnants of the Rechtsstaat: An Ethnography of Nazi Law* (OUP 2018) chapter 9; Jan Christoph Suntrup, 'Between Prerogative Power and Legality: Reading Ernst Fraenkel's *The Dual State* as an Analytical Tool for Present Authoritarian Rule' (2020) 11 *Jurisprudence* 335, 348.

[73] Douglas Morris, 'The Dual State Reframed: Ernst Fraenkel's Political Clients and His Theory of the Nazi Legal System' (2013) 58 *The Leo Baeck Institute Yearbook* 5. However, the traditional account of a normative state allows for the possibility for a liberal

legislation. Kim Lane Scheppele's concept of "autocratic legalism" reminds us that authoritarians can attack the principles of democracy and constitutionalism while being fully compliant with rule-of-law principles, thinly defined, and procedural norms.[74] Singapore's infamous defamation law, for example, belongs to the normative state – its creation and implementation fully comply with legal norms, but it is designed to maintain social stability and target dissenters. An authoritarian may rely on both the normative and prerogative states to assert its powers.

The traditional model of the dual state describes a bifurcated legal order, with one domain (the normative state) being regulated by legal rules, and the other (the prerogative state) governing arbitrarily. While this version of a dual state aptly captures some of the tensions arising from the conflicting visions within a hybrid regime, a further distinction should be made with regard to the normative state in order to better represent a hybrid regime's legal order.

The normative state of a hybrid regime frequently goes *beyond* mere legality. Unlike the normative state of a pure authoritarian dual state, one will almost always find liberal constitutional guarantees in the normative state of a hybrid regime dual state. These guarantees are nontrivial. For example, in Hong Kong, Uganda, and Pakistan, the protection of rights is not limited to private law or politically uncontroversial areas. Political opposition has relied on the normative state to meaningfully challenge the government. Legal mobilization movements and successful constitutional review challenges are routinely observed as well. The liberal part of the normative state, of course, does not govern all areas outside the prerogative state, but its reach can be substantial, and its impact significant.

The normative state of a hybrid regime has liberal tendencies because of its defining characteristics. A hybrid regime's imperative to imitate a democracy necessitates adopting laws, legal structures, and institutions with liberal constitutional contents. As I argued, constitutions in hybrid regimes are not mere shams, and liberal constitutional guarantees are more likely to be enforced in hybrid regimes than in pure authoritarian regimes. Since the degree of political pluralism in a hybrid regime is meaningful, checks on how public power is exercised by the legislature exist. In many cases, there are consequences for constitutional

democratic system. Legality and liberal democratic norms can be, and are oftentimes, compatible.

[74] Kim Lane Scheppele, 'Autocratic Legalism' (2018) 85 *The University of Chicago Law Review* 545.

transgressions, and lots of important questions of law and constitutionality are open to contestation. The authoritarian may be instituting liberal constitutional guarantees for instrumental or disingenuous reasons, but the authoritarian's self-interest is precisely why the liberal part of the normative state is sizable and can meaningfully exist in a hybrid regime. These characteristics of a hybrid regime create an additional and more robust "layer" to the normative state of a hybrid regime.[75]

In short, the normative state of a hybrid regime comprises two layers: the "legality normative state," which fulfils the minimum requirements of rule of law, and the "liberal normative state," which protects liberal constitutional norms. Because of these liberal pockets, the legal order of a hybrid regime is better characterized as a trifurcated, not bifurcated dual state. These three domains – the prerogative state, the legality normative state, and the liberal normative state – combine to form the legal order of a hybrid regime. The existence and size of the liberal normative state is what usually distinguishes the legal order of a hybrid regime from that of a pure authoritarian regime.

While the two layers of the normative state help to legitimate a hybrid regime, the authoritarian essence of a hybrid regime is preserved through the prerogative state. When the regime faces an existential threat, it resorts to the prerogative state for political control instead of revealing its true colors through raw violence. The prerogative state encompasses areas where the authoritarian has absolute discretion. Authoritarians today have learnt to take advantage of their political dominance to conceal arbitrary governance behind the auspices of the "law." Life is unpredictable under the prerogative state. In Uganda and Pakistan, for example, the military has a huge presence and depends on the prerogative state to maintain its political power. The military courts in these countries have routinely been used to try opposition lawmakers[76] and normal civilians.[77] A hybrid regime authoritarian is generally reserved when acting on its prerogative powers, though, at least when compared to a pure authoritarian regime. This is because a hybrid regime cannot

[75] Chan (n 69) 4.

[76] Amnesty International, 'Uganda: Opposition MPs Must Not Be Tried in Military Court,' August 16, 2018, available at www.amnesty.org/en/latest/news/2018/08/uganda-opposition-mps-must-not-be-tried-in-military-court, last visited April 28, 2023.

[77] International Bar Association Human Rights Institute, *Judicial Independence Undermined: A Report on Uganda* (September 2007), available at https://allafrica.com/download/resource/main/main/idatcs/00011366:c4998078afbb451431dc9f210ed92a03.pdf, last visited April 28, 2023.

credibly call itself a democracy when what remains of its legal order is the prerogative state.

A hybrid regime's potential to unleash prerogative power should not be ignored or underestimated, however.[78] This potential is reflected in its political structure. Alongside Hong Kong's liberal constitutional order, for example, exists Beijing's unchecked discretionary power to have final say over the interpretation of the city's mini-constitution. Having issued only five interpretations since the handover, one might argue that Beijing has exercised great self-restraint in intervening in constitutional matters in Hong Kong. However, the selective use of this nuclear option reminds the opposition of what might ensue if they are unwilling to cooperate. This creates coercive effects similar to those when the prerogative state is actually activated. The mere potential to unleash the prerogative state is often enough to subdue the opposition and consolidate political control.

The three domains of a trifurcated dual state interact with one another,[79] and they are "independent yet interrelated."[80] The relative size of the three domains is a function of the formal legal and constitutional provisions, and, more importantly, is also shaped by organic developments in constitutional politics. The prerogative state, for example, might expand when the authoritarian faces a major crisis, crowding out the normative state as a result. There are more subtle and less "transgressive" means for the prerogative state to corrupt the normative state.[81] As authoritarian norms gain ground, state agents such as judges and lawmakers may act with "anticipatory obedience,"[82] exercising discretion in ways that correspond to the will of the authoritarian "in the absence of any directives … from the prerogative state."[83] The corrosive effect of the prerogative state in this instance will undermine the liberal normative state, but not *necessarily* the legality normative state, as anticipatory obedience of such can still be legally justified.

[78] This potential may seem to exist in democracies as well. We might, for instance, find statutory or constitutional provisions conferring similar discretion to the political branches. In reality, this potential is checked in democracies as there are legal and constitutional principles as well as political mechanisms to limit the use of this discretion. This potential is not a free pass in a democracy, but it is real in authoritarian regimes.

[79] Meierhenrich (n 72) 182–7.

[80] *ibid* 245.

[81] *ibid* 183.

[82] *ibid* 184.

[83] Cora Chan, 'From Legal Pluralism to Dual State: Evolution of the Relationship between the Chinese and Hong Kong Legal Orders' (2022) 16 *Law & Ethics of Human Rights* 99, 129.

The authoritarian can reduce the sizes of the two layers of the normative state, but it is also possible for the normative state to resist authoritarian encroachment or even expand. State agents in charge of enforcing the constitution and tensions created as a result of the conflicting ideologies of a hybrid regime can enlarge the normative state. The resilience of the normative state, especially the liberal normative state, depends on the will and capacity of state agents to safeguard liberal constitutional norms. A constitutional court emerges as a crucial actor that can shape the size of the normative state, as it understands the language of the constitution and can adapt to the political circumstances of a hybrid regime. A constitutional court has the power to interpret and apply the constitution in ways that fit the three domains. The boundaries between the domains are porous,[84] and a decision in one domain can affect the other domains. Since these boundaries are defined and determined in practice by judicial interpretation, the scope of the liberal normative state can be expanded by the constitutional court if it handles related constitutional questions properly. Legal reasoning is the practice of argumentation based on similarity and legal principles: a rule established in a prior case will be applied to a subsequent case with similar factual patterns.[85] Equality principles laid down in an LGBTQ rights case, for example, may be developed into equality principles that apply a broader range of circumstances beyond sexual orientation discrimination. Sitting at the fuzzy intersections of the three domains, a constitutional court can exploit the porous nature of a dual state to plant democratic norms. These can be used in the future to undermine the prerogative state and reinforce the liberal normative state.

2.5 Two-Leveled Constitutional Battle

Finally, a hybrid regime creates a particular dynamic within the constitutional order. As suggested earlier, elections in a hybrid regime are autonomous and consequential. Quoting Schedler, "the conflictive interactions that [hybrid regime elections] generate possess a logic of their own, an importance of their own, and effects of their own."[86] The rules favor the regime, but there is sufficient space for the opposition to meaningfully compete within the rules of the game so as to gain political

[84] Mark Tushnet, 'The Possibility of Illiberal Constitutionalism' (2017) 69 *Florida Law Review* 1367, 1375.

[85] Meierhenrich (n 72) 240–2.

[86] Schedler (n 6) 374.

power. An important opposition goal is, however, to change the constitution so as to remove the political asymmetry. As a result, the constitutional dynamics of a hybrid regime occur simultaneously on two levels: *within* constitutional rules and *over* constitutional rules.[87]

A two-level constitutional dynamic is not necessarily unique to hybrid regimes. In a democracy, constitutional actors fight over electoral votes and constitutional rules as well. However, *most* political competition in a democracy happens within agreed-upon constitutional rules. Election is accepted as the only legitimate way of constituting a government and transferring political power. As long as the fairness of the system is not an issue (which normally is the case for a democracy), the constitutional battle remains within the rules of the game. Every so often, there is pressure to alter the constitution to reflect updated norms or correct latent defects, but this occurs relatively infrequently compared to authoritarian regimes. In pure authoritarian regimes, elections are not meant for political competition: they are tools of governance that allow dictators to gather information and co-opt elites.[88] When the results are predetermined, it makes little sense for the opposition to invest significant energy in competing within the constitutional rules. The more pressing problem to be addressed is the constitution itself. The opposition seeks to initiate reforms and instigate fundamental change by changing the constitutional rules or by creating a new constitution.

A perpetual two-level constitutional battle is a necessary feature of a hybrid regime. The possibility of winning an election, though unlikely, offers enough incentive for the opposition to invest in competing within constitutional rules. "As soon as political institutions are granted minimal margins of power and autonomy," Schedler points out, "they can turn against the dictator."[89] Political competition within the constitutional rules will be activated once the electoral game is sufficiently competitive. The rules are unfair, but if the opposition invests enough time and resources in electoral competition and can overcome coordination challenges, they might succeed at the ballot box. This gives the opposition the political power to fundamentally transform politics.

Deciding whether to compete within or over constitutional rules is not a binary choice, though, and in a hybrid regime the two levels of competition co-occur. If the fairness of the game is the real problem, it also

[87] *ibid* chapter 4.

[88] Jennifer Gandhi and Ellen Lust-Okar, 'Elections under Authoritarianism' (2009) 12 *Annual Review of Political Science* 403.

[89] Schedler (n 6) 73.

makes sense for the opposition to compete over the rules. As Schedler puts it, "unwilling or unable to compete within given rules, parties extend their struggle to the rules itself. Rather than focusing their competitive energies on playing the game, they get continually drawn into fights over the basic rules and conditions of the game."[90] The political asymmetry between the incumbent and the opposition stokes conflict over the constitution. Winning on the level of constitutional rules usually requires an even higher degree of public attention and mobilization. Consequently, the opposition may organize mass protests and expose structural irregularities so as to spur public resistance. Other constituencies, such as foreign states and state agents, emerge as potentially important actors on this battlefront. A regime relies on state agents such as the bureaucracy and police to conduct its affairs. But, like any collective entity, a hybrid regime faces agency problems. Successful conversion of state agents into opposition allies can destabilize a hybrid regime, which gives the opposition greater bargaining power. Similarly, the opinion of foreign states may play a major role if the hybrid regime relies on international aid or is closely connected to the international community. International pressure may catalyze constitutional reform.

The challenge faced by the opposition under this two-level constitutional battle is deciding how to allocate their resources. Each strategic choice has an opportunity cost. The two levels are tightly connected, and a decision at one level impacts the options available at the other. For example, the opposition must decide the extent to which they should participate or boycott an unfair election. A higher level of opposition commitment to participation may increase the probability of winning the election, but the underlying asymmetry may already limit that probability. Boycotting an election delegitimizes it and may trigger mass mobilization, capturing the attention of the international community. This option also allows campaigning funds to be invested in other nonelectoral strategies instead. The risk of abandoning the within-constitutional-rule battlefront, however, is losing formal political representation in the legislature, and giving away veto and monitoring powers over public institutions. This challenge also reflects the autocrat's logic of instituting elections: these strategic dilemmas undermine challenge by the opposition. It is difficult for the opposition to make a series of right decisions, while wrong decisions may weaken their challenges on both battlefronts. Compounding the problem further is the fact that the

90 *ibid* 116.

opposition is not a monolithic entity, and there are collective action challenges that need to be resolved as well.

The interconnectedness of the two levels is also illustrated in the tough choices confronting the incumbent. As mentioned, a hybrid regime is characterized by its paradoxical intentions: to pretend to be a democracy while subduing the opposition. As the opposition's popularity grows, the incumbent may be tempted to manipulate the rules further or even resort to naked repression in order to guarantee electoral success. This may unintentionally trigger a backlash from the public and the international community. Assuming that a hybrid regime has not given up on its democratic pretense, the incumbent must also balance its strategies carefully to keep winning elections without corroding its democratic image.

Constitutional courts are crucial constitutional actors with a say at both levels of the constitutional battle. They have the power to determine whether political outcomes are reached in accordance with the rules of the game. This is not about challenging the authority of the rules, but about whether the political outcomes were properly reached given pre-existing rules. Some constitutional courts with jurisdiction over election petition and administrative law questions can apply procedural law, rule-of-law principles, and administrative law doctrines to determine the validity of political outcomes. On top of ensuring actors are playing by the rules, a constitutional court offers one of the most direct means of changing the rules of the game through its determination of the meaning of constitutional rules. When the fairness or constitutionality of the rules are questioned, the court is asked to step in and "clarify." Its decisions may also help raise domestic and international awareness of controversial issues, which can then become focal points for mass mobilization and catalysts for regime change.

Considering the centrality of constitutional courts to dynamics at these two levels, it is no wonder that a constitutional court is a factor in the strategic calculations of both the opposition and the incumbent. The opposition must decide how much it should invest in legal mobilization. Court cases can be costly and time-consuming. The chances of success may also depend on the legal merits of the case and the type of issue being litigated. Even if a favorable judgment is secured, the implementation of the decision depends on the will of the government. Nevertheless, the expected gains of pursuing a legal strategy, which I explore further in Chapter 4, may sometimes be higher relative to competing in the political process. The incumbent must also decide how to balance political control and judicial autonomy. Competent judges may legitimate and improve a hybrid regime's legal system, but these judges may not always be loyal. Even if the regime can control the appointment process, out of self-respect or a concern to protect their own legacy, not all appointed judges are necessarily loyal to the regime. The incumbent may be tempted to resort to ex post means of interference, such as removing judges who challenge the regime, diluting the powers of defiant judges (as in Hungary and Poland), or even assassinating them (e.g. the execution of the chief justice of Uganda, Benedicto Kiwanuka). These more drastic forms of interference will generally backfire on the regime. The lawyers' and judges' movements in Pakistan and Uganda were direct responses to the naked repression of judges, and both movements won the support of the local population and the international community.

2.6 Conclusion

With diverging impulses toward democracy and authoritarianism, a hybrid regime has schizophrenic tendencies: it imitates a democracy while limiting its own democratic potential. The defining features of a hybrid regime have three different implications for its constitution. On an ideological level, a hybrid regime does not have a unifying theory of political legitimacy. Instead, it must cope with two rivalling legitimation stories: democracy and guardianship. On a legal-institutional level, democratic institutions curiously coexist with authoritarian ones, with different conceptions of "legality" competing with one another. In terms of constitutional dynamics, political competition in a hybrid regime takes place at two levels as constitutional actors compete within and over constitutional rules.

These questions inevitably impact the way a constitutional court behaves and how it should act in a hybrid regime, which is the focus of the rest of the book. A constitutional court is conditioned by the sociopolitical context it operates in. The dynamic interplay between democracy and authoritarianism created by the hybridity forces us to reconsider the nature and normative role of a constitutional court. This chapter introduced some of the themes that will be explored in greater depth later on. The next chapter situates a constitutional court in a hybrid regime context. I consider two common ways to think about a constitutional court in a hybrid regime, and develop insights that are relevant to advancing an attractive account of a constitutional court.

3

Constitutional Courts in Hybrid Regimes

3.1 Introduction

The chapter situates constitutional courts within a hybrid regime context. It presents three models of what courts could be like in hybrid regimes. The first two are what I call the Pessimistic Model and the Optimistic Model. They represent two different bodies of literature and two contrasting views of constitutional courts in hybrid regimes.

The chapter begins by examining the Pessimistic Model in Section 3.2. Under this model, a court can do very little to resist an authoritarian, let alone promote democratic norms. It characterizes a constitutional court as part of the authoritarian hierarchy of a hybrid regime, and views the court as an instrument of authoritarian governance. Those attached to this model are skeptical of whether judicial autonomy can truly exist. The regime chooses to institute and maintain a constitutional court for self-serving reasons, and the political environment leaves little space for judicial maneuvering.

While this model rightly highlights how a constitutional court is structurally constrained by a hybrid regime, I argue that the Pessimistic Model tends to overstate the degree of actual control a hybrid regime has over a constitutional court. I highlight the existence of several conditions conducive to the development of judicial autonomy and judicial power that are a consequence of how hybrid regimes are configured.

Section 3.3 proceeds to discuss a more encouraging depiction of a constitutional court. Those who subscribe to the Optimistic Model believe that a court can bring transformative changes to a hybrid regime. It views a constitutional court as the guardian of liberal democratic norms, possessing almost mystical powers that enable it to bring democratic change to a hybrid regime. The Optimistic Model stands for a body of literature that is less concerned with how authoritarian conditions impact a constitutional court, and more with constitutional court's moral responsibility under a hybrid regime.

This model rightly raises important questions about the normative role of a constitutional court in a hybrid regime, and challenges some of the assumptions about constitutional theory that are typically taken for granted in liberal democratic contexts. I argue, however, that the Optimistic Model overestimates the capabilities of a constitutional court. It pays insufficient attention to the prudential and institutional implications of a hybrid regime's political circumstances for the court.

While each model captures distinct elements and raises important issues regarding constitutional courts in hybrid regimes, each has gone too far. Drawing on the lessons learnt from the analyses of the previous two models, Section 3.4 concludes by presenting a more attractive model: the Realistic Model. By "realistic," I do not mean that courts in real life correspond more closely to this model, although it is informed by a nuanced take on judicial-political dynamics in a hybrid regime. Rather, under this model, a constitutional court aspiring to take up meaningful roles in a hybrid regime is a realistic possibility. The Realistic Model serves as the basis for our theoretical inquiries in the coming chapters.

3.2 The Pessimistic Model

The origin of the Pessimistic Model can be traced back to several decades ago when constitutional courts outside democracies were seen as insignificant institutions. This stems from a widely held assumption that judicial politics is conditioned by regime-type politics.[1] Operating in an environment where power was concentrated in the hands of the incumbent, constitutional courts in authoritarian polities were taken as "mere pawns of their rulers."[2] After all, it seems logical to suppose that only loyal judges who dare not challenge the ruler could keep their jobs. It was unimaginable for judges to rule against a regime that had power to threaten the judges' career and personal safety. The historical consensus was that the "judicialization of politics outside democratic polities" was

[1] See Donald W. Jackson and C. Neal Tate (eds), *Comparative Judicial Review and Public Policy* (Greenwood Press 1992); C. Neal Tate and Torbjorn Vallinder (eds), *The Global Expansion of Judicial Power* (NYU Press 1995).

[2] Tamir Moustafa and Tom Ginsburg, 'Introduction: The Functions of Courts in Authoritarian Politics' in Tom Ginsburg and Tamir Moustafa (eds), *Rule by Law: The Politics of Courts in Authoritarian Regimes* (CUP 2008) 1.

"very unlikely."[3] Structurally constrained, constitutional courts in authoritarian regimes were traditionally thought of as being obedient agents of the regime. Anecdotal evidence at the time also seemed to support this view. As Tamir Moustafa observes, "the assumption [that courts in nondemocratic regimes were little more than window dressing for dictators] was so widely accepted that research on judicial politics in nondemocracies was rare prior to the 1990s."[4]

The literature developed over the next thirty years or so as scholars became more aware of the variations in judicial behavior among non-democratic regimes. Some courts, in fact, were found to play a central role in authoritarian politics, enjoying substantial powers to decide on megapolitical questions.[5] There were even courts that successfully challenged and defied authoritarian regimes.[6]

While these more recent studies have significantly advanced debate, many maintain as pessimistic a tone as their predecessors when it came to what courts could do in an authoritarian context. Courts might not be puppets, but they are still largely regarded as authoritarians' instruments of governance, instituted and maintained for their benefit.[7] Judicial independence then becomes a function of the extent to which courts perform certain functions on behalf of the regime. For example, having a constitutional court might bolster the legitimacy of the regime,[8] attract investors,[9] help sideline opposition by enforcing oppressive laws,[10] or

[3] C. Neal Tate, 'Why the Expansion of Judicial Power?' in Tate and Vallinder (n 1) 28.

[4] Tamir Moustafa, 'Law and Courts in Authoritarian Regimes' (2014) 10 *Annual Review of Law and Social Science* 281, 282.

[5] Ran Hirschl, 'The Judicialization of Mega-politics and the Rise of Political Courts' (2018) 11 *Annual Review of Political Science* 93; Tom G. Daly, *The Alchemists: Questioning Our Faith in Courts as Democracy-Builders* (CUP 2017); Tom Ginsburg, 'The Politics of Courts in Democratization: Four Junctures in Asia' in Diana Kapiszewski, Gordon Silverstein, and Robert A. Kagan (eds), *Consequential Courts: Judicial Roles in Global Perspective* (CUP 2013).

[6] For some of the examples, see Eric C. Ip, *Hybrid Constitutionalism: The Politics of Constitutional Review in the Chinese Special Administrative Regions* (CUP 2019) 8 note 69; Yasser Kureshi, 'When Judges Defy Dictators: An Audience-based Framework to Explain the Emergence of Judicial Assertiveness against Authoritarian Regimes' (2021) 53 *Comparative Politics* 233, 251–2 note 1.

[7] Moustafa (n 4).

[8] Raul A. Sanchez Urribarri, 'Courts between Democracy and Hybrid Authoritarianism: Evidence from the Venezuelan Supreme Court' (2011) 36 *Law & Social Inquiry* 854.

[9] Tamir Moustafa, *The Struggle for Constitutional Power: Law, Politics, and Economic Development in Egypt* (CUP 2007).

[10] *ibid*; Jothie Rajah, *Authoritarian Rule of Law: Legislation, Discourse and Legitimacy in Singapore* (CUP 2012).

preserve hegemonic powers more generally.[11] These explanations focus on why incumbents are incentivized to have semi-independent courts.[12] Accordingly, the Pessimistic Model can account for why we might occasionally observe successful judicial challenges to incumbent rule in hybrid regimes. In fact, consistent with the logic of these endogenous explanations, some might even argue that these challenges are sometimes tolerated because they help improve the image of a hybrid regime as they are interpreted as evidence of political contestation.

As an instrument of the incumbent, the court continues to be subjected to its control, with seemingly few limits over how that control is exercised. The literature on court-packing identifies a wide arsenal of tools to discipline a judiciary when the costs of a defiant court outweigh its potential benefits. Some of these techniques are supplied or authorized by the constitution, hence appear soft and lawful to maintain public optics. For example, changing the composition of the court by adjusting the retirement age limit can serve to remove problematic judges without making that objective explicit. Similarly, weakening the judicial support structure[13] and changing access to justice rules[14] are attacks, though not directed at the judiciary, which can prove powerful in limiting a court's effectiveness.

The Pessimistic Model, as we can see, depicts a highly constrained constitutional court. This is perhaps unsurprising, as much of the literature on authoritarian judicial politics focuses on how regime-type politics influence judicial behavior. If the premise is that the strength of a court is associated with regime-type and that governmental powers are centralized in nondemocratic regimes, defeatist conclusions about the democratic potential of constitutional courts in hybrid regimes are to be expected. Judges are thought to be "products of the political divisions and the processes by which they are selected."[15] The judiciary is part of the government structure and necessarily subordinate to the regime. It follows that it is the incumbent that decides the degree of freedom

[11] See generally Ran Hirschl, *Towards Juristocracy: The Origins and Consequences of the New Constitutionalism* (HUP 2004).

[12] See Georg Vanberg, 'Constitutional Courts in Comparative Perspective: A Theoretical Assessment' (2015) 18 *Annual Review of Political Science* 167.

[13] See Charles R. Epp, *The Rights Revolution: Lawyers, Activists, and Supreme Courts in Comparative Perspective* (University of Chicago Press 1998).

[14] See Ceren Belge, 'Friends of the Court: The Republican Alliance and Selective Activism of the Constitutional Court of Turkey' (2006) 40 *Law & Society Review* 653.

[15] Mark Rush, 'Review of Fragile Democracies by Samuel Issacharoff' (2016) 15 *Election Law Journal* 193, 194.

enjoyed by the judges. The power imbalance between the courts and the regime implies that the former are always at the mercy of the latter. The fact that the courts do not advance the authoritarian's interests in a straightforward manner may explain occasional outbursts of judicial defiance. For instance, a court that stabilizes the regime by channeling conflicts may sometimes open space for opposition challenge.[16] Nevertheless, the Pessimistic Model maintains that these instances of judicial defiance are negligible or only mirages that are carefully engineered by the regime for its own benefits. On this view, courts are ultimately inconsequential actors.

This model exposes the complex judicial political dynamics underlying authoritarianism. It highlights the motivations and survival imperatives of an authoritarian, as well as how a court fits into the authoritarian's agenda. However, the Pessimistic Model tends to overstate the power and efficacy of a hybrid regime. That is, it gives insufficient attention to the political costs incurred by the incumbent from interfering with and attacking courts. Behind this model lies the questionable assumption that hybrid regimes are almost always able to successfully realize their intentions. An authoritarian regime is not a monolithic entity. This is especially true for a hybrid regime, which is characterized by ideological tensions and fragmented politics. Individuals who make up the incumbent regime may differ in their intentions and expectations of courts. Some members of the ruling coalition might value the reputational gains of an independent court and tolerate greater judicial autonomy, while more domineering elites may demand direct control over courts. Hence, even those in power may disagree over the role a court should play and the appropriate degree of influence political elites should wield over it. The court may also serve as a forum for disputes within the elite. Even if a regime can express a unified intention, it does not mean it can act at will. Like any other collective entity, a hybrid regime is subject to, among other things, institutional rules (such as internal decision-making procedures), internal resistance (such as infighting among the authoritarian bloc), external resistance (such as risk of sanction from foreign states), the risk of public mobilization, and electoral pressure in states with at least nominally competitive elections.[17] Many of these political constraints are not always as principled or ideal as constitutional rules, but

[16] Moustafa (n 4) 287.

[17] See Robert Barros, *Constitutionalism and Dictatorship: Pinochet, the Junta, and the 1980 Constitution* (CUP 2002); Ip (n 6).

they are effective to the extent that they can restrict the authoritarian's capacity for action. In economics terms, incumbents would have to incur "political transaction costs" to constrain courts.[18] Sanctioning a court involves bargaining, coordination, enforcement, and informational costs for the regime, all of which impair the regime's ability to discipline courts. The higher the political transaction costs, the more likely we will find an independent and strong constitutional court in a hybrid regime.[19] Last, one must not forget that the regime is not infallible. It can make mistakes, for example, by appointing judges who turn out to be less loyal than the incumbent expected. Iftikhar Chaudhry in Pakistan voted in ways that aligned with the incumbent before he was appointed as the chief justice, and Geoffrey Ma, the second chief justice of Hong Kong, represented the government in some of the landmark constitutional cases in Hong Kong before joining the bench. It is fair to say the Chaudhry and Ma courts were not as loyal to the incumbents as originally expected.

What I just described does not necessarily contradict the Pessimistic Model. There is a power imbalance between the regime and the court, and the regime's intentions and expectations shape the behavior and capacity of a court. What tends to be missed in these discussions, though, is the fact that a hybrid regime often cannot act exactly as it wishes. The regime's agency is shaped by a multitude of internal and external factors that diminish its ability to control the court, and may provide the time and space for a constitutional court to pursue its own agenda effectively.

3.2.1 *Features of a Hybrid Regime That Support Judicial Autonomy*

The authoritarian tendency of the hybrid regime is not the sole factor conditioning the identity of the constitutional court. There are also features that create conditions conducive to the development of an autonomous and strong constitutional court. Some features derive from the fact that the high political friction present in the environment of a hybrid regime impedes the regime's ability to act and react. For example, the friction often resurfaces in the community outside of that constitutional order, bringing social volatility to the hybrid state. Other features exploit the regime's incentives and motivations to institute a court in the first place. For example, the need to attract investors is highlighted as a factor conducive to an independent judiciary in authoritarian contexts. Focusing

[18] Ip (n 6).
[19] *ibid.*

on the Egyptian Constitutional Court, Moustafa argues that the regime relies on the judiciary to promote economic growth.[20] The need to maintain a stable and prosperous economy may create spillover effects that contribute to judicial independence. To a certain extent, his theory also applies to Hong Kong, as undermining judicial independence risks discrediting the regime's reputation as an international financial center. Similarly, a number of commentators attribute judicial independence in Uganda to pressure from international and foreign donors.[21] Rachel L. Ellett argues that the incumbent depends on development aid to pay off the regime's allies.[22] Maintaining judicial independence is one important precondition for aid. The regime risks losing an important source of funding if it persistently attacks the courts whenever they issue decisions that are against the government.

To further illustrate how a hybrid regime can actually empower a constitutional court, I identify three features of hybrid regimes that facilitate the development of judicial autonomy and judicial power: semi-competitive elections, political fragmentation, and a claim to democratic legitimacy. The aim is not to provide an exhaustive list of supportive factors, especially since there are possibly many context-specific conditions applicable to particular kinds of hybrid regimes that can equally, if not more significantly, support a constitutional court, such as the needs to attract foreign investors and maintain development aid as I just described.[23] Instead, the hope here is to highlight conditions that stem from the unique political configuration of hybrid regimes.

3.2.1.1 Semi-Competitive Elections

The electoral logic of judicial independence suggests that the political uncertainty generated by elections prompts political actors to adopt an impartial arbitrator.[24] Under electoral uncertainty, political actors from

20 Moustafa (n 9).

21 Rachel L. Ellett, *Pathways to Judicial Power in Transitional States: Perspectives from African Courts* (Routledge 2013); Erica Bussey, 'Constitutional Dialogue in Uganda' (2005) 49 *Journal of African Law* 1, 13.

22 Ellett *ibid.*

23 The factors to be discussed should be treated as weights. That is, the more of these factors are present, the more likely an autonomous court would emerge. It should also be mentioned that these factors are political determinants of judicial autonomy and power. Other more jurisdiction-specific, legal factors that are not discussed can also be significant, such as legal tradition, constitutional design, and formal judicial rules.

24 J. Mark Ramseyer, 'The Puzzling (In)dependence of Courts: A Comparative Approach' (1994) 23 *The Journal of Legal Studies* 721.

different factions have a reasonable chance of defeat. Uncertainty acts almost like the veil of ignorance, enabling political actors with divergent intentions to agree to adopt independent courts. The electoral logic rests on the self-interested nature of political actors and their inability to accurately predict where their interests are going to lie after an election. An independent court is a form of political insurance for conflicting parties that serves as a hedge against future risks. This hypothesis predicts that the higher the degree of electoral competition, the more likely an autonomous court will emerge.

The electoral logic of judicial independence was initially tested in consolidated democracies such as the United States and Japan, as well as new democracies.[25] The theory was thought to be inapplicable to non-democratic regimes because of the lack of electoral competitiveness.[26] One of the problems with this assumption stems from a dichotomous understanding of regime-types, and fails to recognize that elections in some authoritarian regimes can still be sufficiently meaningful and autonomous. The degree of electoral competitiveness in a hybrid regime may be sufficient to activate the electoral logic of judicial independence.

Brad Epperly's work confirms the relevance of the theory to hybrid regimes.[27] Motivated by the need to move away from dichotomies, Epperly's large-N study finds that the electoral logic can apply to non-democratic regimes, and that autocracies that are more electorally competitive tend to have more autonomous courts than those that are politically closed. In other words, moderate levels of political competition result in moderate levels of judicial autonomy. Explaining this phenomenon, he argues that the electoral logic of judicial independence is especially relevant to hybrid regimes because of the autocrat's fear of losing power. As the previous chapter highlighted, elections in hybrid regimes are unfair but sufficiently contested to create uncertainty for the incumbent. Semi-competitive elections increase the probability of the authoritarian losing power in elections. This electoral uncertainty is itself a reason to confer autonomy to courts. More importantly, the risks of losing power are significant for an authoritarian government, which is likely to have accumulated a long list of political enemies during its reign. Unsurprisingly, more than half of all post-tenure authoritarians have

25 *ibid*; Tom Ginsburg, *Judicial Review in New Democracies: Constitutional Courts in Asian Cases* (CUP 2003).

26 Moustafa and Ginsburg (n 2) 28.

27 Brad Epperly, *The Political Foundations of Judicial Independence in Dictatorship and Democracy* (OUP 2019).

been punished, with their political rights stripped, property confiscated, and personal security jeopardized.[28] As a political insurance, an independent court, as he finds, provides the necessary protection to minimize the risk exposure of an authoritarian by safeguarding rights. The anticipated cost of defeat at the ballot box (i.e. the chance of defeat as well as the risks associated with defeat) incentivizes the authoritarian to confer moderate levels of autonomy and power to courts in hybrid regimes.

3.2.1.2 Political Fragmentation

Political scientists posit that divided politics creates opportunities for courts to develop judicial autonomy and judicial powers.[29] Divided politics, or political fragmentation, refers to the number and nature of veto players involved in a decision-making process. Veto players are actors whose consents are necessary to change the status quo.[30] Veto players can be institutional or partisan in nature.[31] Institutional veto players are assigned by the constitution, whereas partisan veto players are outcomes of organic politics. For example, the three branches of government are usually institutional veto players under the separation of powers. In legislatures where multiple majorities are possible, the different majorities are partisan veto players. The more veto players' consent is required, the harder it is to alter the status quo. The nature of the veto players also matters: the more ideologically dissimilar the veto players are, the harder it will be for them to achieve consensus or compromise.[32] A higher degree of political fragmentation makes it harder for all veto players to reach a consensus to change the status quo. Court-curbing actions – as with any other legislation, policy, or constitutional amendment – are only possible when political actors with veto powers can agree. The difficulties of sanctioning courts in divided politics create a wider space for judicial maneuvering. The theory predicts that a politically fragmented environment is more likely to generate independent judiciaries and durable judicial decisions.

[28] *ibid* 34–5.

[29] Rebecca B. Chavez, John A. Ferejohn, and Barry R. Weingast, 'A Theory of the Politically Independent Judiciary' in Gretchen Helmke and Julio Rios-Figueroa (eds), *Courts in Latin America* (CUP 2011). An underlying logic that ties the electoral logic and political fragmentation theories is the diffusion of political powers.

[30] George Tsebelis, *Veto Players: How Political Institutions Work* (Princeton University Press 2002) 19.

[31] *ibid* 19–20.

[32] *ibid* 20.

The ideological tension between democracy and guardianship described in the first chapter manifests at all levels of a hybrid polity, including the governing bloc and civil society.[33] This ideological tension creates political fragmentation across different levels of society. With little in common between the rivalling theories of democracy and guardianship, the ability of a hybrid regime to ensure ideological homogeneity must be weak. Bureaucracies in Pakistan and Hong Kong, for example, have openly resisted the regime and ideologically differentiated themselves from their rulers on several occasions, demonstrating the kinds of internal challenges these regimes must overcome when punishing defiant courts.[34] An authoritarian regime can use top-down techniques to politically indoctrinate elites and state agents, but these techniques are difficult to impose in a hybrid regime, given its more decentralized structure and its need to uphold political pluralism, at least superficially.[35] The regime's inability to maintain ideological coherence results in more space for judicial maneuvering.

The regime and the opposition's struggle to compete for popular support exacerbates the political fragmentation of a hybrid regime.[36] Alliances with elites and the regime's organizational power are unsettled by opportunities for elites to join the oppositional front.[37] Normally, elite defection is unlikely if the ruling party is strong and/or the opposition party is weak. The power balance between the regime and the opposition can shift, however, and the opposition in a hybrid regime can sometimes pose a credible threat, creating attractive opportunities for elites seeking to defect. Or, on other occasions, elites who benefit from abandoning the regime may form their own party, causing infighting that threatens the integrity of the governing coalition.

Following political fragmentation theory, a hybrid regime court is afforded more leeway to exercise judicial powers given the fragmented nature of a hybrid regime. Since conflicting state ideologies permeate all levels of a hybrid regime society, implementing court-curbing actions can be challenging, as the regime needs to convince many ideologically dissimilar veto players within and outside the governing bloc.[38] As

33 Ip (n 6) 47.

34 See *ibid*; Yasser (n 6).

35 Ip (n 6) 47–8.

36 Andreas Schedler, *The Politics of Uncertainty: Sustaining and Subverting Electoral Authoritarianism* (OUP 2013) 49–50.

37 Steven Levitsky and Lucan A. Way, *Competitive Authoritarianism: Hybrid Regimes After the Cold War* (CUP 2010) 68–70.

38 See Julio Ríos-Figueroa, 'Fragmentation of Power and the Emergence of an Effective Judiciary in Mexico, 1994–2002' (2007) 49 *Latin American Politics and Society* 31.

a fragmented state generates more political deadlocks, it follows that there is greater demand for judicial resolution of political questions.[39] A moderately independent judiciary offers a viable alternative for those exhausted by the ineffectiveness of the political arenas, who believe that pursuing a judicial route may result in higher relative net gains. For example, Taiwan entered its hybrid regime era from 1986 to 1996, with electoral politics gradually opening up. Data show that its constitutional court was far more active during this period than previously.[40] The establishment of an opposition party (the Democratic Progressive Party) while the ruling Kuomingtang split into reformist and conservative factions created an environment conducive to the growth of an assertive constitutional court. Partisan disputes and growing support for constitutional reform resulted in room for judicial autonomy. A notable instance of the Taiwanese constitutional court using an opportunity to resolve a political deadlock to advance constitutional democratic norms was the landmark decision Interpretation No. 261. This signified a break with the state's authoritarian past and provided the constitutional foundation for the next election and democratic reforms.[41] Because the incumbent was the dominant party at the time, incumbent infighting also manifested as intra-branch disputes.[42] This led to a significant increase in the number of separation-of-power cases during the same period.[43]

3.2.1.3 The Democracy Claim

As established in the previous chapter, a hybrid regime likes to call itself a democracy. A hybrid regime will do many things to sustain this claim, from instituting formally democratic elections to learning to speak the language of democracy. One important institution that confers

[39] John Ferejohn, 'Judicializing Politics, Politicizing Law' (2002) 65 *Law and Contemporary* 41.

[40] Jiunn-rong Yeh, *The Constitution of Taiwan: A Contextual Analysis* (Hart Publishing 2016) 170.

[41] Chien-Chih Lin, 'Autocracy, Democracy, and Juristocracy: The Wax and Wane of Judicial Power in the Four Asian Tigers' (2017) 48 *Georgetown Journal of International Law* 1063, 1122–3.

[42] Wen-Chen Chang, 'Transition to Democracy, Constitutionalism and Judicial Activism: Taiwan in Comparative Constitutional Perspective' (JSD Dissertation, Yale Law School 2001) chapter 6, 12–13.

[43] Dennis T. C. Tang, 'Judicial Review and the Transition of Authoritarianism in Taiwan' in Taiwan Studies Promotion Committee of Academia Sinica (ed), *Change of An Authoritarian Regime: Taiwan in the Post Martial Law Era* (Academia Sinica 2001) 452.

democratic legitimacy on a hybrid regime is the constitutional court. For one, rule of law and judicial independence have become closely associated with democracy. "Democracy clauses" that demand these guarantees are increasingly common in international trade agreements and aid programs.[44] From policymakers' perspective, adopting judicial independence is democratically fashionable, and it seems to signal to others the regime's commitment to bind itself to rules and curb opportunistic behavior. Furthermore, it adds to the competitive image of a hybrid regime. As Raul Sanchez Urribarri writes, a hybrid regime's "legitimacy and performance resides, to a large extent, on keeping certain contestation arenas open or, at least, preserving the appearance of contestation."[45] An active constitutional court that is willing to resist the regime gives the impression that political pluralism exists in a hybrid regime. Maintaining a moderately autonomous constitutional court helps appease dissenting parties as well as foreign and international stakeholders who are committed to democratic norms.

To derive the legitimacy and instrumental benefits of adopting judicial independence, the regime's commitment to the judiciary must be sufficiently credible. It is one thing to institute a constitutional court and textually guarantee its independence in the constitution, another to actually grant the court the resources and space to perform its duties independently. To function as a legitimizing ideology for a hybrid regime, judicial independence cannot just be an empty expression.[46] A hybrid regime must substantiate its claim to judicial independence. Citizens and other relevant constituencies need to have reasons to believe that the government has tied its own hands in order for judicial independence to provide the expected stabilizing effects.[47] "In politics as elsewhere," Jon Elster writes, "to make a promise and then break it is worse than not making it in the first place."[48] Failing to honor judicial

44 Ozan Varol, 'Stealth Authoritarianism' (2015) 100 *Iowa Law Review* 1673, 1727.

45 Sanchez Urribarri (n 8) 878.

46 As E. P. Thompson famously wrote, "the essential precondition for the effectiveness of law, in its function as ideology, is that it shall display an independence from gross manipulation and shall seem to be just. It cannot seem to be so without upholding its own logic and criteria of equality; indeed, on occasion, by actually being just." E. P. Thompson, *Whigs and Hunters: The Origin of the Black Act* (Breviary Stuff Publications 1975) 263.

47 Barry R. Weingast, 'The Political Foundations of Democracy and the Rule of the Law' (1997) 91 *The American Political Science Review* 245.

48 Jon Elster, *Ulysses Unbound: Studies in Rationality, Precommitment, and Constraints* (CUP 2000) 148.

independence will be perceived as a breach of trust and is guaranteed to be counterproductive.

An implicit bargain between the regime and the constitutional court emerges here. The regime relies on the constitutional court for legitimacy gains, while the constitutional court can only carry out its duties if the regime exercises self-restraint. To uphold this bargain, the regime needs to "find a balance between keeping effective control of the political space and legitimizing its authority."[49] The court must take care not to push its luck too far, else the regime might retaliate in order to preserve its core interests. That said, the regime must tolerate a certain amount of challenge from the constitutional court to show that its intentions are genuine and sincere in order to maintain the impression of a democracy. As mentioned, a judiciary can exploit the regime's motivation for instituting an independent constitutional court to its advantage. The need to maintain a democratic appearance necessarily limits the court-curbing options available to the regime. In some circumstances, discussed in later chapters, the court can rely on the regime's democratic claim to hold the regime accountable as well. The implicit bargain between the regime and the court effectively becomes a shield, and an occasional sword, for constitutional courts to make more assertive decisions.

3.3 The Optimistic Model

Under the Pessimistic Model, a court can do little to bring about democratic changes in a hybrid regime. The Optimistic Model envisages a very different court. The Pessimistic Model focuses on the constraining effects of a hybrid regime, while the Optimistic Model starts by considering the moral responsibility of a constitutional court in a hybrid regime. A court, under this model, is held to be a bulwark against authoritarian oppression as well as leading a hybrid regime toward democracy. The court is regarded as the savior of the oppressed, or the "alchemist" that is capable of turning an autocracy into a democracy.[50]

International policymakers, as well as those living in hybrid regime polities, are attached to the Optimistic Model because of the many kinds of injustice they experience or perceive in a hybrid regime. "People demand justice to escape domination," as Ian Shapiro famously

[49] Sanchez Urribarri (n 8) 859.

[50] Daly (n 5).

writes.[51] Frustrated by how the political process favors the incumbent, the public and opposition in hybrid regimes tend to turn to the judiciary for solutions. After all, judges are commonly seen as justice personified, symbolizing fairness and impartiality. The antidemocratic nature of political institutions in hybrid regimes reinforces faith in formally independent judiciaries, and courts are cast as "beacon[s] of hope."[52] The appointment of Zühtü Arslan as the president of the Turkish Constitutional Court, for example, was described as a potential "safeguard against autocracy and . . . a much-needed glimmer of hope for Turkish democracy."[53] A prominent Pakistani journalist describes the Chaudhry Supreme Court as "the last station on the line, the only forum capable of providing relief."[54] In Hong Kong, some argue that courts are actually better at representing popular will than the political branches.[55] Writing about post-Soviet states, Armen Mazmanyan notes, "while judicialization is conventionally treated as a counter-democratic practice, in non-consolidated democracies it clearly signals success of democratization."[56] The World Bank and other international development organizations project a similar kind of imagery of courts. Rule of law and judicial independence are believed to promote democratic and economic growth. The tremendous faith of international policymakers in the democratic potential of courts is reflected in the billions of dollars spent over the past three decades on legal reform and rule of law projects globally.[57]

The model reflects an aspiration shared by many who live in hybrid regimes, but not many constitutional lawyers have developed these intuitions. Instead, the closest we find to theorizing the views of the

[51] Ian Shapiro, 'On Non-domination' (2012) 62 *The University of Toronto Law Journal* 293.

[52] Ergun Özbudun, 'Turkey's Judiciary and the Drift Toward Competitive Authoritarianism' (2015) 50 *The International Spectator* 42, 53.

[53] Melis Cengiz and Kemal Kirişci, 'A Glimmer of Hope for the Future of Turkish Democracy?' Brookings Opinions, March 9, 2015, available at www.brookings.edu/opinions/a-glimmer-of-hope-for-the-future-of-turkish-democracy, last visited November 5, 2021.

[54] As cited in Shoaib Ghias, 'Miscarriage of Chief Justice: Judicial Power and the Legal Complex in Pakistan under Musharraf' (2010) 35 *Law & Social Inquiry* 985, 993.

[55] Eric C. Ip, 'The Democratic Foundations of Judicial Review under Authoritarianism: Theory and Evidence from Hong Kong' (2014) 12 *International Journal of Constitutional Law* 330.

[56] Armen Mazmanyan, 'Judicialization of Politics: The Post-Soviet Way' (2015) 13 *International Journal of Constitutional Law* 200, 201.

[57] See David M. Trubek, 'The "Rule of Law" in Development Assistance: Past, Present, and Future' in David Trubek and Alvaro Santos (eds), *The New Law and Economic Development: A Critical Appraisal* (CUP 2006).

Optimistic Model are the discussions in the democratization jurisprudence literature on the role of courts in transitional regimes and new democracies. There are two reasons that might explain this gap in the literature on constitutional theory in authoritarian contexts. As the discussion on the Pessimistic Model illustrates, the first is that authoritarian regimes are traditionally thought of as having eliminated all room for plausible discussion of the democratic role of constitutional courts, and are assumed to be too restrictive for the development of any attractive normative account of constitutional courts. The assumption may hold in a pure authoritarian context, but the moderate levels of judicial autonomy existing in hybrid regimes suggests that normative questions about the democratic role of constitutional courts are worth exploring.

Second, one might assume that what constitutional courts should do in authoritarian contexts is obvious and straightforward: decide against the regime or overturn authoritarian policies. Some scholars may even be tempted to equate an antiregime decision with the advancement of democratic norms. These responses simply restate democratic ideals in the abstract, and/or fail to consider the pragmatic challenges and contextual dynamics faced by a court. Moreover, an antiregime decision does not necessarily promote democracy. Developing meaningful normative guidelines suitable for a hybrid regime political context requires properly accounting for the characteristics of a hybrid regime and the ways in which these characteristics normatively and practically affect a constitutional court.

Given the limited theoretical discussion on the normative role of a constitutional court in an authoritarian context, the democratization jurisprudence literature might offer some insights into how the Optimistic Model can be defended. As that literature speaks to a different political context, any insights drawn should be treated with caution. Transitional or new democracies are characterized by their progression toward consolidated democracy, "inordinate pace of change," and a "period of intense flux" for constitutional change.[58] These temporal features are absent in a hybrid regime. Uncertainty over the rules of the game and how constitutional developments will unfold is a hallmark of a transitional regime,[59] but that level of uncertainty is lacking in a hybrid regime, as transformative changes are not expected within the foreseeable

58 Daly (n 5) 152.

59 See Andreas Schedler, 'Taking Uncertainty Seriously: The Blurred Boundaries of Democratic Transition and Consolidation' (2001) 8 *Democratization* 1.

future. Its hybridity persists without a fundamental resolution for a substantial period.

Nonetheless, the incidental fact that some transitional regimes are considered to be or resemble hybrid regimes suggests that the institutional context of the democratization jurisprudence literature is not too dissimilar to that of a hybrid regime. A hybrid regime is analytically distinct from a transitional or new democracy, but they share features that shape constitutional courts in similar ways. Constitutional courts in transitional regimes, for example, have to deal with their authoritarian legacies, while those in hybrid regimes have to manage authoritarian realities.

More importantly, like the Optimistic Model, the democratization jurisprudence literature is interested in the democracy-enhancing prospects of a constitutional court *and* shares the Optimistic Model's high hopes for the transformative potential of a court. Marcus Mietzner, for instance, observes, "that constitutional courts can play a positive role in the stabilization of transitional democracies is not a new theoretical insight."[60] Francesco Biagi's recent study of European constitutional courts finds that, in the context of democratic transition and consolidation, "the role played by the constitutional courts is of the utmost importance."[61] László Sólyom makes a similar point when he says that constitutional courts are "inseparable from democratic changes."[62] Given the similarities in motivations and aspirations, helpful lessons can be drawn from that literature.

3.3.1 *Democracy by Judiciary, and Democratic Hedging*

This part singles out the works of two authors, Kim Lane Scheppele and Samuel Issacharoff, to illustrate the Optimistic Model. Scheppele cogently defends a provocative idea: that constitutional courts can sometimes be more democratic than the elected branches in new democracies. Likewise, a core argument found in many of Issacharoff's works is that transitional or young democracies that are under authoritarian threat

[60] Marcus Mietzner, 'Political Conflict Resolution and Democratic Consolidation in Indonesia: The Role of the Constitutional Court' (2010) 10 *Journal of East Asian Studies* 397, 398.

[61] Francesco Biagi, *European Constitutional Courts in Transition to Democracy* (CUP 2020) 15.

[62] László Sólyom, 'The Role of Constitutional Courts in the Transition to Democracy: With Special Reference to Hungary' (2003) 18 *International Sociology* 133, 135.

justify strong judicial intervention. Both Scheppele and Issacharoff's works are not focused on hybrid regimes per se, even though the political contexts they write about are sometimes substantively similar to hybrid regimes. Reviewing their arguments helps us understand how the Optimistic Model can be theorized. The following paragraphs consider the two authors' works and extract insights that are relevant for a hybrid regime context.

In Scheppele's article "Democracy by Judiciary," she notes that constitutions in many post-authoritarian democracies reflect a substantive vision of democracy.[63] Haunted by their pasts, these third-wave democracies experience "problems with elections" and "problems in communication between elections."[64] Focusing on the experiences of Hungary during the 1990s, Scheppele describes how the representative institutions failed to translate the demands of the people. Electorates were incapable of checking the inadequacies of their representatives due to poor economic conditions.[65] Given the circumstances, it was legitimate, she argues, for the constitutional court to intervene. The constitutional court's duty was to reflect the substantive promises of the constitution by performing political representative functions essential to the proper functioning of a democracy. She depicts the Hungarian Constitutional Court at the time as a highly democratic institution, showing how widely accessible the court was and how it provided a superior avenue for citizens to participate in policymaking.[66] The court famously heard around two thousand petitions a year, struck down one third of all the laws challenged in its first six years of existence, and ordered the legislature to pass laws on certain rights through the "unconstitutionality by omissions" doctrine.[67]

Treating this form of governance as an ideal type, she notes,

> presidentialism and parliamentarism are not the only forms of democratic system on offer, as the political scientists customarily claim. It is logical to think that the third branch – courts – could also be as dominant in some sorts of democratic governments as presidents and parliaments can be . . .

[63] Kim Lane Scheppele, 'Democracy by Judiciary: Or, Why Courts Can Be More Democratic than Parliaments' in Adam Czarnota, Martin Krygier, and Wojciech Sadurski (eds), *Rethinking The Rule of Law After Communism* (Central European University Press 2005) 26, 38.

[64] *ibid* 31–7.

[65] *ibid* 33, 47, 52.

[66] *ibid* 41–2.

[67] *ibid* 33–4, 42, 44.

> [W]hether a court is democratic or not is an empirical question, not an a priori claim.[68]

She calls this idea "democracy by judiciary" or "courtocracy," meaning a government with a "judiciary as the branch with the most power and the final word."[69] A court meets her definition of democratic when its outcomes actually protect democratic rights, with democracy substantively defined.

Issacharoff also advocates for a strong, democratic role for courts in a host of political contexts. The seed of his arguments can be traced back to a famous article he coauthored with Richard Pildes in 1998. In "Politics as Markets," the two authors draw an analogy between the economic market and the political market, arguing that American courts should adopt a jurisprudential approach that increases the cost of political lockups in order to destabilize attempts to monopolize the political market.[70] Just as how American courts at the time considered more structural features in deciding antitrust cases, Issacharoff and Pildes argue that courts should also look at second-order considerations such as the organizational form of politics when determining whether political actors were engaging in anticompetitive behavior under electoral law. Some may be reminded of the antitrust analogy of John Hart Ely's procedural theory of judicial review.[71] Like Ely, the authors argue that as outsiders, courts are well positioned to protect the political market. But while Ely focuses on rights protection, Issacharoff and Pildes focus on political structure.

Over the next two decades or so, Issacharoff developed this insight and applied it to a range of political contexts. For fragile democracies, he is concerned with the threat of antidemocratic groups.[72] There is a need to preserve the structure of a democracy from these internal threats while maintaining a healthy level of political pluralism. Inspired by the economic market analogy, he contends that restrictions are necessary to protect the core of a democracy. The restrictions he suggests are supported by comparative experiences and include, for instance, content restriction on electoral speech and party bans. Importantly, interpreting

[68] *ibid* 44–5.

[69] *ibid* 44.

[70] Samuel Issacharoff and Richard H. Pildes, 'Politics as Markets: Partisan Lockups of the Democratic Process' (1998) 50 *Stanford Law Review* 643.

[71] See John Hart Ely, *Democracy and Distrust: A Theory of Judicial Review* (HUP 1980) 102–3.

[72] Samuel Issacharoff, 'Fragile Democracies' (2007) 120 *Harvard Law Review* 1405.

and enforcing these rules depends on courts. Independent courts were treated as necessary checks against self-serving political actors.[73]

He advocates for a similarly strong constitutional court in a new democracy.[74] Constitutional courts in new democracies, he argues, are responsible for guaranteeing the basic requirements of a competitive democracy. He calls this "democratic hedging." "Precisely when the political branches are immature and the stabilization of democracy is precarious," Issacharoff claims, "courts emerge as central actors in consolidating the constitutional order."[75] This argument resembles Scheppele's, in that the weakness of civil society justifies a strong court. Issacharoff characterizes a constitutional court as an effective and flexible ex post remedy, as it can rely on powerful tools, such as the basic-structure doctrine, to respond to a wide range of circumstances.[76] The court's responsibility here is to buy time for the polity to mature its democratic culture as it safeguards democracy against a strong political party's effort to centralize powers and undermine accountability.[77]

More recently, he extends his argument to consolidated democracies, exploring the role of courts in democracies that are undergoing democratic backsliding.[78] Consolidated democracies, he warns, "may become fragile under excessive pressure on the structural preconditions for democratic governance, at least at times."[79] Courts can play a democracy-enhancing role in consolidated democracies when their integrity and stability begins to be threatened. Consistent with his previous arguments, the role here is a structural one.[80] Courts are capable of playing this role because their arguments are open to public scrutiny,[81] legal reasoning establishes an "indirect electoral link" to the public,[82] rule-of-law metrics exist to help assess the correctness of their decisions,[83] and they are subject to some political accountability, notably through the appointment process.[84]

[73] *ibid* 1467.
[74] Samuel Issacharoff, 'Constitutional Courts and Democratic Hedging' (2011) 99 *The Georgetown Law Journal* 961.
[75] *ibid* 1003.
[76] *ibid* 1002.
[77] *ibid* 965, 1001, 1004.
[78] Samuel Issacharoff, 'Judicial Review in Troubled Times: Stabilizing Democracy in a Second-best World' (2019) 98 *North Carolina Law Review* 1.
[79] *ibid* 26.
[80] *ibid* 9.
[81] *ibid* 42.
[82] *ibid* 49.
[83] *ibid* 43.
[84] *ibid.*

Issacharoff contends that the theories of Jeremy Waldron and Richard Bellamy that emphasize the political side of the constitutional order are based on idealized assumptions as opposed to the "messy reality of lived experience."[85] Recognizing how democratic structures and norms are subverted in real-life democracies, oversight must come from institutions external to the political branches, namely, the courts.[86]

3.3.2 Theoretical Insights Relevant to the Optimistic Model

The extensiveness of Issacharoff's body of work means this chapter cannot do justice to the breadth and complexity of some of the arguments mentioned. Of importance here, though, is the fact that Scheppele's and Issacharoff's work shares certain themes that are relevant to developing the Optimistic Model. These themes allow us to have a closer look at the possible justifications of the Optimistic Model.

3.3.2.1 Source of Authority: Constitutionalism

The Optimistic Model assumes that the court is legitimately exercising its powers against the incumbent. But where does this normative legitimacy come from? Both authors highlight two sources of judicial authority that are relevant to the Optimistic Model. The first is constitutionalism. Constitutions should treat people as constitutional equals. The onus of upholding this falls on the legislature as well as other institutions.[87] However, when the constitution of a hybrid regime fails to treat people equally, judicial intervention is potentially justified so long as the constitutional court acts to support political equality. As Scheppele argues, in circumstances where other constitutional mechanisms are lacking or inadequate, a constitutional court has a greater responsibility to hold the regime accountable.

Issacharoff's argument in relation to constitutionalism is more "formalist."[88] Constitutional courts, he writes, are "little detained by concerns over the authority for judicial review or over the countermajoritarian consequences of constitutional challenge."[89] In this account, the fact that a court is *expressly* granted constitutional jurisdiction under the

[85] *ibid* 6.
[86] *ibid* 15.
[87] N. W. Barber, *The Principles of Constitutionalism* (OUP 2018) 186.
[88] Theunis Roux, 'The South African Constitutional Court's Democratic Rights Jurisprudence' (2013) 5 *Constitutional Court Review* 33, 44.
[89] Issacharoff (n 74) 964.

constitution provides a crucial source of authority for it to be politically interventionist. However, constitutionalism only justifies the existence of the constitutional powers in Issacharoff's account, and he does not say how constitutionalism actually guides the exercise of judicial power. Nevertheless, both accounts suggest that constitutionalism, broadly speaking, is one of the key sources of judicial authority in conceptualizing the democratic role of a constitutional court.

3.3.2.2 Source of Authority: Democracy

A second complementary source of authority is democracy. This reflects the motivations of those who subscribe to the Optimistic Model: in courts we trust when the political process fails us. A lack of democracy leads people to project their faith onto courts and view a court as legitimate when it can somehow shore up democratic ideals. There arises the question of where this type of judicial authority comes from. By defining the state as a democracy and detailing the mechanics of the democracy, the written constitution can be an explicit source of authority. Both Scheppele and Issacharoff, however, seem to assume that democracy is a freestanding higher principle, with Scheppele defining democracy more substantively than Issacharoff. Political culture and socioeconomic conditions are included as part of Scheppele's definition of democracy, while Issacharoff's conception is closer to the procedural account proposed in Chapter 1. Regardless, their arguments rely on a similar intuition that an absence of democracy – that is, when the actual state of affairs falls short of the standards prescribed by the definition of democracy adopted – defines the legitimacy basis of a constitutional court. Whether a constitutional court is legitimate depends on the extent to which its actual performance helps promote democratic ideals.[90]

3.3.2.3 Countering the Counter-majoritarian Difficulty

The Optimistic Model challenges the age-old counter-majoritarian difficulty. The counter-majoritarian difficulty posits that judicial review, or judicial intervention in politics more broadly, is undemocratic. Unelected judges, lacking a democratic mandate, have no authority to veto the outcomes of the democratic process. The Optimistic Model is unbothered by the counter-majoritarian difficulty. For one, many courts

[90] For example, Issacharoff notes that "the legitimacy of these courts subsequent to the founding may turn on the degree that they reinforce the 'democratic hedge' that accompanied the founding." *ibid* 986. And as quoted in text to note 68 in this chapter, Scheppele's view is that whether a court enhances democracy is an empirical matter.

outside democracies seem to enjoy popular support when they overrule the political process. More importantly, the reason why judicial intervention seems legitimate is because the political process of a hybrid regime is not democratic. This is a point raised by Scheppele and Issacharoff. They rightly notice something strange about applying the counter-majoritarian difficulty to nondemocratic contexts or immature democracies. The lack of democratic credentials of the political branches of government raises questions about whether people's interests are properly represented in a hybrid regime. Not only is the gap in democratic credentials between the political branches and a constitutional court significantly narrowed; pathologies linked to a lack of democracy, such as corruption and human rights violations, are also a concern. A change in regime type forces us to reevaluate the normative reasons for and against judicial review in nondemocratic regimes, especially when judicial review is targeting the causes and consequences of authoritarianism.

3.3.2.4 Political Skepticism

Skepticism toward political representatives in hybrid regimes also pervades the Optimistic Model. This sort of skepticism is not unique to hybrid regimes. Both authors point to how messy real-life politics actually is. According to Issacharoff, even consolidated democracies such as the United States and the United Kingdom fall short of the idealized conditions in political theory.[91] The Optimistic Model intuitively appeals to those who share this skepticism of political representatives. Distrust in the political branches motivates arguments for judicial intervention.[92] As Issacharoff argues, "in the manner that foxes should not be posted at the henhouse door, so it is that deference to the legislative process cannot serve as the answer to systematic assaults on the process of electoral accountability."[93] The extent to which a court can compensate for the errors of the political branch is open to discussion, but this skepticism is certainly one that finds an audience in a hybrid regime, where the political process is only pretending to be democratic.

91 Issacharoff (n 78). Ely also famously remarked that "obviously our elected representatives are the last persons we should trust with identification of [political failures]." Ely (n 71) 103.

92 When arguing for a transformative judicial role, Ruti Teitel similarly points to how political actors in transitional regimes tend to lack the experience, legitimacy, and competence to lead the process. Ruti Teitel, 'Transitional Jurisprudence: The Role of Law in Political Transformation' (1997) 106 *The Yale Law Journal* 2009, 2033.

93 Issacharoff (n 78) 16.

3.3.2.5 Democratic Functions

The Optimistic Model, most importantly, is about a democracy-building court. The authors highlight two ways that a court can be democracy-building. Scheppele's account is more intuitive and focuses on individual rights. A constitutional court is often said to be a guarantor of rights, and she offers a variation of this standard account. In addition to enforcing rights set out in the constitution, a constitutional court can safeguard democratic rights by becoming a channel for citizens to participate in policymaking. Issacharoff's account, in contrast, is structural, and holds that a court's role is to preserve the "structural preconditions" of a democracy.[94] He draws inspiration from his antitrust analogy, and perhaps from the comparative experiences on the basic structure doctrine that he cites. A structural role relies on a particular conception of democracy in order to make clear what the structural preconditions of democracy are. Issacharoff adopts a procedural conception of democracy, whose goal is the preservation of pluralistic competition. According to him, a court is not simply tasked with vindicating instances where constitutional rights have been infringed, but must also mitigate the structural deficiencies of a polity and ensure a healthy degree of political competition.

3.3.3 *Overoptimism and Its Dangers*

Both authors make valuable contributions. Their arguments illustrate the potential democratic roles that courts can play in hybrid regimes. Their ideas are intuitively appealing to those who live under hybrid regimes and are desperate for democratic change. The five themes summarized so far suggest ways in which the Optimistic Model can be justified. They raise important normative questions about the legitimacy and function of a constitutional court in a hybrid regime. These questions will be taken up in the next chapters.

The rest of this section explains why the Optimistic Model is overconfident about what a constitutional court can achieve in a hybrid regime. The model reflects what courts hope to achieve in a hybrid regime. Implicit in the model is the notion of a constitutional court that is almost as powerful as the incumbent, capable of standing up to authoritarian encroachment. Yet, as we saw from the Pessimistic Model, this is not an empirically plausible assumption. While courts in hybrid regimes may

[94] *ibid* 26.

not be as weak as the Pessimistic Model suggests, they are certainly not strong enough to live up to the many aspirations of the Optimistic Model. In the following paragraphs I set out four reasons why the Optimistic Model described so far is unworkable or even counterproductive in a hybrid regime. These reasons are not presented as critiques of Scheppele's and Issacharoff's work, but instead focus on the hybrid regime context.

The first objection is that, by overestimating a constitutional court's potential, the model risks overlooking the pragmatic challenges it faces in a hybrid regime. On a moral level, a hybrid regime constitutional court may be justified in acting in ways that are more progressive than conventional theories suggest. On a pragmatic level, pushing a constitutional court too far leads to "risks that run beyond ineffectiveness and even backlash."[95] Not only could the court's decisions be ignored or reversed, but its confrontational attitude may also lead to political responses that undermine the court's institutional integrity. In Scheppele's article, for instance, she observes how the Hungarian court's earlier efforts led to its ultimate downfall. In 1998, in retaliation for the court's assertiveness, the newly elected government replaced the bench with its allies.[96] As valiant as the court was, its inflated self-perception undid its previous efforts at institution-building. This kind of political risk is even more commonplace in authoritarian regimes. Judicial powers were similarly stripped away from constitutional courts in Ukraine, Russia, Egypt, and Turkey after political fallout and confrontations.[97] The harsh institutional terrain of a hybrid regime warrants judicial sensitivity and possibly compromises. To temper ideals, a workable constitutional theory that applies to hybrid regimes must be pragmatic in order to be effective and durable.

Second, the Optimistic Model dangerously borders on the idea of courts as a "surrogate" of elected institutions.[98] A court that supports democratic values is not the same as a court that replaces the democratic process. While judicial decisions can sometimes be consistent with liberal-democratic standards, a democracy run by a judiciary is oxymoronic, as courts are not constructed as elected institutions. We

[95] David Landau, 'Samuel Issacharoff. Fragile Democracies: Contested Power in the Era of Constitutional Courts. Cambridge University Press, 2015' (2015) 13 *International Journal of Constitutional Law* 1082, 1084.

[96] Scheppele (n 63) 53–4.

[97] Adam Chilton and Mila Versteeg, 'Courts' Limited Ability to Protect Constitutional Rights' (2018) 85 *The University of Chicago Law Review* 293, 294–5.

[98] Daly (n 5) 261.

might call a dictator benevolent if his or her decisions uphold individual rights, but a dictatorial state is hardly democratic, as the government's decision-making process disenfranchises the people. Similarly, a hybrid regime led by a court is still not democratic, even if its decisions reflect public opinion. Democracy is not only about outcomes, and proponents of the Optimistic Model should be careful not to take the idea too far. The goal is not to replace a hybrid regime with a rights-conscious court. To avoid creating another form of guardianship, we should instead investigate the ways in which a constitutional court can improve the democratic process of a hybrid regime.

Third, while the Optimistic Model rightly identifies some of the ways in which a constitutional court can support democracy, it is relatively silent about the negative externalities that may arise from expanding the constitutional role of a constitutional court. Courts can perform many functions, but are not necessarily good at all of them. This potentially weakens the arguments in support of the Optimistic Model. The Hungarian court, in Scheppele's characterization, intervened in a number of social policies relating to the *Bokros* package. Due to time constraints, the court bypassed consultations with experts and reviewed "as much of the law as they could."[99] Her example certainly shows that the court can perform some functions of a political representative by allowing civil society to represent their interests through the legal process and checking the quality of the laws. The point about the court's expediency can be self-defeating, though, as it indicates that the judges probably decided consequential policies based on highly questionable empirical assumptions. Institutional concerns are by no means fatal to the search of a democracy-enhancing role, but a theory that demands venturing out of the traditional constitutional boundaries of a constitutional court needs to be honest about some of its possible limitations and be shown why this expansion is justifiable despite some of the new problems it might create.

Finally, the Optimistic Model depends on an idealized vision of judges. Judges under this model are uncorrupted, principled outsiders who have a strong sense of moral responsibility. Many judges in a hybrid regime fall short of this vision, however. The influence of authoritarian politics on the judiciary suggests that there will be judges who hesitate to assert themselves against the incumbent, are indifferent or even opposed to the democratic cause. That is not to say that all hybrid regime judges behave like those portrayed by the Pessimistic Model. The relationship between

[99] Scheppele (n 63) 48.

the regime and the court is never straightforward, and judges are complicated figures. Issacharoff reminds us that even authoritarian regimes need good judges with proper legal training to administer justice in the normative half of the dual state.[100] Bound by their oath to the constitution and the higher principle of justice, these judges may be willing to defy the regime out of moral conscience, self-respect, or simply because they care about their reputation. Examples from places like Hong Kong, Pakistan, and Uganda support this possibility in hybrid regimes. Meanwhile, we must recognize that the actions of even democratically committed judges may be complicated by other legitimate considerations such as personal safety and career security. Accordingly, a workable theory should be sensitive to the human side of judges and the personal or moral struggles they may also face.

3.4 Conclusion: The Realistic Model

This chapter concludes by presenting a more attractive view of constitutional courts called the Realistic Model, which adapts and combines learnings from the two models discussed in this chapter. This model is realistic, not necessarily because it more accurately depicts how constitutional courts in hybrid regimes behave in practice, but because it is realistic about what constitutional courts can achieve in a hybrid regime.

Like the Pessimistic Model, the Realistic Model acknowledges that judicial autonomy in a hybrid regime is limited by authoritarian politics. Those attached to the Optimistic Model are bound to be disappointed, as the sort of judicially led transformative changes promised by that model are improbable. However, the Realistic Model rejects the determinism of the Pessimistic Model and holds that a constitutional court is capable of expanding beyond a marginalized position. In Section 3.2, I outlined three political determinants of judicial autonomy found in most hybrid regimes: semi-competitive elections, fragmented political systems, and the claim to be democracies. That discussion showed how the Pessimistic Model tends to overstate the limits of a constitutional court. Most importantly, it reinforces the Realistic Model's view that meaningful levels of judicial autonomy can exist in a hybrid regime.

[100] Samuel Issacharoff, *Fragile Democracies: Contested Power in the Era of Constitutional Courts* (CUP 2015) 138–9.

The Optimistic Model may be excessively bullish about what courts can accomplish, but the Realistic Model shares its democratic motivations. It allows for the possibility that a constitutional court's scope for action is wider than what might be expected under the Pessimistic Model. This opens up the space for courts to play a democracy-enhancing role in a hybrid regime. Some justifications for a democracy-enhancing role were introduced in the discussion of the Optimistic Model. The political challenges arising from a hybrid regime complicate this debate by forcing us to take authoritarian realities seriously when theorizing the normative role of a constitutional court. Nevertheless, through the Optimistic Model, we can start to imagine ways in which a constitutional court can enhance democracy. What exactly a democracy-enhancing role entails is the subject of the coming chapters. The themes highlighted in Section 3.3 – judicial legitimacy, the counter-majoritarian difficulty, and institutional limitations – serve as a theoretical foundation for us to build upon.

Finally, the Realistic Model views the relationship between a constitutional court and regime politics as a dialectical and ongoing process. This has significant implications, as it opens up a more fundamental discussion about how judicial politics in a hybrid regime should be understood.[101] This contrasts with the unidirectional approaches underlying the Pessimistic Model, wherein regime politics is conceived as a one-way, independent causal factor explaining variations in judicial behavior, and the Optimistic Model, whose primary focus is on how a constitutional court can impact constitutional politics.

Under the Realistic Model, the court and the regime are interdependent. A constitutional court relies on a hybrid regime for resources and implementation, but a hybrid regime also needs a constitutional court for political legitimacy and other instrumental gains. While the interdependence is not necessarily symmetrical – the balance of power usually favors the regime more – the constitutional court is uniquely positioned within this interdependent relationship to change the power balance in and the constitution of a hybrid regime. As a result, neither the court nor the regime has sole control over the development of constitutional politics. Repeated interactions between the constitutional court and other political actors determine constitutional change. This dialectical perspective better accounts for the complex and dynamic developments of authoritarian judicial politics. It also underscores the fact that a court is simultaneously constrained by *and*

[101] See Michael McCann, 'Causal Versus Constitutive Explanations (or, On the Difficulty of Being so Positive . . .)' (1996) 21 *Law & Social Inquiry* 457.

constitutive of constitutional politics: A constitutional court internalizes some of the norms and expectations posed by a hybrid regime, but, most importantly, the hybrid regime is simultaneously shaped by the decisions of the constitutional court. Once again, the dialectical perspective of the Realistic Model explains why it might be realistic for a constitutional court to play a democracy-enhancing role in a hybrid regime.

4

Five Democratic Roles

4.1 Introduction

The previous chapter concluded with a realistic account of a hybrid regime constitutional court. A hybrid regime imposes constraints on a constitutional court, but a constitutional court also enjoys some agency to shape the political environment. The regime and the constitutional court are mutually dependent, and their relationship is dynamic and interactive. Given that a moderate level of judicial autonomy exists in a hybrid regime, it is plausible for a constitutional court to play a democratic role in a hybrid regime, however modest that role may be.

This chapter furthers this argument by offering a perspective on constitutional courts in hybrid regimes that reveals their democracy-enhancing potential. Courts, I claim, should play a role in protecting and promoting democratic values in a hybrid regime. This chapter lays out how that can and should be done. Some of the discussion in this chapter stretches beyond democratic settings and addresses pathologies associated with a lack of democracy, such as poor governance and corruption.

Section 4.2 opens the discussion with the familiar counter-majoritarian difficulty. The debate centers on whether judicial review can be justified under democratic theory, given the constitutional court's lack of democratic credentials. This debate highlights the issues that need to be addressed when a democratic role is claimed for a court. Section 4.2 argues that the counter-majoritarian difficulty is severely blunted in a hybrid regime because the democratic conditions necessary for it to hold are weakened or absent. The different ways in which those democratic objections are undermined by a hybrid regime are then illustrated.

The fact that the counter-majoritarian objection is relatively irrelevant in a hybrid regime context does not automatically imply that a constitutional court has the moral authority to take on a democratic role in a hybrid regime. It does, however, give us greater room to consider how a constitutional court can support democratic ideals in a hybrid regime. Five different democracy-enhancing roles of a constitutional court are proposed, alongside tools that would help facilitate the realization of these roles. Each role contributes to democracy in different ways and relies on a particular aspect of a constitutional court. The five democratic roles include: (1) the referee role, (2) the interpretative role, (3) the participatory role, (4) the quasi-representative role, and (5) the educative role. They will be examined in Section 4.3.

The democracy-enhancing roles I propose are not necessarily unique to a hybrid regime. As the first chapter points out, some degree of fluidity exists among regime types. Democracies typically call for judicial restraint, but can occasionally experience political failures similar to those we encounter in hybrid regimes, which may necessitate creativity on the part of judges or a greater degree of judicial intervention.[1] Conversely, while it would normally be unwise, or even impossible, for constitutional courts to challenge pure authoritarian regimes, windows of opportunity may occasionally open for courts to develop judicial power and press on against the authoritarian. The democratic roles presented in this chapter may be relevant to both these scenarios. This is not necessarily a weakness of the overall argument, as it only extends the applicability of the judicial roles.

Crucially, though, the roles described are customized for constitutional courts in hybrid regimes. Each role addresses the democratic deficit inherent within hybrid regimes and the recurring political problems they experience. While the democratic roles and the accompanying tools may guide and assist courts outside hybrid regimes, they are intended for constitutional courts in hybrid regimes because of the types of challenges those courts encounter. Furthermore, these roles and tools are best suited to constitutional courts in hybrid regimes given what these courts can realistically achieve. For instance, demanding that courts replace the political branches in authoritarian contexts is not only impractical, but also imprudent because of the near certainty of political backlash. For similar reasons, the fashionable basic structure doctrine or unconstitutional constitutional amendment doctrine is excluded from the discussion because the required level of judicial

[1] For how courts can sometimes counter political malfunctions in a democracy, see e.g. Rosalind Dixon, 'The Core Case for Weak-form Judicial Review' (2016) 38 *Cardozo Law Review* 2193.

power and autonomy to meaningfully apply the doctrine is usually absent in a hybrid regime context.[2] On the other hand, these roles are very unlikely to be realized in a pure authoritarian political setting due to the limited space for judicial maneuvering. In short, the democratic roles are framed for a hybrid regime and are sensitive to the potential and limitations of constitutional courts in hybrid regimes.

Section 4.4 of this chapter addresses how competency concerns impact the democratic roles proposed. The roles are democratically legitimate, not because constitutional courts are electorally representative, but because they show how courts can and should support and advance democracy. Nevertheless, there are two limiting principles to address, institutional competence and judicial power, which impose normative and prudential limitations respectively on the democratic roles a hybrid regime court can take up. The topic of judicial power is discussed fully in the coming chapters, while Section 4.4 of this chapter addresses the issue of institutional competence. Questions of competency should not be taken lightly, but are not absolute arguments and must be assessed in a comparative institutional manner. I argue that these roles are justifiable because there is a lack of better alternatives in a hybrid regime. Courts are a second-best solution: they may not normally be the best institution to tackle certain political failures, but the inadequacies of the political process in a hybrid regime offer reasons for a constitutional court to take up greater responsibility. Limited departure from the normative boundaries posed by competency concerns is, as a result, justifiable.

[2] There are instances where hybrid regime courts have applied these doctrines, but the conditions for *meaningful* deployment of them are often missing. For example, in 2018 the Constitutional Court in Uganda ruled unconstitutional a constitutional amendment that sought to extend the term of parliamentary office. The same case however upheld the amendment to remove the age limit for presidential candidates, effectively allowing Museveni to run for another term. While the court had adopted the basic structure doctrine in the case, the decision was widely criticized as wrongly applying the doctrine. The Supreme Court upheld the lower court's decision. This case needs to be read in the context of Museveni's hawkish attitude toward the Ugandan judiciary. For the Constitutional Court's decision, see: Male Mabirizi & Ors v. Attorney General [2018] UGCC 4 (July 26, 2018). See also: Karoli Ssemogerere, 'Uganda's Age Limit Petition: Constitutional Court Demurs on Substance, Cautious on Procedure,' Constitution Net, August 14, 2018, available at https://constitutionnet.org/news/ugandas-age-limit-petition-constitutional-court-demurs-substance-cautious-procedure, last visited November 5, 2021; The Observer, 'Museveni Attacks Judges over Age Limit Petition Ruling,' July 30, 2018, available at https://observer.ug/news/museveni-attacks-judges-over-age-limit-petition-ruling/, last visited January 12, 2026.

4.2 The (Ir)relevance of Democratic Objections

Coined by Alexander Bickel, the famous counter-majoritarian difficulty describes the normative legitimacy challenges encountered by an unelected institution that exercises political power in a democratic society.[3] Critics of judicial review argue that the delegation of (quasi-) lawmaking power to the court is in tension with popular self-government. To allow democratically made laws to be reversed by those who are not electorally accountable is counter-majoritarian. At its core, the counter-majoritarian difficulty is based on the idea of political equality. The authority to resolve political disputes should be left to the people and its elected representatives, not unelected judges.

Democratic objections to judicial review can be supported by different conceptions of democracy and are not necessarily limited to a majoritarian conception. Hence, the term counter-majoritarian difficulty can be misleading. Here, I use the term "democratic objections" to refer to democracy-based arguments against judicial review.

Broadly speaking, there are three types of democratic objection: the intrinsic objection, the instrumental objection, and the cultural objection. These will be outlined briefly as they are already well known and widely discussed elsewhere. The discussion in this section will condition how a court in a hybrid regime should approach its democratic role and, more broadly, shape and inform the second half of the chapter.

4.2.1 Intrinsic Objection

The intrinsic objection contends that judicial review violates the right to equal political participation. As noted in the first chapter, reasonable disagreement about morality and the meaning of rights is present in any society. Democracy is arguably the best way to resolve disagreements and reach collective decisions in society while preserving the value of political equality. Democracy ensures people's equal political input through equal and universal suffrage, and facilitates the equal treatment of such input through its deliberative process. The political process of a democracy enjoys superior lawmaking authority as it confers roughly equal rights on citizens to decide on matters of law and policy. Judicial review gives the constitutional court a power similar to that wielded by the political branches of government. Constitutional courts establish new social or

[3] Alexander M. Bickel, *The Least Dangerous Branch: The Supreme Court at the Bar of Politics* (YUP 1986).

political norms, for instance, by disapplying statutes or giving a new meaning to a constitutional provision. Judges are unelected, however, and do not enjoy the formal democratic mandate of the people. Hence, critics contend that judicial review undermines democracy by displacing the decision-making authority of the people. The decision-making process of judicial review disenfranchises the democratic will.[4] Or, as argued more radically by Richard Bellamy, it is a form of political domination or arbitrary power.[5]

4.2.2 *Instrumental Objection*

Critics also argue that judicial review is undemocratic because it generates bad political outcomes. Political outcomes can be democratically bad in two ways. The first is that judicial decisions do not represent the political will of the people. As opposed to the intrinsic objection, which is rights-based, the instrumental objection is more focused on the nature of the outcomes produced by courts. The standard account of this objection is that the political branches of government decide and vote according to the preferences of the people. Facing the prospect of electoral defeat, politicians are incentivized to act in ways that accord with the views of their constituents. Politicians also are in close proximity to their constituents and have the tools to learn their likes and needs. In contrast, some argue that unelected judges sitting in their chambers are insulated from popular pressure and cannot properly ascertain the views of society. Judges are limited by the law and to the evidence and arguments put forward by the litigants. Their decisions, as result of their inability to gauge public opinion, counter the democratic will.[6]

An objection similar in spirit is that judges lack the capacity to make political decisions correctly. The political branches of government are set up in ways that ensure better expertise and information-gathering power in policymaking.[7] For example, legislatures are much larger in size than courts so that they can accommodate a broader range of views during

[4] Jeremy Waldron, 'The Core of the Case Against Judicial Review' (2006) 115 *The Yale Law Journal* 1346.

[5] Richard Bellamy, *Political Constitutionalism: A Republican Defence of the Constitutionality of Democracy* (CUP 2007).

[6] See Or Bassok, 'The Two Countermajoritarian Difficulties' (2011) 31 *Saint Louis University Public Law Review* 333, 340–1.

[7] See Paul Yowell, *Constitutional Rights and Constitutional Design: Moral and Empirical Reasoning in Judicial Review* (Bloomsbury Publishing 2018).

lawmaking; experts can assist the democratic process to compensate for the knowledge gap on more technical issues; and the political branches in general are equipped with more flexible solutions to address complex or polycentric problems. These branches of government are created for different purposes, and John Finnis calls this the "asymmetry of aims."[8] Demanding that the judicial branch to take on a political role would, as a result, lead to "serious long-term bad consequences."[9] While a court lacks the institutional strength of the political branches of government, some might counter that judges are at least better at getting the correct meaning of rights.[10] Judges may be poor policymakers, but constitutional judges are not asked to make policies; instead, they decide whether the law or policy in dispute violates a constitutional right. Judges are legally trained and apply the relevant interpretative techniques to determine the meaning of the constitution. In response, critics maintain that questions of rights involve or are no different to questions of morality. Given how we disagree on politics, courts do not have privileged access to the truth on questions of rights. There is no reason to believe that courts will get rights questions correct, and good reason to suspect that they may get them wrong because of their institutional deficiencies.

4.2.3 Cultural Objection

Critics are also worried about the negative impact judicial review might have on the political culture of a democracy. These social effects are more subtle and indirect. A healthy democracy relies on a robust political culture where, among other things, the citizenry is politically engaged, tolerant of reasonable disagreements, willing to speak to reason, and respectful of constitutional norms. Court skeptics argue that the existence of an active constitutional court, or what Mark Tushnet terms the problem of "judicial overhang,"[11] will gradually subvert the political foundations of a democracy in several ways.

[8] John Finnis, 'Judicial Power: Past, Present and Future,' Judicial Power Project, October 20, 2015, available at http://judicialpowerproject.org.uk/wp-content/uploads/2015/10/John-Finnis-lecture-20102015.pdf, last visited November 5, 2021.

[9] *ibid* 11.

[10] Ronald Dworkin, *Law's Empire* (HUP 1986).

[11] Mark Tushnet, *Weak Courts, Strong Rights: Judicial Review and Social Welfare Rights in Comparative Constitutional Law* (Princeton University Press 2009) 98.

First, it may "promot[e] legislative disregard of the constitution,"[12] or what Wojciech Sadurski identifies as "legislative apathy."[13] Political representatives, officials, and the people may feel alienated from the constitution when a constitutional court always has the final word. This resulting lack of motivation and responsibility distances political actors from the constitution.

Second, the expansion of the judicial realm takes the constitution away from the people and their elected representatives. Political constitutionalists argue that the meaning of the constitution should be the product of an ongoing political deliberation.[14] This form of constitutionalism is inherently democratic and guarantees equality, openness, and inclusivity in constitution-making. Political constitutionalists believe that judicial dominance over the constitution denies the people meaningful opportunities to participate in making the constitution. Judicial review, they argue, is undemocratic because it stifles popular political participation and public deliberation.[15] This goes against the aim of building a "democratic public culture."[16]

Third and relatedly, some scholars suggest that a constitutional court may promote "pure interest-based politics"[17] as opposed to a more value-based or deliberative form of politics. Lacking a sense of responsibility and connection to the constitution, political actors might view constitutional rules as impositions by an elitist constitutional court, perceiving them as mere rules of a political game. To these political actors, the imposed rules derive legal authority simply because they happen to be the law decided by the court, and the constitution becomes devoid of moral substance. For instance, Tushnet argues that strong-form judicial review encourages mere position-taking by politicians. That is, lawmakers can "get political mileage out of taking a position on this question, without worrying that anything actually will happen, because the courts will find the statute unconstitutional anyway."[18] In the long run,

12 *ibid.*

13 Wojciech Sadurski, 'Judicial Review and the Protection of Constitutional Rights' (2002) 22 *Oxford Journal of Legal Studies* 275, 286.

14 Bellamy (n 5).

15 See Larry D. Kramer, *The People Themselves: Popular Constitutionalism and Judicial Review* (OUP 2004); Tushnet (n 11). For a critique of the idea of popular constitutionalism, see Robert Post and Reva Siegel, 'Popular Constitutionalism, Departmentalism, and Judicial Supremacy' (2004) 92 *California Law Review* 1027.

16 Bellamy (n 5) 7.

17 *ibid* 44.

18 Tushnet (n 11) 82.

the existence of a constitutional court might lead to an unattractive, Schumpeterian form of politics that is characterized only by self-interest and competition.

4.2.4 *Democratic Objections in a Hybrid Regime?*

Those defending judicial review have put forward a number of rebuttals.[19] A common counterargument is to justify judicial review by reconceptualizing democracy. Democracy, some say, cannot only be about majoritarianism (or majority preferences) given the dangers of the tyranny of the majority. Under this approach, liberalism is built into the definition of democracy. Judicial review reinforces democracy by protecting minority rights and reducing majoritarian biases.[20] Some rely on empirical evidence to show that the counter-majoritarian difficulty is, in reality, exaggerated.[21] These arguments are descriptive and point out how judicial outcomes in some jurisdictions actually follow public opinion despite the courts' alleged limitations. Others have considered how weaker or dialogic forms of judicial review can ameliorate the tension between democracy and constitutionalism by preserving the gains of a constitutional court while retaining the people's final decision-making authority.[22] Lowering constitutional amendment requirements is an institutional response with a similar effect. There are also those who insist that the democratic objections should not be framed in universal terms and that questions of normative judicial legitimacy are highly contingent on local contextual factors. As Tom Daly remarks, "though often couched in universal language, [the counter-majoritarian difficulty] tends to speak in many ways to the very particular development of strong judicial review in the United States as a polity."[23] With express grants of judicial review powers and shorter judicial tenure in many parts of the world outside the States, the legitimacy of many constitutional

[19] For a comprehensive discussion of how the debate is framed in different ways, see Nimer Sultany, 'State of Progressive Constitutional Theory: The Paradox of Constitutional Democracy and the Project of Political Justification' (2012) 47 *Harvard Civil Rights-Civil Liberties Law Review* 371.

[20] See e.g. Dworkin (n 10).

[21] See e.g. Barry Friedman, *The Will of the People: How Public Opinion Has Influenced the Supreme Court and Shaped the Meaning of the Constitution* (Farrar, Straus and Giroux 2009).

[22] See e.g. Dixon (n 1).

[23] Tom G. Daly, *The Alchemists: Questioning Our Faith in Courts as Democracy-Builders* (CUP 2017) 250.

courts tends to be less contentious than depicted by an American-centric scholarly debate.

This chapter takes no strong view on the points raised, which have been thoroughly debated by others for decades. Instead, my aim here is to test the strength of the democratic objections in a hybrid regime context. In the previous chapter we briefly touched on how it seems intuitively strange to apply the democratic objections to polities other than well-functioning democracies. Intriguingly, however, to the best of my knowledge, the relevance of these democratic objections outside democracies have only been examined episodically.[24] Perhaps this is because it is assumed that these objections simply do not apply, or because courts are thought to be weak and irrelevant in authoritarian regimes and there is no point in considering those courts' moral responsibility. Given the growing number of authoritarian regimes in the world and the varying patterns of judicial behavior among them, the strength of the democratic objections in a hybrid regime context deserves more attention.

Here, I take a careful look at how a change in political context affects the democratic objections that many take for granted in a democracy. I show that the democratic objections do not apply with full force or are of limited relevance to a hybrid regime. Some of the objections may not even be valid in democracies. I start with a general argument, and then address the three types of democratic objections introduced so far individually.

Let us begin with an obvious point: the democratic objections are framed explicitly or implicitly for polities with well-functioning democratic institutions. The democratic objections presuppose a certain kind of political environment, one that is, by definition, improbable in a hybrid regime. Judicial review is illegitimate when it is juxtaposed against a democratic process that is in "good working order,"[25] or

[24] Jeremy Waldron, it will be discussed, is open to the possibility that a case for strong judicial review can be made outside well-functioning democracies. There are others who raised suspicion in passing remarks about the applicability of the counter-majoritarian debate, or asserted that it is inapplicable, outside democracies. See e.g. Armen Mazmanyan, 'Judicialization of Politics: The Post-Soviet Way' (2015) 13 *International Journal of Constitutional Law* 200; Kim Lane Scheppele, 'Democracy by Judiciary: Or, Why Courts Can Be More Democratic than Parliaments' in Adam Czarnota, Martin Krygier, and Wojciech Sadurski (eds), *Rethinking The Rule of Law After Communism* (Central European University Press 2005); Paul Gewirtz, 'Approaches to Constitutional Interpretation: Comparative Constitutionalism and Chinese Characteristics' (2001) 31 *Hong Kong Law Journal* 217.

[25] Waldron (n 4) 1362.

"maturely self-determined polities with a discursively deliberative legislature."[26] Democratic institutions in a hybrid regime fail to meet these criteria.

Stepping back momentarily, even those studying constitutionalism in democracies have questioned whether real-life democracies actually satisfy these criteria. For instance, poor economic conditions have undermined people's political rights and ability to access quality information; well-organized interest groups have exercised disproportionate political power in important policy areas; and all sorts of political horse trading has led to inefficiency that impairs the government's ability to deliver public goods. Even with equal and universal suffrage, real-life democracies are still a long way from the ideal of political equality assumed by the theorists who argue against judicial review.

The reason for this gap is partially due to human nature and the messiness of reality, and partially because political equality is only an ideal. Questioning how the counter-majoritarian debate is commonly framed in the literature, Jerry Mashaw rightly observes that, "if the suggestion is that courts reviewing statues confront the true will of the people, then the image is surely false. Not only do we not have popular democracy in the sense that this vision of the 'countermajoritarian difficulty' suggests, we could not have it."[27] One lesson offered by public choice theory, as Mashaw and other economists have demonstrated, is that democracy is an ideal that cannot be fully attained in reality. There is no such thing as the general will of the people, and the preferences of the people can never be accurately aggregated. Any method of reaching collective decisions is limited by cyclic preferences and some level of arbitrariness of the agenda-setter. There is no real-life system that can give equal political weight perfectly. A lot of the democratic objections are, as a result, misguided as they juxtapose a rosy picture of democracy with a real-life version of a constitutional court.

For the sake of theory building, some critics would understandably relax the standard. Jeremy Waldron notes that the democratic condition does not "demand perfection" and only asks for "electoral and legislative arrangements [to be] in reasonably good shape."[28] Even with less stringent democratic conditions, however, a hybrid regime – with its blatant and intentional violation of political equality – still clearly misses the

[26] Finnis (n 8) 20.

[27] Jerry Mashaw, *Greed, Chaos, and Governance: Using Public Choice to Improve Public Law* (YUP 2008) 202.

[28] Waldron (n 4) 1402.

target. Indeed, Waldron expressly leaves open the possibility that the "costs of obfuscation and disenfranchisement [relating to judicial review] are worth bearing for the time being" under circumstances outside the conditions he specified.[29]

The "core" debate about the legitimacy of judicial review and constitutional courts may be limited to democracies, but the terms of the debate can provide us with a basic framework to approach our question of interest. I have yet to show how a constitutional court can be democratic, but understanding the problems of applying the different democratic objections to a hybrid regime will illuminate our later discussion.

Consider the intrinsic objection, which is premised on the notion that the political process confers an equal political right. Under this argument, the normative superiority of the political process derives from how it is structured in an open and inclusive way. As discussed in Chapter 2, the political process in a hybrid regime is defined by its uneven playing field and a lack of electoral competitiveness. The system is designed to disenfranchise dissidents and the opposition, while giving disproportionate power to the incumbent and its allies. The ability to participate and contest in hybrid regime politics depends largely on one's political status. People have unequal access to political channels, and social groups targeted by the incumbent are systematically excluded from the political process. The political process of a hybrid regime is itself a form of domination and arbitrary rule. The normative superiority of the political process assumed in the procedural-based objection is missing in a hybrid regime context.

Two instrumental objections were raised: one based on the representativeness of a judicial decision and another based on institutional competence. The first kind of argument is inherently dangerous, as it assumes that the only point of a government is to mirror the views of the people. It takes a narrow understanding of democratic representation and applies it as the only yardstick across all governmental institutions, including the court. Democratic representation is one of the tenets of democracy, but is not the only value of a democracy. There should be a strong presumption of political equality, but departures are sometimes justifiable in the pursuit of other goals. For example, central banks and courts are both unelected and not designed to be "representative" like legislatures, but they provide expert services that improve policymaking (for the case of

29 *ibid* 1401, 1406.

central banks) and ensure fairness in adjudication (for the case of courts).[30]

Aside from the questionable intrinsic validity of the representation-based instrumental objection, there is the additional question of whether a constitutional court is really antidemocratic when it is overruling unrepresentative or even antidemocratic outcomes. Political representatives in hybrid regimes are not democratically elected and many of them lack the formal authority to represent the people.[31] They might not be viewed as legitimate representatives given how the rules favor the incumbent.[32] The incumbent may even seek to distort and suppress the views of certain constituencies. Information channels are blocked to bury dissenting voices. The views of certain social groups may never make it into the political process. Meanwhile, allies of the regime are given disproportionate weight. The representation-based instrumental objection hinges on the idea that the political branches of government are necessarily better at political representation than a constitutional court. The analysis here suggests that this may not always be the case in a hybrid regime. In fact, the political branches of government in hybrid regimes may deliberately skew political representation in order to entrench the incumbent's power.

As for the competency-based instrumental objection, political branches in nondemocratic regimes are not necessarily less capable than those in a democracy. In fact, it might be argued that some authoritarian regimes appear to perform well at delivering basic goods: a lack of democratic oversight can result in greater efficiency. Consequently, this democratic objection can hold true even for a hybrid regime. However, a hybrid regime is prone to certain kinds of political failures because of how the regime is structured. There is plenty of evidence in the political science literature that shows that the democratic deficit and one-party dominance impact, or are associated with, economic performance[33] and

[30] See Paul Tucker, *Unelected Power: The Quest for Legitimacy in Central Banking and the Regulatory State* (Princeton University Press 2019).

[31] See Hanna Pitkin, *The Concept of Representation* (University of California Press 1967) chapter 3 on "formal representation."

[32] See Andrew Rehfeld, 'Towards a General Theory of Political Representation' (2006) 68 *The Journal of Politics* 1 for a perception-based concept of representation.

[33] See Siddharth Chandra and Nita Rudra, 'Reassessing the Links Between Regime Type and Economic Performance: Why Some Authoritarian Regimes Show Stable Growth and Others Do Not' (2015) 45 *British Journal of Political Science* 253; Gabriella R. Montinola and Robert W. Jackman, 'Sources of Corruption: A Cross-country Study' (2002) 32 *British Journal of Political Science* 147; John F. Helliwell, 'Empirical Linkages between Democracy and Economic Growth' (1994) 24 *British Journal of Political Science* 225.

quality of governance.[34] A lack of democracy can lead to an array of problems, including weaker government accountability, state capture, endemic corruption, less transparent decision-making, and arbitrariness. Hence, while the political branches of a government in a hybrid regime are not necessarily less competent than those in a democracy, there is a much greater tendency for those in a hybrid regime to deviate from their intended functions. Democracy has no direct relation to this, but a lack of democratic accountability may incentivize corruption and poor governance, thereby impairing the competency of the political branches. These are reasons to suggest that the competency-based instrumental objection does not always hold in a hybrid regime. The question of institutional competence will be further discussed toward the end of this chapter.

There were also three kinds of cultural objections relating to how a constitutional court might subvert democratic culture. When exported to a hybrid regime, however, those arguments are radically weakened, given the difference in starting points. Political constitutionalists suggest that judicial intervention prevents or hinders the emergence of a democratic culture. They argue that, without a strong constitutional court, lawmakers and officials will be incentivized to take responsibility for the development of the constitution. With or without a constitutional court, however, the people in a hybrid regime lack the devices to effectively and easily hold the incumbent electorally accountable. Political constitutionalism without democracy cannot guarantee responsive constitutional engagements. Similarly, political participatory rights are limited in a hybrid regime to begin with. The people in a hybrid regime are distanced from the constitution, as ordinary channels for political and constitutional participation are clogged. If anything, as I explain later in this chapter, a constitutional court may provide an additional and invaluable channel for many who are frozen out of the political process to participate in the constitution.

It is also hard to see how a constitutional court would further encourage interest-based politics in a hybrid regime when a very unattractive form of interest-based politics already appears to be a defining feature of

[34] See Christopher Clague et al., 'Property and Contract Rights in Autocracies and Democracies' (1996) 1 *Journal of Economic Growth* 243; John D. Griffin, 'Electoral Competition and Democratic Responsiveness: A Defense of the Marginality Hypothesis' (2006) 68 *The Journal of Politics* 911; Michael K. Miller, 'Elections, Information, and Policy Responsiveness in Autocratic Regimes' (2015) 48 *Comparative Political Studies* 691.

a hybrid regime. Political scientists have long argued that a function of elections in authoritarian regimes is to allow those in power to "hold onto power."[35] Summarizing the literature on authoritarian electoral politics, Jennifer Gandhi and Ellen Lust-Okar identify several important functions of elections in authoritarian regimes, including "spread[ing] the spoils of office broadly among members of the elite," "aid[ing] incumbents in maintaining their ties with elites by deterring defection among members of the ruling coalition," and "serv[ing] to co-opt the opposition."[36] What these tested explanations have in common is an important assumption that authoritarian politics is, to a large extent, premised on interest-based politics. By sustaining and developing interest-based networks within the authoritarian camp, unfair elections exploit the self-interested nature of political actors to help the incumbent stay in power. Again, if anything, the existence of a democratically committed constitutional court may help destabilize these interest-based networks and instill constitutional-democratic norms back to hybrid regime politics. How a constitutional court impacts the political culture of a hybrid regime depends not on its mere existence but on how it behaves.

4.3 Five Democratic Roles

The strength of the democratic objections is conditional upon the status and health of a political process. The fact that a hybrid regime is undemocratic and tends to behave in antidemocratic ways does not automatically justify a judiciary's democracy-enhancing role. Nonetheless, it invites us to consider how a constitutional court can protect and promote democratic values given the democratic deficit of a hybrid regime. As I have already noted, the democratic objections might even condition the way a constitutional court should act in a hybrid regime. For instance, a constitutional court may have a role in creating a democratic culture and exerting pressure on the state to treat people as constitutional equals in a hybrid regime.

A constitutional court is not an inherently democratic institution. It is not democratically elected, and, as mentioned in the first chapter, its legal dimension functionally distinguishes it from the political institutions of government. Nevertheless, by virtue of its constitutional location and

35 Jennifer Gandhi and Ellen Lust-Okar, 'Elections under Authoritarianism' (2009) 12 *Annual Review of Political Science* 403, 404.

36 *ibid* 405.

some of its functions, a constitutional court, I argue, has a role to play in supporting democratic ideals in a hybrid regime.

Five democracy-enhancing roles are presented here. Certain roles target specific democratic values – such as rule of law (referee role), political participation (participatory role), and political representation (quasi-representative role) – while others are more general. And, as noted at the beginning of this chapter, the roles address pathologies associated with a lack of democracy as well.

The democracy-enhancing roles to be presented come with costs and risks, but I show that they can be mitigated and are potentially worth bearing considering the democratic returns. These roles are not particularly novel; each stems from a familiar aspect and function of a constitutional court. By introducing a proper frame, we can see how a constitutional court can shore up democratic norms and/or inhibit the development of authoritarianism. As I have mentioned, these roles may not be unique to a hybrid regime, but they are designed for constitutional courts in hybrid regimes. The ways in which a constitutional court can enhance democracy are multifaceted: they not only address antidemocratic laws and policies, but also seek to empower the opposition, strengthen the democratic structure, and reinforce the democratic culture. The five roles are not mutually exclusive, and each has its own place and time. They will be supported by comparative experiences to highlight the plausibility of the normative claims.

4.3.1 *Refereeing Role*

The first role envisages a court as a referee that applies clear limits on political powers and ensures dominant political forces are playing by the rules. This is principally a rule-of-law argument: democracy requires the rule of law to operate, and a constitutional court is responsible for upholding the rule of law. The referee role is limited to enforcing unambiguous and unarguable political-constitutional rules, that is, when the law is clear. This is arguably the most modest of the five roles, but is still important as it connects the court to its adjudicative function. The referee role not only provides clarity and certainty to the constitution, but also improves the accountability of the incumbent in a hybrid regime and restores temporary speed bumps within the constitutional order.

4.3.1.1 Ely and Process Theory

John Hart Ely's renowned process theory of judicial review inspires three of the roles proposed (the referee role, the interpretative role, and the quasi-representative role), so it is helpful to outline aspects of his argument first. In his seminal book *Democracy and Distrust*, Ely proposes a theory of judicial review that is "participation-oriented, representation reinforcing."[37] Courts, according to his theory, enhance participation and reinforce representation by "polic[ing] the process of representation."[38] The purpose of judicial review, Ely writes, is to "ensure that the political process [i]s open to . . . all viewpoints, on something approaching an equal basis."[39]

His argument is motivated by his distrust of the political process. His theory's central idea, as Stephen Gardbaum describes, is that the "protection of a system of representative democracy against erosion or degradation by elected representatives cannot be left exclusively in their hands."[40] Malfunctions within the political process are incapable of self-correction when those problems are created by political representatives themselves. According to Ely, there are two ways for a court to fulfil this role: by upholding rights key to the democratic process such as freedom of expression and voting rights, and by protecting the rights of minorities.

Process theory sounds attractive, as it aims to offer a novel way out of the counter-majoritarian difficulty. Compared with Ronald Dworkin's interpretivism, Ely argues that process theory is more democratically legitimate as courts under his theory need not engage with substantive norms and values. According to Ely, judicial review is justified as it improves democracy without removing the democratic authority of the people. His work is also driven by a strong skepticism of political actors that is commonly found in contemporary constitutional scholarship.[41] The fact that this political distrust still resonates with us today is perhaps one reason why his work remains highly relevant.

A question many have had about Ely's work, however, is whether his theory is actually value- or substance-free.[42] Interpretations of democratic

37 John Hart Ely, *Democracy and Distrust: A Theory of Judicial Review* (HUP 1980).
38 *ibid* 73.
39 *ibid* 74.
40 Stephen Gardbaum, "Comparative Political Process Theory" (2020) 18 *International Journal of Constitutional Law* 1429, 1430.
41 Pierre Rosanvallon, *Democratic Legitimacy: Impartiality, Reflexivity, Proximity* (Princeton University Press 2011) 85.
42 See e.g. Laurence H. Tribe, 'The Puzzling Persistence of Process-based Constitutional Theories' (1980) 89 *The Yale Law Journal* 1063.

rights and minority rights clearly have substantive dimensions and involve moral disagreements. This line of critique makes one wonder if Ely can completely sidestep the counter-majoritarian difficulty faced by other theories that support judicial review. Nevertheless, this critique is not necessarily fatal. Ely's theory is process-based because it aims to improve the democratic process, not because it focuses only on judicial review of process rights or procedures. In fact, Ely's theory is arguably better characterized as a particular interpretative approach with a democratic orientation. Or as Aileen Kavanagh describes, his theory is "substance oriented towards, and emanating from, the American system of representative democracy."[43] While some of the arguments presented later are inspired by Ely's process theory, these objections do not matter in the context of the thesis, as will shortly be clarified.

4.3.1.2 Courts as Referees

The first role discussed is a literal interpretation of what Ely calls "court as referee."[44] This phrase is borrowed from the title of one of his chapters, where he argues that the role of a court is to police the political process. Echoing Ely's justifications, my arguments throughout this book share a strong distrust of political representatives and seek to orient a hybrid regime toward a more democratic constitutional structure. Departing from Ely, the first role proposed here adopts a narrow understanding of "process" to mean constitutional "rules," with rules meaning directives with unambiguous triggers.[45] These rules include but are not limited to procedural requirements and clear-cut legal-constitutional boundaries. The clarity of a rule is obviously a matter of degree, as some rules can be more unarguable than others. However, within every legal community, common standards for determining the meaning of legal and constitutional provisions exist, and there are inevitably rules that lie closer to the "unambiguous" end of the spectrum. The referee role is most applicable to rules close to that unambiguous end. A sports referee is only in the business of enforcing the rules of the game. It is not their job to question the inherent fairness of the rules. Similarly, the role of a court as referee is not to evaluate the substance or constitutionality of government policies or laws, but to guard against rule-breaking

43 Aileen Kavanagh, 'Comparative Political Process Theory' (2020) 18 *International Journal of Constitutional Law* 1483, 1484.

44 Ely (n 37) 73.

45 See Pierre Schlag, 'Rules and Standards' (1985) 33 *UCLA Law Review* 379.

activities and procedural irregularities. With their constitutional jurisdiction and ancillary powers, courts have the tools to ensure that the constitutional rules and political processes are followed and obeyed.

By limiting a court's role to unambiguous rules and procedures, the referee role largely escapes the substance versus process criticism that haunted Ely's process theory. As a corollary, however, this role seems weak as one might ask how democracy-enhancing a constitutional court is without engaging with questions of value and substance. Furthermore, some might argue that since the rules are created by authoritarians, many rules are actually unattractive. The referee role might, then, have authoritarian effects when the court is asked to uphold antidemocratic laws as well.

I make four points in response to these concerns. First, I am not ignoring substantive approaches. In fact, judicial roles with a more substantive dimension are explored in the next subsections. The refereeing role is only one of five roles; courts should consider all of them whenever they are appropriate under different conditions. While fairness of the law and its democratic pedigree is normally beyond the purview of a constitutional court, the ways in which a constitutional court can challenge the constitutionality and validity of authoritarian laws and policies are explored later in this chapter. Not to mention, it is also occasionally possible to couch questions of fairness, democracy, and justice as questions of constitutionality and validity.

Second, while the referee role might sound modest, it is of crucial importance, as it strengthens constitutional legal accountability in a hybrid regime. Capturing perfectly how hybrid regime incumbents today behave, Erin Jenne and Cas Mudde write, "authoritarian leaders typically undermine democratic institutions by not respecting the law. Rather than changing the rules, they bend or break them, relying on patronage and low administrative capacity to get away with it."[46] This nature of hybrid regime incumbents provides the necessary impetus for the referee role. Given the incumbent's higher default chance of winning elections and the reduced political cost of dislodging various kinds of oversight, constitutional rules with normative substance are easily ignored or disregarded without repercussions or public knowledge. The referee role compels the incumbent to answer to the law by limiting the

[46] Erin K. Jenne and Cas Mudde, 'Hungary's Illiberal Turn: Can Outsiders Help?' (2012) 23 *Journal of Democracy* 147, 148.

exercise of arbitrary powers and imposing legal and reputational costs for legal noncompliance.

The Pakistani courts provide an excellent illustration of the referee role. Two political failures that the Chaudhry court focused on tackling were the abuse of executive powers and governmental corruption. This is reflected in the kinds of cases selected by the court[47] as well as some of the high-profile challenges it made against the incumbent. Perhaps the most famous case in this regard is *Watan Party v. Federation of Pakistan*,[48] more commonly known as the Pakistan Steel Mills case. The case involved the privatization of state-owned steel mills, where the opposition and labor unions as claimants argued that the enterprise was sold at an excessively low price and alleged corruption. Annulling the privatization agreement, the Supreme Court described the process as "reflecting serious violation of law and gross irregularities with regard to sale of the first and the biggest steel mill that this country has."[49] The many glaring irregularities included grossly understating the valuation by excluding the value of the land,[50] a mismatch between the name of the buyer and the name of the bidder,[51] dubious credentials of the real buyer,[52] and failure to complete the transaction within the prescribed period of time.[53] While the incident was only one of many corrupt dealings occurring in Pakistan at the time, the judgment symbolized the court's determination to crack down on public corruption. The constitutional court helped advance good governance and tackle pathologies related to a lack of democratic oversight.

Elections in a hybrid regime are another process in particular need of a referee. As previously described, incumbents win elections in hybrid regimes through a variety of questionable tactics, many of which are unlawful, and are occasionally able to evade liability due to the lack of public admonishment. In Hong Kong, for example, opposition candidates have been disqualified from running for election because they are deemed by the incumbent to not be patriotic enough. In disqualifying these candidates, the government did not offer any opportunity for the

47 Asher Qazi, 'Suo Motu: Choosing Not to Legislate, Chief Justice Chaudhry's Strategic Agenda' in Moeen H. Cheema and Ijaz S. Gilani (eds), *The Politics and Jurisprudence of the Chaudhry Court 2005–2013* (OUP 2015) 302.

48 PLD 2006 SC 697.

49 *ibid* para 78.

50 *ibid* para 63.

51 *ibid* para 78, 89.

52 *ibid* para 85.

53 *ibid* para 69.

candidates to explain or defend themselves. On procedural fairness grounds, the courts held that the disqualifications were against "the principle of natural justice" as the government had failed to provide the candidates with a reasonable opportunity to respond.[54]

The Ugandan courts' historical record as a referee may be mixed, but there was a "dramatic rise in the accountability functions of the judiciary" during the 2000s, as Siri Gloppen observes.[55] The courts played their referee role in some of Uganda's most well-known cases. A notable one involved a referendum. Prior to 2000, Uganda operated as a one-party system under the banner of Museveni's Movement System or no-party democracy. Article 271(3) of the Ugandan constitution, however, stipulated that a referendum determining "the political system the people of Uganda wish to adopt" must be held within four years after Uganda's first election in 1996. With restrictions on opposition parties and the incumbent's systemic advantage over the existing political structure, the opposition argued that there was no way that the referendum could have been held fairly. The result of the 2000 referendum favored preserving the current political system. Seeking to overturn the referendum, the opposition took the matter to court. The Constitutional Court held that the Referendum Act was unconstitutional as it was passed without the constitutionally mandated quorum.[56] A new Referendum Act that was supposed to replace the old one was also ruled unconstitutional by the Supreme Court on similar procedural grounds. The result of the referendum was, however, maintained, likely because the Supreme Court did not want to trigger a constitutional crisis.[57]

The kind of accountability offered by a constitutional court in its role as referee differs from democratic accountability. Constitutional legal accountability is based on the idea of determining whether a law or action

[54] *Chow Ting v. Teng Yu Yan Anne (Returning Officer)* [2019] 4 HKLRD 459, para 27. After Hong Kong's electoral system was overhauled by Beijing in 2021, all electoral candidates now have to be vetted by a government-appointed Candidate Eligibility Review Committee and the Committee's decision on a candidate's eligibility is nonjusticiable. See Hong Kong Basic Law, Annex 2, Art. 5.

[55] Siri Gloppen and others, *Courts and Power in Latin America and Africa* (Palgrave Macmillan 2010) 85.

[56] Rachel Ellett, *Pathways to Judicial Power in Transitional States: Perspectives from African Courts* (Routledge 2013) 144.

[57] Erica Bussey, 'Constitutional Dialogue in Uganda' (2005) 49 *Journal of African Law* 1, 13. In *Oloka-Onyango v. Attorney General* [2014] UGCC 14, the Constitutional Court had also invalidated the infamous Anti-Homosexuality Act in 2014, similarly on the ground that the law was not passed with the constitutionally prescribed quorum. The law sought to criminalize same-sex relations, with penalty up to life imprisonment.

violates a constitutional or legal norm, while democratic accountability is based on a principal–agent relationship between the government and the people.[58] The government, as a principal, has a duty to act on behalf of, report to, and justify its decisions to its people. As an agent, the people are empowered to sanction the government through elections and other established political means when the government falls below a certain standard.

However, the benefits of constitutional legal accountability overlap with those offered by democratic accountability.[59] The government must explain itself to the people in the legal process, as constitutional legal accountability forces the state to confront issues that are otherwise ignored because of the incumbent's political dominance. A constitutional court's expressive and public character flushes out the dubious intentions of those in power, improves the transparency of the government, and allows the people to better monitor the state. By reminding the incumbent that rules have to be taken seriously, constitutional legal accountability promotes political responsiveness, at least regarding the issues being challenged.

Third, on top of providing constitutional legal accountability and partially compensating for the lack of democratic accountability, the referee role supports rule-of-law values through the social effects it creates. Rule of law requires society's internalization of constitutional legal norms. This begins with the public *and* government officials' acceptance that powers must be exercised in accordance with established rules.[60] Taking the law seriously is a basic requirement of rule of law. In authoritarian regimes, government decisions are sometimes made on a whim, and the law is distorted or ignored to realize the incumbent's self-interested agenda. A constitutional court can help restore the fundamental values of rule of law by showing that rules need to be respected by everyone, including the incumbent. In sports, the referee is "a symbol of fair play, integrity and sportsmanship."[61] A similar symbolic power is at play here, which has potentially far-reaching effects on the constitutional culture of a hybrid regime. The social effects of a constitutional court will be discussed later in this chapter.

[58] Jeremy Waldron, *Political Political Theory: Essays on Institutions* (HUP 2016) chapter 8.

[59] See Jeff King, *Judging Social Rights* (CUP 2012) 60–2.

[60] See Brian Tamanaha, 'Law's Evolving Emergent Phenomena: From Rules of Social Intercourse to Rule of Law Society' (2018) 95 *Washington University Law Review* 1149.

[61] This is a provision reproduced in many guidelines or codes of conduct for sports referee.

Finally, the referee role is justifiable when the rules being applied are attractive ones. Sometimes, despite the unambiguous language of the rule, it may be possible for courts to make exceptions by creating contextual requirements for the application of an unattractive rule. A certain degree of selective enforcement is defensible given the authoritarian effects that would ensue as a result of a completely neutral application of the referee role. Selective enforcement, however, depends on judges' ability to legitimately carve out exceptions despite the unambiguous language of a rule. Furthermore, the risk of being selective is that the court might be seen as politically biased and ignoring the demands of the law. There is consequently a limit as to how selective courts can be if they want to preserve their image of impartiality and minimize the risks of political backlash. True to the spirit of a referee, this role inevitably requires a constitutional court to sometimes enforce rules with authoritarian effects.

Despite this, the net effect of the referee role is likely to be democratic in most hybrid regimes. Whether this role ultimately leads to democracy-enhancing effects depends on whom this role impacts the most. The answer here is rule-defiant actors, most notably the incumbent and elites in a hybrid regime, who are able to act with impunity because of their electoral and political dominance. A rule being the product of an undemocratic process does not mean that it is inherently unattractive. In fact, in an attempt to free-ride on the reputation of liberal democracies, hybrid regimes oftentimes import constitutional provisions and political rules from other democracies.[62] A referee role will revive many constitutional breaks and constrain authoritarian aggrandizement.

4.3.2 Interpretative Role

The first role explains how a constitutional court should approach clear directives. In contrast, the interpretative role discussed here applies when a court enjoys a greater degree of discretion.

This role requires courts to adopt an interpretation or reason that is more closely aligned with constitutional democratic values whenever legal discretion permits. While it would rarely be sensible to enforce democracy as a freestanding principle, judges should use democracy to *guide* their interpretation of the constitution and law. I adopt a broad

[62] See Rosalind Dixon and David Landau, *Abusive Constitutional Borrowing: Legal Globalization and the Subversion of Liberal Democracy* (OUP 2021).

conception of interpretation, referring not only to how constitutional provisions should be read (such as widening the ambit of a rights provision), but more generally to how judicial discretion should be exercised (such as giving more weight to liberal democratic rights).

This role is consistent with Ely's democracy-enhancing goal, but goes beyond process theory, as it is not limited to the process rights that he refers to. This interpretative role is an abstract approach that has implications for how different constitutional doctrines should be applied. This role, I show, guides how judges should choose between competing jurisprudential ideas, how the proportionality doctrine should be applied, and how judges should consider the quality of the legislative debate in determining questions of constitutionality. These are not the only examples of giving effect to the interpretative role, but they illustrate the different possibilities for folding democratic norms into existing jurisprudential techniques.

4.3.2.1 Discretion and Value Judgment

Most problems presented before a constitutional court involve constitutional and/or statutory interpretation. This can happen in a number of ways. The text of the law, especially constitutions, are frequently open-textured and indeterminate. Relying on the text alone or even precedents may be insufficient to control a legal outcome.[63] A constitutional text that protects freedom of speech, for instance, does not specify whether pornography or appropriation art are protected speech under the constitution. We may also need social and/or moral facts to answer the question. The open-textured nature of the law is not necessarily a defect. Relying on legal concepts such as "fairness," "reasonableness," and "necessity," the language of a legal provision or doctrine invites discretion in order to adapt to different social circumstances. Partly because of how laws are usually drafted in such a manner in a public law context, a legal issue can attract closely balanced legal arguments which have diverging, and sometimes irreconcilable, conclusions.

A key assumption here is that the law, particularly constitutional law, often accommodates reasonable disagreements. This is partially attributable to the nature of legal language, but, to a greater extent, to the fact that many constitutional cases involve moral and/or policy considerations.

[63] This assumption is shared and defended by many. Ronald Dworkin's thesis in *Law's Empire*, for example, implies that judges enjoy a lot of discretion especially in what he calls "hard cases."

The assumption here is not that law is simply politics or the result of judges' personal preferences. The attitudinal model of law, once very popular among political scientists, obscures the legal dimension of a constitutional court and fails to account for interactions and deliberations within the courtroom.[64] Nevertheless, the law is usually not a mathematical equation that renders unequivocally right or wrong answers. The standards of the legal community impose normative limitations on what kinds of legal methodologies are acceptable. Within the parameters of the law, though, broadly speaking, there can be a number of legal arguments and legal outcomes in a given case that are considered legally persuasive or at least reasonable under accepted standards of legal argumentation.

4.3.2.2 Adopting a Democracy-Enhancing Route

The interpretative role does not dismiss the importance of the law, but relies on a characteristic of law that is especially common in constitutional law. In these instances, the ultimate decision of a court must involve a degree of value judgment. Consciously or subconsciously, judges need to choose among competing outcomes based on the norms inherent in the different legally plausible arguments that are available to them.

The difference in judicial treatment of defamation against public officials or public institutions in Hong Kong and Singapore exemplifies how a constitutional right can give rise to almost opposing lines of jurisprudence depending on judicial interpretation. While both courts operate in hybrid regimes, those in Hong Kong adopted a path that is much more consistent with liberal democratic values than their counterparts in Singapore. In the first landmark case after the handover, *Ng Ka Ling & Ors v. Director of Immigration*,[65] the Court of Final Appeal in Hong Kong established the approach of giving rights-protective provisions a generous interpretation.[66] This is not empty rhetoric. In *Cheng Albert v. Tse Wai Chun Paul*,[67] the Court of Final Appeal decided that the defamation defense of fair comment can only be defeated if the defendant does not genuinely hold the view he or she expressed. Departing from the common-law position at the time, the court ruled that the motive of the

[64] See e.g. Jeffrey Segal and Albert Cover, 'Ideological Values and the Votes of US Supreme Court Justices' (1989) 83 *American Political Science Review* 557.

[65] [1999] 1 HKLRD 315.

[66] *ibid* para 77.

[67] [2000] 3 HKLRD 418.

speaker, however improper it may be, became irrelevant. Reiterating its rights-protective interpretative approach, the court held that "the Courts should adopt a generous approach so that the right of fair comment on matters of public interest is maintained in its full vigour."[68] In striking a balance between freedom of expression and protecting private reputation, the Hong Kong courts prioritized the prior. In recent years, the defense of fair comment has become especially valuable as Hong Kong witnesses an increased number of defamation claims (or the threat thereof) launched by the incumbent and its allies against the media and dissidents. At the time of writing, none of these defamation claims have eventuated or succeeded, probably because of how difficult it is for a defamation claim to succeed in court as a result of the *Cheng* case.

Contrast this with the Singaporean approach. Scholars observe that defamation suits are routinely weaponized by the authorities to silence critics and censor opposition.[69] The Singaporean courts have adopted a more speech-restrictive position than courts in Hong Kong. Leaders of the incumbent party regularly win in these defamation suits.[70] Such suits are not only brought against individuals, but also the press. Foreign press and online columnists are particularly targeted.[71] As one critic observes, "the Singapore judiciary has hardened its position in rejecting the arguments that defamation actions and contempt of court committals could constitute unlawful interference with the fundamental right of free speech."[72] While the Hong Kong courts have effectively disarmed the authoritarian in this respect, the Singaporean courts have chosen a path that tilts the balance toward the authoritarian in the name of protecting private reputation. It is well known that defamation laws have significant chilling effects on the political community of Singapore.

Another rights-protective interpretative example can be found in Uganda, where the Supreme Court made a particularly bold move in 2004 by ruling unconstitutional a law that criminalizes "false news," more

[68] *ibid* para 3.

[69] See e.g. Cameron Sim, 'The Singapore Chill: Political Defamation and the Normalization of a Statist Rule of Law' (2011) 20 *Pacific Rim Law & Policy Journal* 319; James Gomez, 'Restricting Free Speech: The Impact on Opposition Parties in Singapore' (2006) 23 *The Copenhagen Journal of Asian Studies* 105.

[70] See e.g. Cassandra Chan, 'Breaking Singapore's Regrettable Tradition of Chilling Free Speech with Defamation Laws' (2003) 26 *Loyola of Los Angeles International and Comparative Law Review* 315, 318.

[71] Tsun Hang Tey, 'Confining the Freedom of the Press in Singapore: A Pragmatic Press for Nation-building' (2008) 30 *Human Rights Quarterly* 876, 898.

[72] *ibid.*

commonly referred to as fake news.[73] With the rise of social media and the difficulty of detecting false or misleading content, fake news has become a problem faced by states around the world. Authoritarians have, however, reserved the power to determine what is "fake" or not to themselves. These laws have been abused to silence critics and censor the press. In Uganda, fake news was broadly defined by legislation as "any false statement, rumour or report which is likely to cause fear and alarm to the public or to disturb the public peace," with a maximum penalty of two years for publishing such content. The law was challenged in court and eventually struck down. The Supreme Court was well aware of the problems caused by fake news, but the court was more skeptical about leaving "unfettered discretion" to the authorities. The judges also repeatedly emphasized the importance of freedom of expression and freedom of press, and reminded the government of its constitutional commitments as a "free and democratic society."

These cases illustrate the interpretative choices that are typically available to judges in constitutional cases, as well as the choices they must make in light of their own assessments of what morality requires. While these courts operate in environments with similar legal traditions and political constraints, the Hong Kong and Ugandan courts have demonstrated that it is possible to find and adopt jurisprudential routes that correspond to constitutional democratic norms more closely.

There might be concerns about what a democratically friendly interpretation is in practice. Different understandings of democracy might affect, on a more granular level, which democracy-enhancing route should be adopted. But consistent with my approach in the first chapter, a thin conception of democracy is already sufficient to activate this approach. In other words, there may be many interpretations in each case that satisfy the requirements of this role. More importantly, the choices available to a hybrid regime constitutional court are rarely two closely democratic routes. Rather, one is quite clearly authoritarian in character and defended by the incumbent, while the other is the challengers' route that mitigates the antidemocratic tendency of the law or policy in question.

4.3.2.3 Proportionality Doctrine

The interpretative role affects how doctrines that structure judicial discretion should be applied. Take, for example, the proportionality test,

[73] *Onyango-Obbo and Anor v. Attorney General* [2004] UGSC 81.

which is arguably the most prominent doctrine in constitutional jurisprudence in recent decades.[74] Replacing ad hoc balancing exercises, the proportionality test offers a systematic framework that allows courts to assess the extent to which a derogation of rights is constitutional, or, to use the terminology of the test, proportionate.[75] Providing an "analytical structure,"[76] the doctrine has allowed courts to adjudicate rights cases more systematically, effectively, and transparently. There is an ongoing and robust debate over how the test and its application can be perfected. An oft-repeated observation is that even with the proportionality test, there remains considerable latitude for judicial discretion.[77] The language and the different stages of the proportionality test provide the "discursive frame for norm-based argumentation that enables the litigating parties and the judge to bridge the domain of law and the domain of interest-based conflict."[78] A function of these legal frames is to constrain judicial discretion, but the test remains sufficiently malleable to accommodate competing arguments.

The test helps judges identify relevant goals and interests in conflict and points toward considerations that should be given weight to, but it remains the judges' task to apply the framework and fill in the gaps, which involves considerable discretion. To what extent is an aim legitimate? What does it mean for a policy to be a proportionate response to such an aim? How should judges factor in alternative options in assessing proportionality? These are questions that invite value judgments. My intention here is not to critique the test, but instead to show how the test offers room to prioritize constitutional democratic norms.

For one, the intensity of review when applying the proportionality test should be turned up when constitutional democratic norms are threatened. Because constitutional democratic norms are particularly weak and vulnerable in a hybrid regime, there is a necessity for the constitutional court to be extra vigilant in adjudicating cases that concern these rights. Heightened scrutiny increases the threshold for deference to the

74 See Alec Stone Sweet and Jud Mathews, *Proportionality Balancing and Constitutional Governance: A Comparative and Global Approach* (OUP 2019).

75 For normative justifications for the proportionality test, see Paul Craig, 'Proportionality, Rationality and Review' (2010) *New Zealand Law Review* 265, 271–3.

76 Mattias Kumm, 'The Idea of Socratic Contestation and the Right to Justification: The Point of Rights-based Proportionality Review' (2010) 4 *Law & Ethics of Human Rights* 142, 147.

77 Finnis (n 8) 20–3.

78 Alec Stone Sweet and Jud Mathews, 'Proportionality Balancing and Global Constitutionalism' (2008) 47 *The Columbia Journal Transnational Law* 72, 86–7 note 33.

government and requires closer inspection of the justifications relied upon by the government in order to ensure that the rights in question are given extra protection.[79] Likewise, courts should give extra weight to rights that are missing or weak in a hybrid regime when engaging in balancing exercises, such as the right to political participation, political equality, freedom of expression, and freedom of assembly.

4.3.2.4 Reducing the Presumption of Constitutionality

An even more ambitious technique that is similar in spirit is to reduce the presumption of constitutionality or validity as applied to all laws and policies being challenged in a hybrid regime.[80] Courts normally presume that the law made by the democratic process is constitutional. This presumption, which manifests in different ways in different jurisdictions, emerges from the separation of powers, which implies that the judiciary ought to respect the legislative function of the political process and the will of the people. Nevertheless, the presumption is tenuous in a hybrid regime, as its political process does not enjoy the same degree of democratic legitimacy. This does not mean that all laws should be presumed to be unconstitutional, but rather that the reduction in the presumption supports a higher degree of scrutiny generally. In practical terms, this might mean, for example, that a government should be required to adduce additional evidence to prove that the adoption of the policy in question is justified and to make comparative assessments between alternatives, instead of the court merely accepting the government's assertion of competency in policymaking areas and any kind of empty rhetoric.

4.3.2.5 Semi-procedural Review

Another way the interpretative role can be implemented is to use the quality of the legislative debate or the consultative process as grounds for adjusting the level of deference, or even use these as an independent reason to strike down laws. The superior democratic legitimacy of the political branches of government is a commonly cited reason for judicial deference. There has been much academic discussion regarding how and the extent to which this factor should affect the degree of judicial scrutiny.[81] These

[79] Cora Chan, 'Deference, Expertise and Information-gathering Powers' (2013) 33 *Legal Studies* 598.

[80] For a similar suggestion, see Roberto Gargarella, 'In Search of a Democratic Justice – What Courts Should Not Do: Argentina, 1983–2002' (2003) 10 *Democratization* 181, 184.

[81] See e.g. Chan (n 79); Alison Young, 'In Defence of Due Deference' (2009) 72 *The Modern Law Review* 554; Aileen Kavanagh, 'Deference or Defiance? The Limits of the Judicial Role

debates have theoretical implications for a hybrid regime, as many laws and policies being challenged lack the same democratic pedigree and democratic approval scholars assume exist in liberal democracies. The argument here is that poor legislative deliberation or failure to engage with those impacted by a decision or a law should result in a more assertive constitutional adjudicative approach. Ittai Bar Siman Tov calls this approach semi-procedural judicial review.[82] It is semi-procedural because it is substantive in nature (as a court is determining the constitutionality of a law based on its substance), but the examination of the legislative and consultative process (i.e. the procedural look) complements its substantive judgment. Procedural defects are taken to indicate a substantive flaw or the presence of unconstitutional motivations.

Scholars are still considering whether the quality of the legislative debate or consultative process should be used as a separate doctrine or incorporated into the proportionality doctrine. The latter appears to be the more popular option at present. Nevertheless, this form of review is not as novel as it sounds: the European Court of Human Rights, as well as constitutional courts in Germany, Belgium, Israel, South Africa, and Colombia, for instance, have all, through different doctrinal means, relied on the quality of the legislative debate or consultative process to intervene and strike down laws.[83]

The most notable case in this area is arguably *Hirst (No 2)*, where the Grand Chamber found that the UK government's "general, automatic and indiscriminate" ban on prisoners' voting violated the European Convention on Human Rights' provision on free elections.[84] Arriving at its decision, the Grand Chamber noted that there was "no evidence that Parliament [had] ever sought to weigh the competing interests or assess the proportionality of a blanket ban on the right of a convicted prisoner to vote."[85] Another exemplar is the South African case *Doctors for Life*.[86] The South African Constitutional Court decided that the

in Constitutional Adjudication' in Grant Huscroft (ed), *Expounding the Constitution: Essays in Constitutional Theory* (CUP 2008).

82 Ittai Bar-Siman-Tov, 'Semiprocedural Judicial Review' (2012) 6 *Legisprudence* 271.

83 *ibid*; Liora Lazarus and Natasha Simonsen, 'Judicial Review and Parliamentary Debate: Enriching the Doctrine of Due Deference' in Murray Hunt, Hayley Hooper, and Paul Yowell (eds), *Parliament and Human Rights: Redressing the Democratic Deficit* (OUP 2014) chapter 19, 385.

84 *Hirst v. The United Kingdom (No. 2)* (2006) 42 EHRR 41, para 82.

85 *ibid* para 79.

86 *Doctors for Life International v. Speaker of the National Assembly and Others* 2006 (6) SA 416 (CC).

government has a duty to facilitate public involvement in the law-making process. Determining whether the government had acted reasonably to discharge this duty, the court examined the nature and importance of the law in question, as well as its impact on the public.[87] Practical concerns, such as saving time or money, were not accepted by the court as legitimate excuses.[88] "What is ultimately important is that the legislature has taken steps to afford the public a reasonable opportunity to participate effectively in the law-making process," the court wrote.[89] A similar approach can be found in the Colombian constitutional jurisprudence, where a "minimal public deliberation" is required in order to justify deference to the government.[90] A lack of engagement with the interests of the rights-holders, as evidenced by the congressional record, was used by the Colombian Constitutional Court to justify striking down the law in question.[91]

The political branches in hybrid regimes do not always rubber-stamp legislation, but weak democratic accountability gives good reason to question their decision-making processes. Semi-procedural review promotes deliberative and responsive decision-making. Regardless of the precise doctrinal vocabulary used, the approaches adopted by the courts surveyed ask similar questions, including: whether the authorities thoroughly examined alternative choices, whether lawmakers spent sufficient time and effort reviewing relevant options, whether rights-holders were represented and consulted, whether their views were engaged, and to what extent are those impacted by the law in question were given an opportunity to participate in the decision-making process. These questions are informed by democratic principles such as democratic participation, democratic deliberation, and democratic representation. Courts are developing ways to improve this approach, for example, by proposing minimum standards and experimenting with more dialogic remedies that seek to work along with the political branches. Bar Siman Tov has suggested that courts should focus on ensuring "a minimal level of deliberation" and the "possibility for participation."[92] The ultimate goal is not to replace the judgment of the political branches, but to increase the

[87] *ibid* para 128.
[88] *ibid.*
[89] *ibid* para 129.
[90] David Landau, 'Political Institutions and Judicial Role in Comparative Constitutional Law' (2010) 51 *Harvard International Law Journal* 319, 363.
[91] *ibid* 363–4.
[92] Bar-Siman-Tov (n 82) 297.

transparency of the political process and weed out substantive flaws and dubious intentions.

Semi-procedural review comes with undeniable costs. It may increase the complexity of cases, with judges having to spend longer examining legislative materials. Some may be worried about a court's lack of expertise. However, courts are accustomed to examining and referring to legislative materials given that they are routinely asked to ascertain the legislative intent of the law. Moreover, there is a growing body of comparative jurisprudence for courts to learn from. Courts already have the analytical tools to apply and hone this technique. Echoing the conclusions of Liora Lazarus and Natasha Simonsen, the democratic gains realized by introducing the quality of democratic deliberation as an evaluative criterion outweigh the implementation considerations that others might have.[93] This is especially the case in a hybrid regime, where political rights are weakly protected and political processes deliberately undermine representative and deliberative values.

4.3.3 Participatory Role

The global rise in judicial power has created new opportunities for individuals to participate in politics through the legal process. These opportunities, as Rachel Cichowski explains, do not necessarily diminish democracy, as the legal process does not seek to replace the traditional avenues of political participation such as voting, lobbying, and protesting.[94] Instead, the expansion of judicial power opens up an alternative means for political participation and to channel disagreements. The legal mobilization literature generally shows how activists and civil society organizations in all kinds of regime types have used domestic courts and supranational ones to express their opinions and shape policy outcomes.[95]

The general point about courts as complementary participatory channels lends particular credence to a hybrid regime. A central problem of

[93] Lazarus and Simonsen (n 83) 401.

[94] Rachel Cichowski, 'Courts, Rights, and Democratic Participation' (2006) 39 *Comparative Political Studies* 50.

[95] See e.g. Waikeung Tam, *Legal Mobilization under Authoritarianism: The Case of Postcolonial Hong Kong* (CUP 2012); Freek Van der Vet, '"When They Come for You": Legal Mobilization in New Authoritarian Russia' (2018) 52 *Law & Society Review* 301; Lynette Chua, 'Legal Mobilization and Authoritarianism' (2019) 15 *Annual Review of Law and Social Science* 355.

a hybrid regime is the arbitrary clogging of political participatory channels and systemic disenfranchisement. Social groups such as the opposition and dissidents face significantly higher costs of political participation because of their ideology and political backgrounds. Voices that challenge status quo are suppressed, muted, or even excluded from the political market. Certain views and interests are consequently not properly or never represented in formal political processes. A hybrid regime may maintain a façade of fair public contestation, but as long as the incumbent and its allies have privileged access to resources, networks, and positions of power, challengers are handicapped or even wholly excluded from the political process.

The participatory role facilitates democracy by providing additional participatory opportunities to those who are disenfranchised in a hybrid regime. The argument is not primarily concerned with a reliance on courts to directly change the outcomes of certain laws and policies. Rather, a court, as a participatory channel, is intrinsically valuable as it expands the space for public participation and breathes life into the voices that are left out in the political market of a hybrid regime.[96] The participatory potential of a court is "grounded in procedural features that are essential characteristics of judicial institutions per se."[97] The adjudicative nature of the legal process, or, more precisely, the right to hearing and the right to grievance, can be thought of as a novel way of enhancing the right to political participation. The legal process does not promise a claimant success, but it does guarantee his or her right to assert a legal claim and the opportunity to make his or her case using legal reasoning, legal justifications, and evidence.

Also relevant is the expressive function that comes with the legal process. Legal proceedings and judgments are often public in nature. Interactions within the courtroom, including what is said and argued by the claimant, are reported on by the press and can carry weight in the public discourse. Judicial decisions, especially in common law decisions, also explicitly set out the factual accounts and reasoning offered by the parties, formally documenting the different narratives.

By taking advantage of the procedural features of the legal process and its public nature, those who are persecuted and silenced in a hybrid regime can use courts as a platform to make their voices heard. A claimant may

[96] Rosanvallon (n 41) 145. See also Aileen Kavanagh, 'Participation and Judicial Review: A Reply to Jeremy Waldron' (2003) 22 *Law and Philosophy* 451.

[97] Alon Harel, *Why Law Matters* (OUP 2014) 192.

face all sorts of challenges if he or she expresses similar views through other political channels. In fact, opposition and dissidents are often censored or jailed *because* of their political expressions. Typical avenues for political participation may simply be unavailable to certain social groups. Seen in this light, constitutional courts, or courts in general, provide a lower-risk avenue for these groups to participate in politics, as the legal process is a channel that is formally sanctioned by the state. A court's expressive function in this regard may not be as good as a well-functioning legislature, but is nonetheless desirable if a well-functioning legislature is not present.

4.3.3.1 A Second-best Participatory Channel

As a participatory channel, the legal process is limited in many ways. To activate the legal process, one must become a claimant by framing the grievance as a right and finding the appropriate cause of action. The political message the claimant wishes to make may be distorted or diluted as a result of being reformulated as a legal claim. The claimant may also need the assistance of lawyers to translate a political claim into a legal one. Aside from the gap in expertise, there is also a financial barrier. In many jurisdictions, litigation can be costly. On top of lawyers' fees and the costs of case preparation, one might have to also pay for the legal costs of the adversary (especially in common-law jurisdictions). Making oneself heard through the legal process can consequently be an expensive endeavor, and only those who can overcome these barriers can participate in the legal process. Accordingly, some might argue that the legal process is self-selecting as it only represents the voices of the wealthy. Finally, due to court backlogs and a high caseload, the legal process in some jurisdictions can be very slow and may not be as flexible as more traditional channels for political participation in adapting to changing circumstances.

Consistent with the theme of this chapter, the argument here is a second-best one. As I made clear at the beginning, the idea here is not for the legal process to replace or replicate the traditional avenues of participation, but to complement them. This complementary effect is especially valuable in a hybrid regime given the lack of participatory opportunities to begin with. For some constituents, the participatory role is more accessible than the political branches of government, and provides a rare opportunity for these social groups to express claims that compete with or counter the regime's. While the legal process is not without its challenges, the hostility posed by the incumbent government through the political channels may be absent from the legal process. The court is not a democratic forum, but a court can realize some of the participatory values that are typically instantiated through the political branches. A claimant enjoys a right to participate in the legal process, and he or she can use the legal process in ways that resemble a formal political channel. The legal process reveals and/or amplifies expressions that are left out in the political process. Assuming that the claims are framed properly in court, the government is forced to acknowledge the existence of different political ideologies and kinds of reasoning, and address them with the level of respect they deserve by defending against these claims with accepted modes of legal argumentation and facts.

This role, I emphasize, does not depend on the substantive outcome but on the potential of the legal process to descriptively represent different voices.[98] Though the law might ultimately be on the government's side, the legal process can, at the very least, provide a platform for views that would have otherwise been ignored or trivialized by the incumbent in the political arenas. The monopolization of "truth" is one of the most effective ways to maintain authoritarian control. Courts counter this Orwellian nightmare by allowing the people to challenge the incumbent regime's claims. The market of ideas theory posits that the "truth" will reveal itself so long as voices within society are allowed to compete freely. The "truth" is not determined by a single arbiter such as a court, but rather by the political market, that is, the people. Courts facilitate the revelation of the "truth" by making the public aware of the lost voices and respecting these voices through formal recognition. These voices, institutionalized by the adjudicative process, may destabilize the dominant narrative so carefully curated by the regime. The court enriches the democratic space by surfacing views that are suppressed or hidden by the authoritarian.

4.3.3.2 Overcoming Barriers

Furthermore, the limitations identified so far do not render the participatory role obsolete. The fact that a political claim needs to be translated into a legal claim is something that can and is often overcome by litigants in authoritarian regimes, as evidenced by how legal mobilization movements are prevalent in both common-law (such as Hong Kong, Pakistan,

[98] This is not the same as Pitkin's concept of "descriptive representation," which refers to representatives who share similar attributes with their representees. See Pitkin (n 31) chapter 4. Representation is descriptive here in the sense that the court can bring into public existence voices that have existed all along but are suppressed.

and Uganda)[99] and civil-law (such as Russia, Ukraine, and Turkey) authoritarian jurisdictions.[100] Many lawyers in these jurisdictions are willing to take on public-interest cases at a significantly lower cost or even on a pro bono basis. It is not uncommon to find lawyers leading opposition movements and formulating political and legal strategies to challenge the incumbent. Creative solutions have also been devised to help raise funds for litigations. Aside from the more traditional methods such as forming political parties and lobbying private donors, opposition in jurisdictions such as Russia, Ukraine, and Hong Kong have experimented innovatively on online crowdfunding to finance political campaigns as well as defense and public-interest litigation.[101]

By controlling the fluidity of legal traffic, courts have the tools to mitigate the aforementioned challenges as well. Generally, access to justice rules and constitutional rights are judicially enforced and tend to be malleable. A generous interpretation may well expand this alternative space for public participation. Article 184(3) of the Pakistani constitution provides the Supreme Court with original jurisdiction to take up cases of public importance and related to the enforcement of fundamental rights. This provision offers considerable room for legal interpretation. The power of original jurisdiction, or also known as *suo moto* actions, has been interpreted broadly, especially during the Chaudhry court era. Chaudhry's more progressive use of *suo moto* actions provided "direct" and "faster" access to justice to "the most underprivileged segments of society."[102]

The Ugandan courts, in contrast, adopted a more cautious and gradual approach to expanding the accessibility of the courts. The infamous Rule 4 of the Constitutional Court Rules (1996) provided that a petition must be filed within thirty days of the alleged constitutional breach. Important

[99] Tam (n 95); John Mubangizi, 'Strategic Litigation in South Africa and Uganda: Shared Perspectives and Comparative Lessons' (2020) 13 *African Journal of Legal Studies* 351; Sahar Shafqat, 'Civil Society and the Lawyers' Movement of Pakistan' (2018) 43 *Law & Social Inquiry* 889.

[100] See Van der Vet (n 95); Sophia Wilson, 'Cause Lawyering in Revolutionary Ukraine' (2017) 5 *Journal of Law and Courts* 267; Ceren Belge, 'Friends of the Court: The Republican Alliance and Selective Activism of the Constitutional Court of Turkey' (2006) 40 *Law & Society Review* 653.

[101] Alexander Sokolov, 'Russian Political Crowdfunding' (2015) 23 *Demokratizatsiya: The Journal of Post-Soviet Democratization* 117; Natalia Khoma, 'Technologies of Political (Socio-political) Crowdsourcing and Crowdfunding: World Experience and Steps Towards Implementation in Ukraine' (2015) 1 *Toruńskie Studia Międzynarodowe* 149; Julius Yam, 'Political Crowdfunding of Rights' (2020) 50 *Hong Kong Law Journal* 395.

[102] Qazi (n 47) 304.

constitutional challenges in the earlier days had been time-barred by the thirty-day rule.[103] The justices themselves noticed the "irony" of this: that even applicants involved in a contractual breach or a tort action had "far more time to bring [an] action" than in a constitutional breach.[104] In around half a decade, the courts fixed the problem in incremental fashion, first by construing that the thirty-day period commences after the claimant perceives the alleged breach,[105] and finally declaring that the rule violates the right of access to the constitutional court.[106]

The attitude of the Hong Kong courts is similarly liberal when it comes to legal access rights. To establish standing in judicial review in Hong Kong, one must demonstrate "sufficient interest" in the disputed matter. Courts generally give this requirement a broad interpretation: an applicant need not necessarily be the aggrieved person directly affected by the policy or decision to qualify for standing. In the absence of an obvious or direct interest, courts have also granted standing when the proper context arises.[107] Relaxing access norms invites a broader range of individuals and groups to make use of the legal process. A less rigid understanding of rights reduces the difficulty of translating a political expression into a judicially enforceable claim.

4.3.4 Quasi-representative Role

The quasi-representative role promotes political representation by applying legal tests favorable to litigants suffering from authoritarian bias or neglect.[108] The kind of political representation I am referring to here approximates to Hanna Pitkin's account of "substantive representation," which means acting in the interest of those represented.[109] But, of course, the court is not exactly a political representative, as it lacks the formal

[103] See e.g. *James Rwanyarale and Anor v. Attorney General* [1997] UGCC 1 (18 December 1997); *Ismail Serugo v. Kampala City Council and Anor* [1999] UGSC 23 (11 June 1999).

[104] *Uganda Association of Women Lawyers and Ors v. Attorney General* [2004] UGCC 1 (10 March 2004).

[105] See e.g. *Joyce Nakacwa v. Attorney General and Ors* [2002] UGCC 1 (11 October 2002).

[106] *Uganda Association of Women Lawyers* (n 104).

[107] Karen Kong, 'Public Interest Litigation in Hong Kong: A New Hope for Social Transformation?' (2009) 28 *Civil Justice Quarterly* 327, 341.

[108] The test to be proposed draws on an argument by Jeff King in *Judging Social Rights*, which will be discussed in detail later.

[109] Pitkin (n 31) 209.

mandate (such as the act of voting) that connects the representee with the representative.

I call this role quasi-representative for two reasons. First, this role supports political representation of those who are politically disadvantaged under a hybrid regime. Not only should a court remove barriers to political participation by acting as an alternative political participatory channel (as required by the participatory role), but the quasi-representative role requires tilting the playing field toward vulnerable litigants. Second, because of how the role is designed, the quasi-representative role may sometimes engender surprisingly majoritarian or democratically responsive patterns of judicial decision-making.

In practice, the quasi-representative role and the interpretative role share overlapping features, as both require courts to use democratic values to guide their applications of judicial doctrines. A crucial difference, however, is that the quasi-representative role has a distinct focus on the status of the litigants.

The quasi-representative role builds on Ely's process-based theory and Jeff King's refinement of Ely's theory. This section begins by discussing each in turn.

4.3.4.1 Representation-reinforcing: Ely

In *Democracy and Distrust*, Ely identifies minority discrimination as one of the most notable forms of political malfunction occurring in the United States at the time he was writing, and devotes one whole chapter to explaining how process theory can facilitate the representation of minorities. He explains that political malfunctions can occur because of concentration of powers in the majority groups. In these circumstances, minority groups cannot truly protect themselves even if they are guaranteed an equal vote.[110] His proposal focuses on unconstitutional motives. That is, laws that are passed with illicit motives or impermissible reasons should be prohibited. His concern is not with the substantive benefits brought upon by a law or policy, but the reasons for depriving a certain group of their entitlements.[111] He acknowledges the forensic difficulties of finding illegitimate motives (such as political representatives may not be open about their motivations), but argues that motives can be inferred from impact and pattern.[112]

110 Ely (n 37) 135.
111 *ibid* 145.
112 *ibid* 136–45.

A main challenge of applying Ely's approach is correctly identifying the particular social groups that are worthy of extra judicial protection. Unconstitutional motives, he argues, can be more easily ascertained by applying the doctrine of suspect classifications.[113] What this means is that the government will bear a higher burden of proof, or be subjected to more rigorous scrutiny, if the law or policy in question is directed against a suspect class or group. Common standards for identification at the time included, the discrete and insular minority approach, the historical discrimination suffered by the group, and the immutability of the group's defining trait. Arguing that those standards are insufficient, he identifies "stereotyping" as more on point.[114] Not all forms of stereotyping are impermissible, as stereotyping can simply be a form of generalization. The kind of stereotyping he has in mind is one that results in a significantly higher chance of legislative misapprehension.[115] This kind of stereotyping is more likely when the stereotyping is one that "serves the interests of the decision-makers."[116]

4.3.4.2 Majoritarian Bias or Neglect: King

King has sought to refine Ely's approach by proposing the "particularly vulnerable to majoritarian bias or neglect" test.[117] He argues that the unconstitutional motivation standard sets too high a bar, and that Ely fails to address subtler instances of discrimination, such as neglect.[118] To address these concerns, he suggests that strong judicial restraint would be inappropriate when the claimant is from a group that is particularly vulnerable to majoritarian bias or neglect. A group is a vulnerable one if it is "at substantial risk of bias or neglect."[119] This naturally excludes minority groups such as corporations, which might be objects of majoritarian bias but are not subjected to the "harm" of bias. King departs from the unconstitutional motive requirement and relies on majoritarian bias instead. This is a broad notion that describes "a form of proactive hostility towards the group, or of disadvantage created by unfair preference for the interests of the majority."[120] By adding majoritarian neglect,

113 *ibid* 145.
114 *ibid* 155–7.
115 *ibid* 157.
116 *ibid* 158.
117 King (n 59) 181.
118 *ibid* 180.
119 *ibid* 182.
120 *ibid* 182.

King accounts for the possibility of harm caused not by proactive prejudice but by an inertia to disregard as result of the majority's position.

King is aware of the challenges of identifying the group in court but argues that these can be addressed. Courts today have ready access to a wide range of materials to help identification, such as government reports, social science studies, and opinions of international and civil society organizations.[121] He also accepts that proving majoritarian bias involves some level of substantive discussion, but his argument is a circumscribed one that focuses on "group or status-based disadvantage."[122] Errors may arise in applying the test, but he argues that, with an appropriate degree of restraint, the error costs can be kept low while reaping the modest benefits offered by courts.

4.3.4.3 Quasi-representative Role: Incumbent Bias or Neglect

While King was addressing the adjudication of social rights in a democracy, his approach can be altered in ways to reinforce political representation in a hybrid regime.

Building on King's approach, the argument here is that: (1) if the claimant is from a group that is particularly vulnerable to *incumbent* bias or neglect, and (2) if that bias or neglect can be linked to the law or policy in question, (3) legal tests that are more favorable to the litigants should be adopted. This approach provides extra legal protection to social groups that are vulnerable to authoritarian bias or neglect in a hybrid regime. As mentioned, this approach resembles some of the techniques under the interpretative role, but its benefits are directed toward disadvantaged social groups in a hybrid regime.

The first step in adapting King's test to the circumstances of hybrid regimes is to recognize that the concept of majoritarian bias is of limited relevance to a hybrid regime, because the hostile group is the incumbent. It is hard to classify whether an incumbent is a majority or minority group, as electoral results are distorted due to unfair elections. Though it is possible, or even probable, that an incumbent possesses majority support, that is not always the case, hence the concept of majoritarian bias rarely applies in the current context.

Instead, the concern is incumbent bias. We have already discussed the biases generated by a lack of electoral accountability and democratic oversight. It follows that the typical victims of incumbent bias are not

121 *ibid* 183.
122 *ibid* 183.

necessarily minority groups. Both majority groups (such as the opposition) and minority groups (such as religious groups and sexual minorities) can be targeted by the incumbent if these groups, because of their ideologies or organizational capacity, pose a threat to the incumbent's power.

Neglect is an equally relevant issue in a hybrid regime. Elections are used by authoritarian incumbents to better gauge public opinion and social sentiment, but elections are poor information-gathering devices if they are unfair and self-selective. A lack of electoral connection to the people means the incumbent may be blindsided by or ignorant to what is happening in society and the views of the less prominent social groups. Unlike the bias situation described in the previous paragraph, neglect here is an unintentional consequence of unfair elections.

Proving (the risk of) harm caused by bias or neglect is probably easier in a hybrid regime due to the severity of the bias or neglect. In a democracy, minority groups are at least able to participate in an open political process. They might not be able to defeat majority groups with entrenched powers, but they can at least compete in the political process. In a hybrid regime, oppressed groups have limited opportunities for political participation, and lack the opportunities to protect themselves through the political channels that exist in a democracy. Given that the views of the incumbent can sometimes go unchecked and unchallenged in a hybrid regime, there is an even greater chance and a potentially higher degree of legislative misapprehension.

A possible response here might be that a lack of democracy might be blamed for many things, and this might give courts a free pass to wield broad judicial review powers. This scenario is not necessarily problematic as long as a court's intervention in each instance can be justified. Additionally, establishing linkage between the harm done to a minority group or groups and the incumbent's bias or neglect will be difficult if the incumbent has engaged in responsive law-making. While some social groups may not have a say through the ballot box, if the incumbent is willing to, there are devices that function as proxies for elections that enable more responsive and representative law-making. Like the political branches of government in democracies, those in hybrid regimes can make use of consultation committees and public opinion polls to compensate for the information loss that results from a lack of free and fair elections. Expert reports and academic research would also enable better policymaking. A committed incumbent has the capacity to make good policies that are respectful of different constituents, even if he or she is not democratically elected. The fact that a disenfranchised social group is dissatisfied with a policy in this instance does not necessarily justify judicial intervention, as it could be that the incumbent has already proven that it made reasonable efforts to engage with impacted constituents and accurately balanced competing interests. Good policies can occur in nondemocratic settings. Proving linkage between (the risk of) harm and incumbent bias is ultimately a contextual and evidential question.

A final important difference between my approach and King's concerns the implications of our tests. Under King's approach, the government would be subjected to a higher standard of proof if majority bias or neglect is proven. My approach has wider implications. If a claimant can prove authoritarian bias or neglect and its linkage to the law or policy in question, judges should consider all sorts of ways to support them in court. This includes not only adjusting the burden of proof, but also providing greater legal protection in other areas that the court has control over, such as standing, remedies, legal procedures, costs, and so on. In more concrete terms, this may involve, for example, adopting a higher degree of scrutiny, according less deference to the government, a more flexible application of standing rules, the issuance of stronger remedies, greater leniency toward the claimant with regard to court deadlines, and cost judgments that are more sympathetic to the claimant's motivations. The quasi-representative role alters the power balance in favor of those who are handicapped in the political arenas.

4.3.4.4 Politically Representative Effects?

Earlier, I mentioned that one reason why this role is termed "quasi-representative" is because the approach proposed may sometimes create decision-making patterns that seem politically representative. This is due to the quasi-representative role potentially benefiting vulnerable groups in a hybrid regime who are majority groups or represent interests that enjoy majority support.

An illuminating example is the spate of cases in Hong Kong relating to LGBTQ rights. In Hong Kong, the community is generally in favor of LGBTQ rights. Studies and surveys in the past decade consistently find that a majority of people support the protection of the LGBTQ community.[123] LGBTQ rights in Hong Kong are considered more liberal

[123] A survey conducted in 2005 found that the majority of the public was generally accepting of homosexuals, and the public tended to be in favor of using legislation to tackle lesbian,

than in many other Asian societies with similar social underpinnings, such as China and Singapore.[124] Hong Kong's courts, as opposed to the political branches of its government, have been a key engine for these developments.[125] Despite popular support for the development of LGBTQ rights, the pro-incumbent parties' voter base has conservative inclinations. Because of pro-incumbent parties' dominance in the legislature and the systemic political advantages they enjoy, ordinary political channels were never productive avenues for developing LGBTQ rights. There was not an openly gay lawmaker in Hong Kong until 2012, and there was, and is, little incentive for the incumbent's allies to invest in these issues.

In contrast, Hong Kong's courts appear to have tracked social sentiment and expanded the right to equality to include the prohibition of discrimination on the ground of sexual orientation. From decriminalizing buggery[126] and legalizing transgender marriage[127] to the recognition of marriage or civil partnership status of same-sex couples for dependent visa purposes[128] and the extension of spousal benefits to same-sex married couples,[129] the signs for social change

gay, bisexual, transgender, and queer (LGBTQ) discrimination issues. MVA Hong Kong Limited, Survey on Public Attitudes towards Homosexual (2006), available at www.cmab.gov.hk/doc/en/documents/policy_responsibilities/public_consultation/public_homosexuals_eng.pdf, last visited November 8, 2021. Studies conducted by the University of Hong Kong in 2013 and 2017 found that there was growing support for LGBTQ rights – from 58 percent support for sexual orientation antidiscrimination law in 2013 to 69 percent in 2017 and from 38 percent support for same-sex marriage in 2013 to over 50 percent in 2017. Holning Lau and others, *Support in Hong Kong for Same-Sex Couples' Rights Grew over Four Years (2013–2017): Over Half of People in Hong Kong Support Same-Sex Marriage* (Centre for Comparative and Public Law at the University of Hong Kong 2018).

124 Carole Petersen, 'International Law and the Rights of Gay Men in Former British Colonies: Comparing Hong Kong and Singapore' (2016) 46 *Hong Kong Law Journal* 109.

125 *ibid.* Peterson attributes Hong Kong's relative success in protecting LGBTQ rights to the rights-protective constitutional framework and the incorporation of international law jurisprudence. While undeniably important, those laws alone do not guarantee liberal outcomes. Authoritarian states that regularly violate human rights such as Libya and Egypt are parties to the International Covenant on Civil and Political Rights. James Hollyer and Peter Rosendorff also found that some authoritarian regimes actually torture more after signing conventions against torture in order to signal their dominance and power. James Hollyer and Peter Rosendorff, 'Why Do Authoritarian Regimes Sign the Convention against Torture? Signaling, Domestic Politics and Non-compliance' (2011) 6 *Quarterly Journal of Political Science* 275.

126 *Secretary of Justice v. Yau Yuk Lung* [2007] 3 HKRD 903.

127 *W v. Registrar of Marriages* [2013] 3 HKLRD 90.

128 *QT v. Director of Immigration* [2018] 4 HKC 403.

129 *Leung Chun Kwong v. Secretary for Civil Service* [2019] 4 HKC 281.

through the legal process have been very promising. The local community, international organizations, and multinational corporations have celebrated many of these decisions.[130]

I am not arguing that the Hong Kong courts have decided these cases based on public opinion. Their judgments are filled with elaborate reasoning supported by case law from all around the world. What is interesting, though, is that the courts have afforded a greater degree of judicial protection to the LGBTQ community by explicitly recognizing them as a protected class. This is in stark contrast to how the incumbent has treated these groups in the political process, where they were given limited representational opportunities. Most intriguing is the fact that the courts were actually more majoritarian on this issue than the political process, as sexual rights issues tend to have the backing of the majority of Hong Kong people. This represents one of many cases in Hong Kong where the courts appear to have followed public opinion.[131]

A similar pattern can be found in the constitutional development of women's rights in Uganda. Partly due to Uganda's colonial history and partly due to local customs, gender equality has not been reflected in many of the laws of the country.[132] Because of its "non-democratic framework," as Erica Bussey observes, "the political system in Uganda is structured in such a way that there is little opportunity of full and free debate about any controversial political issue."[133] As a result, the "only place" where "issues of national importance" can be debated is the courts.[134] Accordingly, women rights organizations such as the Uganda Association of Women Lawyers and Law and Advocacy for Women in Uganda have leveraged the legal process to fight for gender equality.[135] Relying on broadly framed constitutional provisions, the Constitutional Court and the Supreme Court of Uganda have struck down legislation that treated women unfairly on issues of divorce, succession, and adultery, and ruled that the practice of female genital mutilation and the government's

[130] See e.g. Mike Ives, 'Gay Official Wins Court Battle for Spousal Benefits in Hong Kong,' *The New York Times*, June 6, 2019.

[131] Eric C. Ip, 'The Democratic Foundations of Judicial Review under Authoritarianism: Theory and Evidence from Hong Kong' (2014) 12 *International Journal of Constitutional Law* 330.

[132] See Manisuli Ssenyonjo, 'Women's Rights to Equality and Non-Discrimination: Discriminatory Family Legislation in Uganda and the Role of Uganda's Constitutional Court' (2007) 21 *International Journal of Law, Policy and the Family* 341.

[133] Bussey (n 57) 22.

[134] *ibid.*

[135] Mubangizi (n 99).

nonprovision of basic maternal healthcare were unconstitutional.[136] Again, these cases have striking representational overtones as they are reflective of the fundamental rights and interests of the entire female population of the country. The quasi-representative role does not require courts to follow public opinion, but may create an image of a politically representative court because of the extra legal protection afforded to vulnerable groups who are sometimes representative of majority interests.

4.3.5 *Educative Role*

Finally, the educative role aims to strengthen the constitutional democratic culture of a hybrid regime. This role focuses exclusively on the indirect or "extralegal effects"[137] generated by a constitutional court. Sociolegal scholars have long identified the potential of courts beyond the courtroom.[138] These indirect effects have been called many different names, such as radiating effects,[139] educational effects,[140] ripple effects,[141] and catalytic effects.[142] They highlight the constitutive power of a court, that is, its ability to shape public meanings.[143] The constitutive power of a constitutional court is derived from the law's expressive nature. The law – be it constitutions, legislations, the legal process, or legal decisions – relies on its expressiveness for its many functions: from coordinating behavior in society to expressing an ideology on behalf of the state.[144] Legal and political changes are a function of the many competing claims constantly made by constitutional and political actors.

136 See Ssenyonjo (n 132); Joseph Oloka-Onyango, *When Courts do Politics: Public Interest Law and Litigation in East Africa* (Cambridge Scholars Publishing 2017) 127–30; *Center for Health, Human Rights and Development (CEHURD) & 3 Ors v. Attorney General* [2020] UGCC 12 (August 19, 2020).

137 Dieter Grimm, 'Integration by Constitution' (2005) 3 *International Journal of Constitutional Law* 193.

138 See Michael McCann, 'Causal Versus Constitutive Explanations (or, On the Difficulty of Being so Positive . . .)' (1996) 21 *Law & Social Inquiry* 457; Marc Galanter, 'The Radiating Effects of Courts' in Keith Boyum and Lynn Mather (eds), *Empirical Theories about Courts* (Longmans 1983); Sally Engle Merry, 'New Legal Realism and the Ethnography of Transnational Law' (2006) 31 *Law & Social Inquiry* 975.

139 Galanter *ibid.*

140 Sadurski (n 13) 286.

141 Celeste Arrington, 'The Mechanisms behind Litigation's "Radiating Effects": Historical Grievances against Japan' (2019) 53 *Law & Society Review* 6, 7.

142 Tamir Moustafa, *Constituting Religion: Islam, Liberal Rights and the Malaysian State* (CUP 2018) chapter 1.

143 *ibid*; McCann (n 138).

144 Richard McAdams, *The Expressive Powers of Law: Theories and Limits* (HUP 2015).

A constitutional court is one of these actors. It shapes identities, rights, narratives of social events, and constitutional culture more broadly through its decisions, language, and the adjudicative process. Moreover, social media and the internet enable the constitutive power of a court to travel further and penetrate deeper than ever before.

The educative role is made possible because of the constitutive power of a court. A court can play the educative role through the messages it sends, and by acting as a medium through which other parties can send messages. The latter version of the educative role is similar in practice to the participatory role, though the focus of the participatory role is on political participation as opposed to the social effects the court creates. The rest of this section explores the wide range of educative effects courts can produce, and underscores a few principles that can guide judges in taking up the educative role.

As argued in this chapter, a goal of the referee role is to bolster rule-of -law values. One of the ways the referee role can achieve this is through *demonstrating* that the law matters. The educative effect here derives from the visible aspect of the referee role. Using the well-known maxim, justice needs to be seen to be done. Public displays of abuse and impunity create the impression that powers to be can "get away with it." The referee role has a secondary effect of demonstrating to the public that rule of law as an ideal is achievable and is to be taken seriously. The indirect impact of the referee role is to socialize the people and the incumbent into rule-of-law norms.

The words chosen and the reasoning adopted by a constitutional court shape the language used in the constitutional landscape. Judges need to be aware of the potential power of rhetoric, and adjust their language in ways that promote a more attractive understanding of the constitution and rights. As Alec Stone Sweet notes, within the cycle of the judicialization of politics, "legislators absorb the behaviour norms of constitutional adjudication, and the grammar and vocabulary of constitutional law, into those repertoires of reasoning and action that constitute political agency."[145] Similarly, Sadurski argues that judicial review has the effect of "promot[ing] the 'right' understanding of constitutional rights among the legislators and the general public."[146] Political actors' adoption of a set of constitutional language might lead to their internalization of

[145] Alec Stone Sweet, *Governing with Judges: Constitutional Politics in Europe* (OUP 2000) 202.

[146] Sadurski (n 13) 286.

constitutional norms. The rhetoric of the court structures the behavior of the incumbent and could potentially trigger a cognitive shift in how those in power should understand their responsibilities as political representatives.

Constitutional courts should also supply discursive frameworks and communicative resources to democracy activists and other allies outside the courtroom. Through their experience with the adjudicative process and by observing judgments, oppositional groups and dissidents can learn to transform grievances into rights-based claims. This change of frame – from a narrow political demand to a generalizable right – potentially legitimizes their claims, widening the appeal of their political message and increasing its relevance.[147] Protestors from Hong Kong have relied on concepts found in the city's mini-constitution, international conventions, and judicial decisions to frame their demands and appeal to the international community. This kind of educative effect does not necessarily depend on the final outcome of a judicial decision. Case studies have shown how merely granting standing can already endow political claims with credibility and legitimacy.[148] In Pakistan, while anticorruption cases were not always obeyed, they were, as Moeen Cheema observes, "reported with considerable excitement in the domestic press" and had "weaved a narrative of endemic corruption and crony capitalism" that "belied the [incumbent's] claim of good governance."[149]

The court and its decisions can act as focal points to destabilize the authoritarian as well. The incumbent intentionally makes coordination by the opposition difficult through a range of political tactics, such as banning political parties and imposing harsh conditions for public gatherings. The legal process, as noted earlier, is public in nature, and important court cases frequently attract media attention. By ruling against the government, a court's decision that brings constitutional violations to the public's attention could potentially mobilize the public against the incumbent.[150] Legal defeats might also spark public outrage against authoritarian policies.[151] For instance, even though the

[147] Arrington (n 141) 21–2.

[148] Arrington (n 141) 22.

[149] Moeen Cheema, 'Two Steps Forward One Step Back: The Non-linear Expansion of Judicial Power in Pakistan' (2018) 16 *International Journal of Constitutional Law* 503, 517.

[150] David Law, 'A Theory of Judicial Power and Judicial Review' (2008) 97 *Georgetown Law Journal* 723.

[151] See Douglas NeJaime, 'Winning Through Losing' (2011) 96 *Iowa Law Review* 941.

Constitutional Court of Uganda struck out an initial application challenging the government's failure to provide adequate maternal healthcare, the Museveni government decided shortly after to improve hospital conditions and emergency services, possibly because it had to appease growing dissatisfaction of its public healthcare system.[152] Focal points can also be created by other events related to legal proceedings. Even court dates, as Celeste Arrington observes in the context of Japan, "entail an element of public performance and institutionalized ritual that provides moments to rally supporters and media attention."[153]

A constitutional court might also act as a conduit for messages, and a constitutional court can control the reach of these messages. Politicians in Israel, for example, have used legal proceedings to gain media exposure and change popular discourse, even though they are aware that they are likely to lose in court.[154] The educative role entails amplifying the attractive aspects of those messages, which might mean adopting the challengers' concerns, putting greater emphasis on rights-protective elements, and exposing gaps in the laws.

4.3.5.1 Principles in Applying the Educative Role

The examples given so far contain some lessons for how a constitutional court can play this educative role effectively. First and foremost, the court needs to be aware of and sensitive to its audiences. As Mark Galanter observes, "[the outward influences of a court] cannot be ascertained by attending only to the messages propounded by the courts. It depends on the resources and capacities of their various audiences and on the normative orderings indigenous to the various social locations where messages from the courts impinge."[155] Given this role's emphasis is on its expressive nature and the communicative resources it offers, a constitutional court needs to anticipate who will be reading the judgment, their motivations, and potential responses. The coming chapter elaborates further on the importance of courts remaining sensitive to their audiences.

152 Oloka-Onyango (n 136) 267. The case was dismissed based on the political question doctrine. Upon appeal, the Supreme Court decided that the courts do have jurisdiction. And subsequently, the constitutional court decided the omission was unconstitutional.

153 Arrington (n 141) 25.

154 Yoav Dotan and Menachem Hofnung, 'Legal Defeats–Political Wins: Why Do Elected Representatives Go to Court?' (2005) 38 *Comparative Political Studies* 75.

155 Galanter (n 138) 118.

Second, a constitutional court must closely attend to the language it uses. Legal decisions that are crafted in overly technical or open-ended ways invite competing interpretations. Political actors seeking distortion may claim a different understanding. A court cannot simply reissue another decision to clarify what it meant. If there is a clear message or tone that a court wishes to convey, it should aim to contextualize its message and minimize room for distortion.

Third, and most importantly, a constitutional court needs allies outside the courtroom to facilitate its educative role. Galanter's observation above reveals an inherent limitation of this role: the creation of meaning is a dynamic process, and courts cannot determine public meaning on their own, at most being able to shape and influence its formation. A court can minimize distortion through careful writing, but how a court's behavior and decisions are interpreted are ultimately left to the audiences external to the courtroom. In most cases, however, decisions do not reach audiences directly. More commonly, "sophisticated intermediaries"[156] such as the press, professional organizations, and the academy interpret the decisions and provide a more layperson-friendly narrative. These intermediaries help "translate" the law and amplify the decision. It then becomes important for the court to nurture friendly relations with these intermediaries, as they directly affect a constitutional court's constitutive power. They are not simply transmission vessels, but powerful middlemen who can apply interpretive frames to induce certain kinds of social behavior. The state may seek to undermine the court and its allies by co-opting media outlets, but a court can also enhance freedom of information and other organizational rights to counter authoritarian intermediaries. A court needs trusted mediums, and trusted mediums need the constitutional protection of the court. A symbiotic relationship between the courts and its intermediaries is essential to the effective implementation of the educative role. In the penultimate chapter, we will examine more closely the ways in which courts can build relationships with allies outside the courtroom.

Last but not least, similar to what was argued under the participatory role, it is important for a court to remain accessible. This is not because of the intrinsic value accorded by this alternative participatory channel. Instead, a court must be accessible so that its political allies can rely on the legal process to disseminate their messages. Some of the educative effects of a court already discussed are impossible if the legal process is

[156] Law (n 150) 751.

too restrictive. A court can also set its own agenda in this regard by exercising its discretionary power regarding which kinds of cases get through and when to hear them.

4.4 Institutional Competence

So far, I have argued that a constitutional court should protect and promote democratic values in a hybrid regime. The five roles discussed in this chapter set out different ways for courts to achieve that goal. The roles sometimes also address pathologies associated with unfair elections and a lack of democratic oversight.

Democratic theory is used to justify these roles, but there is also a question of institutional legitimacy. The roles perhaps demand more of a constitutional court than what would be expected in a democratic political system, hence institutional competency concerns might be magnified. Constitutional lawyers may question whether a constitutional court has the capacity to perform the democratic roles outlined in this chapter and the extent to which those roles are limited by competency concerns.

While acknowledging the institutional limitations of a constitutional court, I argue that the democratic roles are defensible for three reasons. First, institutional competency concerns are not absolute arguments and must be assessed on case-by-case and role-by-role bases. Second, the democratic roles are not an excessive stretch of a constitutional court. Third, and most importantly, some level of departure from competency considerations is warranted, given a hybrid regime's lack of democracy and the political dysfunctionality associated with this. Questions of institutional competency are relative and depend on the extent to which the political branches of government are functioning according to their intended goals. A mature democracy with well-functioning political institutions calls for a more deferential constitutional court due to the democratic objections discussed. Exceptional circumstances, such as when the constitution is being disputed or undergoing transition, might require a more creative and activist court, as a court may have "no option" but to transcend the law to preserve the constitutional order.[157] Similarly, what I argue is that some of the risks associated with pushing

[157] See N. W. Barber, and Adrian Vermeule, 'The Exceptional Role of Courts in the Constitutional Order' (2016) 92 *The Notre Dame Law Review* 817.

the normative boundaries imposed by competency considerations are worth bearing because of the democratic benefits it might yield.

Institutional competency captures the idea that authority is allocated according to the institution's likelihood of reaching good outcomes.[158] Is a question suitable for the court to consider given its institutional qualities? A court is considered legitimately exercising its power if it has the necessary capacity to do so.[159] Judges are professionally trained in the law. The adjudicative process provides opportunities for the parties to offer reasoned arguments. Judges, after hearing the relevant arguments, arrive at a decision based on preexisting legal and constitutional norms and accepted modes of reasoning.

Different questions call for different standards of decision-making. It is often argued that a court is not best equipped to deal with polycentric questions given their complexity and potential to disrupt relations far beyond the suit.[160] The focused nature of adjudication does not allow courts to address the more layered issues involved. There are also disputes whose resolution lies beyond the expertise of the professionally trained judges: questions of morality or pure preferences might be best left to the masses for public deliberation and voting, while social distribution problems will benefit from technocratic expertise that judges lack.[161] Judges also may not have the necessary information to arrive at a proper decision since the adjudicative process is limited to the evidence and arguments provided by the litigating parties. Facing empirical uncertainty, judges are incapable of evaluating the precise effects of their decisions with the possibility of creating unintended adverse effects.[162] Conversely, a legislature, with its ability to consult people and cater for a multitude of interests, is designed for policymaking.[163] Presumably, even legislatures in hybrid regimes can gather more information and have access to better political solutions than the courts. Whether the political branches of a hybrid regime actually use their institutional competence for the betterment of society or for authoritarian entrenchment is another issue that I set aside for now. As discussed, institutional

[158] King (n 59) 130. See also Kavanagh (n 81).

[159] Lorne Sossin, *Boundaries of Judicial Review: The Law of Justiciability in Canada* (Carswell 1999) 292.

[160] Lon Fuller, 'The Forms and Limits of Adjudication' (1978) 92 *Harvard Law Review* 353.

[161] Donald Horowitz, *Courts and Social Policy* (Brookings Institution Press 1977).

[162] Adrian Vermeule, *Judging Under Uncertainty: An Institutional Theory of Legal Interpretation* (HUP 2006). See also Yowell (n 7).

[163] N. W. Barber, *The Principles of Constitutionalism* (OUP 2018) chapter 3.

competence is not necessarily related to regime type, and the same limitations exist in courts in hybrid regimes. Transgressing a court's institutional boundaries increases the chances of arriving at wrong decisions. A court can never act like an elected institution because judges are typically unelected and the court lacks some of the institutional advantages of the other branches.

Some may treat competency challenges as general and decisive arguments. However, they are only possible *weights* against the democratic roles. Expertise and information-gathering capacity, for instance, must be proven on an issue-by-issue basis, and not be generally assumed from the political branches' position or the subject matter involved.[164] Not every constitutional case poses the same kinds of obstacles to a constitutional court. The fact that a case's impact may be far-reaching and uncertain, for example, does not automatically justify judicial restraint. Judges lay down legal principles; it is a collateral effect of this duty that these principles will affect many people and relationships beyond the litigants.[165]

More importantly, the strength of those arguments must be tested against each of the democratic roles suggested individually. A closer examination of each role shows that the competency concerns are not as pronounced as some might assume.

Among the five roles described, capacity concerns are least relevant for the referee role and the participatory role. The referee role relies on the inherent expertise of courts in adjudication and procedural justice. The rule-based nature of the referee role sets out clear limits for the extent of judicial intervention. The participatory role, in contrast, begins to blur the line between law and politics by allowing political claims to be expressed through the legal process. While the participatory role calls for a generous interpretation of access rules and constitutional rights, it does not suggest that all political claims should be allowed in the courtroom. As argued in this chapter, those looking to use the constitutional court as a participatory channel must translate a political claim into a legal claim by first reframing their political demands using legal language and by complying with the relevant rules of legal access. Satisfying these criteria is not necessarily challenging, but access rules limit the scope of the participatory role. The efficacy of the participatory role is also independent of substantive outcomes. Its benefits are procedural in

164 Chan (n 79).
165 King (n 59) 193.

nature, providing those who are frozen out of the political process opportunities to express their views.

While the interpretative and quasi-representative roles have a heavy substantive dimension, they rely on and are limited by what King calls the "basic interpretative approach" of a court. The "basic interpretative approach" checks the "acceptability of the justifications put forward for interferences with or denials of interests in question."[166] The interpretive role does not give a constitutional court a free pass to actively fix every political problem in a hybrid regime. The role is conditioned by the principles that structure the adjudicative process, the standards of the legal community, and the kinds of arguments leveled by the litigants. The process of reaching decisions under the basic interpretative approach is what defines the legal dimension of a constitutional court and distinguishes the interpretative role fundamentally from the political roles of the legislature and the executive branches. The authoritarian effects of what is being challenged help determine the strengths of the government's defense and the plausibility of its premises. The interpretative role has political effects, but the manner in which decisions are reached under the interpretative role is still largely consistent with how a constitutional court normally decides.

Similarly, the court is not asked to track public opinion under the quasi-representative role, but to afford extra judicial protection to certain kinds of social groups. The basic interpretative approach is retained. Drawing on Ely and King, I have proposed a workable standard to identify these groups and the necessary elements to activate this role. To address questions of competency, a court can be assisted by all kinds of extrinsic materials to trace the impact of incumbent bias or neglect.

The educative role highlights the social effects created by a court, some of which may be considered secondary in nature, but those effects are derived from the adjudicative process. In fact, the educative role is functionally similar to the traditional watchdog role of a constitutional court (through the signaling effects it creates), complemented by a higher degree of democratic sensitivity when crafting the contents of the judgments. Some might be concerned about the far-reaching social effects this role might have. It is the duty of a constitutional court to lay down fundamental principles that govern society. As I have previously pointed out, the fact that the effects it creates are far-reaching is not necessarily a problem. The real question is whether the messages the court sends are

[166] *ibid* 97.

legitimate, and the activities carried out under the educative role – such as the adoption of rights-based language, spotlighting constitutional transgressions, and making democratically attractive parts of the judgment accessible – are justifiable under democratic theory.

Perhaps the real discomfort lies in the fact that the interpretative role, the quasi-representative role, and the educative role require judges to consider democratic norms during constitutional adjudication. I have four responses to this. First, democracy is constitutionally good and there is no shame in the judicial advancement of democratic values. Second, a thin conception of democracy can already activate these roles. Third, the courts are not asked to develop and put forth their own theory of democracy, but to focus on the elements that would promote democratic values during constitutional adjudication. Last, I have relied on familiar aspects of the adjudicative process and offered specific guidelines under each role to structure their application.

Finally, and perhaps most importantly, these roles are justifiable from a comparative institutional perspective because they address problems that occur in hybrid regimes as a consequence of how their political branches are structured. Comparative institutional analysis assesses institutions based on *relative* institutional competence.[167] Neil Komesar explains how comparative institutional approaches should be applied to the study of law.[168] Different institutions are "alternative mechanisms by which societies carry out their goals."[169] In deciding how to allocate authority, comparative institutional competence cannot be avoided. Each institution presents different sets of strengths and flaws, and there can be multiple institutional pathways to reach a particular goal. Institutions should always be assessed relative to each other against a uniform standard. The fact that an institution seems to be performing suboptimally does not necessarily imply that an alternative institution must be superior. However, it may be a strong reason to consider alternatives. Komesar reminds us that, "we must confront the reality that the best choices will be highly imperfect and that the relative merits of institutions will vary across different settings."[170]

167 See Daniel H. Cole, 'The Varieties of Comparative Institutional Analysis' (2013) *Wisconsin Law Review* 383.

168 Neil K. Komesar, *Imperfect Alternatives: Choosing Institutions in Law, Economics, and Public Policy* (University of Chicago Press 1994); Neil K. Komesar, *Law's Limits: Rule of Law and the Supply and Demand of Rights* (CUP 2001).

169 *ibid Law's Limits*, 31.

170 *ibid* 189.

A constitutional court is an imperfect solution to the political problems of a hybrid regime, but there are also limited alternatives in a hybrid regime. Elections are rigged, space for public mobilization is restricted, and the media is subjected to a substantial level of state control. As noted previously, the competency concerns relating to stretching the role of a constitutional court are only weights. They must be weighed up against the potential gains of the democratic roles and the available alternatives. In the absence of alternatives *and* if a sufficient level of judicial autonomy can be guaranteed, a constitutional court can and should act as a second-best solution to the democratic failures of a hybrid regime. The very reason for arguing for those roles is that the political branches in a hybrid regime tend to bc unable to fulfil many of their intended functions. The utility of the referee role, for instance, rests on the rule-breaking tendency of an authoritarian; the participatory role and the quasi-representative role look to supplement the lack of participatory opportunities and reinforce political representation; and the interpretative role and the educative role help restore and protect democratic norms on a more general level. True to the comparative institutional spirit, the democratic roles may only be a temporary remedy, as opposed to a permanent fix. Holding the court constant, if the political branches begin to improve and reform or if the political process is capable of self-correction, the competency considerations should be given more weight and the constitutional court should start taking a back seat.

4.5 Conclusion

In the first half of the chapter, we considered the extent to which democratic objections against judicial review apply to a hybrid regime. I showed that the democratic objections do not hinder the pursuit of democracy-enhancing judicial roles, as the conditions for them to apply to a hybrid regime are missing or weakened. The considerations raised by those objections paved the way for us to consider how a constitutional court can and should support democratic ideals in a hybrid regime.

Five democracy-enhancing roles were discussed. Each role highlights a different aspect of a constitutional court and contributes to enhancing democracy in a different way. The referee role seeks to preserve rule-of-law values by enforcing rules impartially; the interpretative role requires exercising judicial discretion in ways that are consistent with democratic values; the participatory role asks the court to act as an alternative political participatory channel; the quasi-representative role promotes political representation by protecting disadvantaged groups in a hybrid regime; and the educative role reinforces the democratic culture of a hybrid regime through judicial rhetoric and the court's expressive functions.

This chapter acknowledged the limitations that a constitutional court faces in undertaking these roles, but argued that a constitutional court is an attractive second-best solution, given the democratic deficit in a hybrid regime, and considering the lack of viable alternatives and the positive impact exercising these roles can have on embedding democratic values. The chapter has also considered ways of addressing competency issues with regard to each of the democratic roles. Those concerns are answerable and, to some extent, already factored into the roles themselves.

Another consideration at play is their feasibility. An assumption here is that a constitutional court must enjoy a sufficient degree of judicial autonomy. This, as the previous chapters have shown, is a realistic possibility. However, there is the question of whether these democratic roles are sustainable, and how the authoritarian climate of a hybrid regime might affect the application of the democratic roles. These issues will be taken up in the coming chapters.

5

The Legitimacy Paradox

5.1 Introduction

In the previous chapter, we explored ways in which a constitutional court can and should contribute to democratic values in a hybrid regime. Toward the end of the chapter, I also highlighted the extent to which questions of competency might limit the democracy-enhancing roles of a constitutional court. While democratic theory may justify the roles suggested, we must also engage with another question: whether it is *feasible* for a constitutional court to play those roles under the political climate of a hybrid regime. Empirical evidence, as laid out in Chapter 3, generally shows that constitutional courts in hybrid regimes enjoy some degree of judicial autonomy. Those findings give us prima facie reasons to believe that the democratic roles are possible. This chapter takes a closer look at how the hybridity of a hybrid regime impacts the conditions under which a constitutional court exercises its powers and applies the roles. This issue is explored through the lens of perceived legitimacy.

This chapter argues that courts in hybrid regimes face a legitimacy paradox: An activist court risks attracting backlash from the authoritarian, whereas a deferential court may undermine the trust of a democracy-supporting population. The paradox emerges from the competing ideologies of a hybrid regime mentioned in Chapter 2. Consequently, the way the judiciary navigates politically salient cases will have huge effects on its institutional health. As explained later in the chapter, the nature of the dilemma is philosophical, but this problem has practical implications for courts.

One of the earlier scholars to identify the legitimacy paradox was Martin Shapiro.[1] Relying on sociological theories of judicial legitimacy and a relational framework, this chapter develops and unpacks Shapiro's

[1] I borrow the term from Shapiro. See Martin Shapiro, 'Courts in Authoritarian Regimes' in Tom Ginsburg and Tamir Moustafa (eds), *Rule by Law: The Politics of Courts in Authoritarian Regimes* (CUP 2008) 334–5.

legitimacy paradox in a hybrid regime. A court must be able to navigate the legitimacy paradox to play the democratic roles effectively and sustainably. Guidelines regarding how the challenges posed by the paradox can be addressed are discussed in subsequent chapters. This chapter aims to identify and understand the paradox, as well as highlight the challenges it brings.

Legitimacy is conceptualized in either sociological or philosophical/moral terms. This chapter focuses on the sociological conception of judicial legitimacy, or what I refer to as "perceived legitimacy." In the words of David Beetham, the topic of legitimacy is curiously "suspended between two separate bodies of literature."[2] Social scientists focus on the descriptive and empirical dimensions of legitimacy, while political and legal theorists are interested in its moral conditions. The discussion in the previous chapter addressed many questions relating to the normative legitimacy of a constitutional court in a hybrid regime.[3] There are some overlapping concerns between the two conceptions of legitimacy – sociological and normative – since they both relate to the broad concept of legitimacy.[4] Nevertheless, they need to be distinguished, especially since there is a tendency in our daily usage to conflate normative legitimacy with perceived legitimacy. While normative legitimacy relates to the actual justifications of the court as an institution and its actions, perceived legitimacy describes whether people believe and treat a court as if it were legitimate. Perceived legitimacy echoes Max Weber's notion of legitimacy as well as what Joseph Raz terms "de facto authority."[5] The utility of perceived legitimacy is commonly understood to be closely connected to the electoral incentives of democratically elected representatives.[6] As will become evident later, however, the hybridity of

2 David Beetham, *The Legitimation of Power* (Palgrave Macmillan 1991) 7.

3 In particular, it engaged questions of democratic legitimacy and institutional legitimacy of a constitutional court.

4 They are not contrary conceptions of legitimacy as they approach the topic from different angles and can inform one another. Perceived legitimacy is conceptually parasitic on normative legitimacy. Perceived legitimacy describes people's belief of legitimacy. We must at least be aware of what people's normative views of legitimacy are in order to describe this social fact. Perceived legitimacy can also feedback into normative legitimacy. A widely held perception that a court is legitimate suggests that the court at least has some capacity to coordinate society effectively. This perception gives us a reason, though not a decisive reason, to regard it as actually legitimate.

5 Beetham (n 2); Joseph Raz, *The Morality of Freedom* (OUP 1988) chapter 2; Arie Rosen, 'The Normative Fallacy Regarding Law's Authority' in Wil Waluchow and Stefan Sciaraffa (eds), *Philosophical Foundations of the Nature of Law* (OUP 2013) 75.

6 See Georg Vanberg, *The Politics of Constitutional Review in Germany* (CUP 2005); Clifford James Carrubba, 'A Model of the Endogenous Development of Judicial Institutions in

a hybrid regime forces us to rethink how regime-type should affect how we understand the concept of perceived legitimacy.

While judicial power and perceived legitimacy are closely connected concepts, they remain analytically distinct. Judicial power broadly refers to the consequentiality of a court as an actor within the constitutional order.[7] A powerful court is one that has social impact, which means its decisions or opinions are obeyed and respected by the relevant parties. Power can, of course, be used in different ways, and the previous chapter offered direction regarding how that power, if gained, should be exercised. A common function of judicial power is the formal powers enjoyed by a court. For instance, the Polish, Hungarian, and Ugandan constitutional courts are empowered to address legislative omissions, while the South African and Kenyan constitutional courts can issue nonbinding advisory opinions in the absence of a dispute.[8] The range of formal powers courts enjoy is only part of the equation, however.[9] Other factors that shape judicial power include, for example, the formal authority granted by the constitution, the extent to which the political culture is committed to rule-of-law norms, how political powers are distributed, and the perceived legitimacy of a court. The latter is the central focus of this chapter. As such, maintaining perceived legitimacy is not just for the sake of popularity; this perception helps the court maintain its effectiveness. Although perceived legitimacy is only one factor affecting judicial power, it is a particularly salient one in a hybrid regime. More importantly, as the next two chapters demonstrate, judges have some degree of control over its perceived legitimacy.

The rest of the chapter is divided into two parts. Section 5.2 lays out the conventional view of perceived legitimacy, including the mechanisms behind it and its utility. The conventional view is premised upon the political dynamics of a democracy; this requires modification in order to be applicable to a hybrid regime.

Section 5.3 then takes on this task by introducing a relational angle. An audience-based framework is shown to help us identify the key audiences that are relevant to judicial legitimacy in different regime-types. The

Federal and International Systems' (2009) 71 *The Journal of Politics* 55; Gregory A. Caldeira and James L. Gibson, 'The Etiology of Public Support for the Supreme Court' (1992) 36 *American Journal of Political Science* 635.

[7] Stephen Gardbaum, 'What Makes for More or Less Powerful Constitutional Courts?' (2018) 29 *Duke Journal of Comparative and International Law* 1.

[8] See Adem Kassie Abebe and Charles Manga Fombad, 'The Advisory Jurisdiction of Constitutional Courts in Sub-Sahara Africa' (2013) 46 *George Washington International Law Review* 55.

[9] And formally strong courts are not always substantively strong.

audience-based framework is then applied to a hybrid regime to set out the legitimacy paradox. The paradox is a logical outgrowth of the irreconcilable ideologies that define a hybrid regime. The effects of the paradox are practical, as exemplified by the tensions between the expectations different political actors within a hybrid regime have of a constitutional court. It will be explained how these conflicting expectations create challenges for judicial maneuvering in a hybrid regime.

5.2 Perceived Legitimacy: The Conventional View

5.2.1 The Court and the Public

The sociological conception of judicial legitimacy is traditionally linked to public support, or as political scientists call it, "diffuse support."[10] It refers to the people's "confidence in institutions to make, in the long run, desirable public policy."[11] Perceived legitimacy describes whether courts are believed to be and treated as legitimate institutions. Perceived legitimacy seeks to capture a social phenomenon, instead of prescribing standards for determining what legitimacy should mean. As a result, perceived legitimacy is morally agnostic and accommodates different conceptions of normative legitimacy.

Perceived legitimacy matters because it reflects people's deference to a court's decisions and affects its ability to command authority.[12] This is especially so for constitutional courts. As James Gibson and his colleagues note, "since judges often make decisions contrary to the preferences of political majorities, courts, more than any other political institution, require a deep reservoir of good-will."[13] Constitutional courts' inevitable involvement in politics and their potential to decide against the people and political representatives opens them to attacks and public scrutiny. Courts lack the sword and the purse, and do not have the coercive power or resources to ensure compliance. Perceived legitimacy is an important asset of the court, as it "helps members to accept or tolerate outputs to which they are opposed or the effects of which they see as damaging their wants."[14]

10 Caldeira and Gibson (n 6).

11 James Gibson and others, 'The Effects of Judicial Campaign Activity on the Legitimacy of Courts: A Survey-based Experiment' (2011) 64 *Political Research Quarterly* 545, 546.

12 Tom R. Tyler, *Why People Obey the Law* (YUP 1990).

13 James L. Gibson, Gregory A. Caldeira, and Vanessa A. Baird, 'On the Legitimacy of National High Courts' (1998) 92 *American Political Science Review* 343.

14 Caldeira and Gibson (n 6) 637.

Legitimacy is largely a question of degree, and the consequences of its absence become particularly acute below a certain threshold. There is no general answer as to where that threshold is, exactly, as this depends on contextual factors, but perceived legitimacy does not necessarily mean majority support. What is required is a "sufficient base of support" for a court to exercise its powers effectively.[15] At best, the decisions of a court perceived to be illegitimate will be ignored by the political branches of government and the public; at worst, enemies of the court may take advantage of the gap to "reform" the court. On the other hand, a court that is trusted by the people will likely "stand against the winds of public opinion"[16] and also be able to induce compliance of the political branches, even when political actors find the decisions disagreeable.

Disagreement with a ruling does not necessarily suggest perceived illegitimacy. Legal discontent differs from a lack of legitimacy.[17] Judges are entrusted to decide what they think is best according to the constitution and the law. Courts regularly issue decisions that the public, legal community, and academy disagree with. The fact that judges arrive at conclusions we might not like should come as no surprise, as this is simply a facet of their duty. Notwithstanding the strict legalist school of thought, it is understood that there can be reasonable disagreements regarding legal ideas, especially in constitutional cases involving moral and policy considerations. While persistent, sharp disagreements may lead to a decline in perceived legitimacy, dissatisfaction with the outcome of a decision does not necessarily lead to a lack of confidence in the institution. It may be generally accepted that, sometimes, a legitimate court reaches conclusions with which we disagree.

In fact, the possibility of legal disagreement underlines the utility of perceived legitimacy. Perceived legitimacy provides a "reservoir of good will."[18] A high level of perceived legitimacy suggests enduring and favorable attitudes of the court. Consequently, the people will be more forgiving of decisions by a legitimate court. Criticism of a court does not necessarily reduce the public's confidence in it. Having the general support of the public improves the chances of the court surviving the repercussions of its controversial decisions. With it, the court can play the "legitimacy" card to influence the regime, or motivate other constitutional actors to accept the authority of the court.

[15] Tom S. Clark, *The Limits of Judicial Independence* (CUP 2010) 262.

[16] Caldeira and Gibson (n 6) 635.

[17] Richard Fallon, *Law and Legitimacy in the Supreme Court* (HUP 2018) 6.

[18] David Easton, *A Systems Analysis of Political Life* (John Wiley 1965) 275.

Studies find that the reservoir of goodwill tends to be durable.[19] Over longer horizons, though, the level of public support of a court does shift. And, once a court goes reputationally bankrupt, recovery becomes especially difficult. A court's image of neutrality is compromised when the people begin viewing it with distrust and skepticism. These attitudes desacralize the court and a "wrong" decision in this instance will feed their suspicion. This creates a tricky situation for the courts, because there are bound to be decisions that some part of a polity finds disagreeable. Unlike the elected branches, which can "re-establish their legitimacy every few years via electoral processes,"[20] periodic cycles for replenishing perceived legitimacy are unavailable to most courts, or occur less often than the elected branches.[21] The reservoir of goodwill cannot be filled overnight, and once it begins to dry out, political backlash is likely to ensue. People might not only ignore the rulings of the court, but also demand a reduction in the judiciary's power. The confidence of the public is not only intrinsically important to any public institution, but also instrumental to a court's ability to maintain its institutional health.

To maintain the public's support, courts must,[22] according to the conventional view, appear impartial[23] and be careful not to diverge excessively from the will of the majority.[24] In other words, while courts must look like they are applying the law in a professional manner, they also need to be sensitive to public sentiment. Studies find that some courts are actually quite good at tracking public opinion and some judges are highly attuned to the views of the political community and signals that are indicative of public opinion.[25] By suggesting that courts are indirectly accountable to the public, these findings are perhaps at odds with the more traditional conception of the judicial role. As Tom Clark writes, "The irony is that in order to protect its image as a neutral,

[19] Caldeira and Gibson (n 6) 637.

[20] Vuk Radmilovic, 'Strategic Legitimacy Cultivation at the Supreme Court of Canada: Quebec Secession Reference and Beyond' (2010) 43 *Canadian Journal of Political Science* 843, 845.

[21] Some courts that are elected or with shorter tenure may have mechanisms similar in function to the political branches in replenishing legitimacy.

[22] There are factors affecting diffuse support that are beyond the control of the court, such as the public's general level of confidence in the political system. A decline in the public's trust in the government may have spillover effects on the judiciary.

[23] Caldeira and Gibson (n 6); Tyler (n 12).

[24] Robert Dahl, 'Decision-making in a Democracy: The Role of the Supreme Court as a National Policy-maker' (1957) 6 *Journal of Public Law* 279.

[25] Dahl *ibid*; Clark (n 15) 73–5.

independent decision-making body, the Court must in fact pay close attention to what will be deemed acceptable by the populace and sometimes yield from any neutral perspective to avoid overstepping the bounds imposed by perceptions of what is legitimate."[26] As uncomfortable as the conclusion might be, the conventional view described sets out a convincing case about how public opinion indirectly shapes judicial power.

5.2.2 Outside Democracies?

The conventional view rightly captures the utility of perceived legitimacy to courts, but the mechanisms behind the conventional view are limited to a democracy. The conventional view assumes that a nexus can be established between the public and the elected branches. Public opinion matters to courts because the people, through elections, shape the incentives and behavior of the political representatives. Or, as Georg Vanberg argues, the "principal inducement" for why the political branches would respect the judiciary's decisions is the "threat of a loss of public support for elected officials who refuse to be bound by them."[27] The conventional view is predicated upon the assumption that a court-supporting public punishes political actors who seek to undermine the court by voting them out of office.[28] Under this model, the potential to suffer real "electoral consequences"[29] convinces political representatives to exercise self-restraint even when the court is an assertive one that challenges their policies.

This assumption very often holds in democracies.[30] In nondemocratic regimes, however, the nexus between public opinion and electoral pressure is severely weakened, if not completely broken. The conventional view would certainly be inapplicable to a pure authoritarian regime. The lack of electoral competition suggests that the public cannot discipline the incumbent at the ballot box in the same way as democratic publics do. In cases where the authoritarian fully controls the press and the flow of information, the public cannot even monitor the incumbent's behavior.[31] Nor may there be a strong enough opposition to credibly challenge the

[26] Clark *ibid* 22.
[27] Vanberg (n 6) 14.
[28] *ibid*; Carrubba (n 6).
[29] Vanberg (n 6) 14.
[30] Vanberg makes it clear that his theory is limited to advanced democracies. *ibid* 20.
[31] *ibid* 21.

incumbent either.[32] When the public cannot threaten the incumbent's power, it becomes much easier for the incumbent to control its courts, even if the courts command public support. Hence, the role of public opinion in protecting the courts is drastically reduced in a pure authoritarian regime.[33]

For similar reasons, the conventional view cannot fully explain how public opinion contributes to judicial legitimacy in a hybrid regime. The relevance of the public in a hybrid regime is not exactly straightforward. In contrast to the public in authoritarian regimes, those in hybrid regimes enjoy some opportunities and freedoms to participate and compete in elections. Unlike democracies, though, hybrid regime elections are flawed and favor the incumbent. The public still seems to matter, but to a lesser extent than a democracy. The introduction of an unfairly elected government complicates the conventional model. On top of the public, should a court be sensitive to the incumbent's preferences as well? What if there are sharp disagreements between the incumbent and the public? How would the ideological and political tensions between the incumbent and a democracy-supporting population impact the approach taken by a hybrid regime court? The conventional view fails to answer these questions, because the inducement function of the public it posits presumes a functioning democratic system with a democratically accountable government.

5.3 Perceived Legitimacy in a Hybrid Regime

The conventional view is appropriate for mature democracies where democratic norms are entrenched and the political rules are clear and well established. In a hybrid regime, however, elections are less competitive, and informal and authoritarian political norms play a larger role in everyday politics. Given some of the limitations of the conventional view outside democracies, this part develops an audience-based framework to better understand the political foundation of perceived legitimacy in a hybrid regime. The audience-based framework maintains some of the insights of the conventional view but supplements it with a relational angle.

[32] Brad Epperly, *The Political Foundations of Judicial Independence in Dictatorship and Democracy* (OUP 2019) 129.

[33] This does not mean the public is irrelevant. Rather, it means that the public may have to incur greater costs in order for it to have an impact.

The proposed framework resonates with a broader call for what Bjorn Dressel, Raul Sanchez-Urribarri, and Alexander Stroh term a "relational approach" to studying judicial politics.[34] An increasing number of scholars have highlighted the significance of relational networks involving judges to studying judicial patterns outside mature democracies. Learning about formal rules and institutional structure when studying courts in authoritarian contexts is not enough. As Dressel and his colleagues observe: "Formal practices are interwoven with informal ones and that day-to-day personal interactions are central to all parts of a polity, including the judiciary."[35] Given the prominence of authoritarian politics in hybrid regime constitutional law, one must be especially sensitive to power relations outside the courtroom in order to build a better picture of how judicial power is developed. The proposed audience-based framework helps us select the relevant audiences that shape judicial power in a hybrid regime and explores how and why these stakeholders matter. This part begins by developing the audience-based framework. Next, the framework is applied to understand the legitimacy paradox faced by a hybrid regime constitutional court, as well as the challenges of navigating this paradox.

5.3.1 An Audience-Based Framework

Perceived legitimacy is a perception of something that needs to be demonstrated to the perceiver. The emphasis is on "perceived": A court must be able to show its qualities. More importantly, perceived legitimacy is fundamentally a relational concept. The qualities of a court must be demonstrated *to* – that is, be seen, be felt, or be heard by – someone in order for those qualities to have legitimizing effects. Perceived legitimacy is, as Nienke Grossman calls it, "agent relative,"[36] and depends on whom the legitimation is addressing.[37]

It seems increasingly clear that judges are aware of those who pay attention to their actions, that is, audiences, and that the regard of these

[34] Björn Dressel, Raul Sanchez-Urribarri, and Alexander Stroh, 'The Informal Dimension of Judicial Politics: A Relational Perspective' (2017) 13 *Annual Review of Law and Social Science* 413.

[35] Björn Dressel, Raul Sanchez-Urribarri, and Alexander Stroh, 'Courts and Informal Networks: Towards a Relational Perspective on Judicial Politics Outside Western Democracies' (2018) 39 *International Political Science Review* 573, 575.

[36] Nienke Grossman, 'The Normative Legitimacy of International Courts' (2013) 86 *Temple Law Review* 61, 80.

[37] Beetham (n 2) 11.

audiences directly or indirectly shapes judicial norms and preferences. As mentioned earlier in this chapter, an avenue of research looks at how the decision-making patterns of courts sometimes actually tracks with public opinion. These works examine public attitudes by treating the public as a monolithic entity. In practice, many judges are sensitive to a variety of social groups, and their attentiveness to actors outside the courtroom can be far more nuanced. A survey on judges from common-law apex courts reveals that judges do regard actors other than litigants, such as government agencies and the international community, as part of their audience.[38] More importantly, the results of the survey indicate that some judges consciously respond to their audiences' attitudes when writing their judgments.[39]

These findings fit well with Lawrence Baum's audience-based theory of judicial behavior, which was developed more than a decade ago.[40] Baum's hypothesis is that judges value their audiences' regard and are motivated to decide in ways that gain their audiences' approval. A lower court judge might, for example, try to please his or her seniors by writing judgments that increase the chances of a promotion. Alternatively, judges who hope to leave a legacy in an area of law might be particularly sensitive to the opinions of the legal academy. His theory has been developed and applied recently to explain varying levels of judicial assertiveness against different authoritarians in Pakistan.[41]

The works outlined in previous paragraphs rely on an audience-based approach to partially explain how judges *actually decide* in real life. An audience-based approach can also be used to theoretically explain the political foundation of a court's perceived legitimacy. An audience-based approach complements the conventional view of judicial legitimacy by disentangling the roles of the different kinds of audiences faced by a court. With various audiences creating different expectations, the

[38] Brian Flanagan and Sinéad Ahern, 'Judicial Decision-making and Transnational Law: A Survey of Common Law Supreme Court Judges' (2011) 60 *International & Comparative Law Quarterly* 1, 15.

[39] *ibid.*

[40] Lawrence Baum, *Judges and Their Audiences* (Princeton University Press 2009). Similar in spirit, Nuno Garoupa and Tom Ginsburg argue that judges are responsive to reputational mechanisms and that these internal and external mechanisms can explain judicial behavior. See Nuno Garoupa and Tom Ginsburg, *Judicial Reputation: A Comparative Theory* (University of Chicago Press 2015).

[41] Yasser Kureshi, 'When Judges Defy Dictators: An Audience-Based Framework to Explain the Emergence of Judicial Assertiveness against Authoritarian Regimes' (2021) 53 *Comparative Politics* 233.

audience-based approach enables us to trace whose perception matters to the court and how linkages to certain audiences affect how a court *should* decide.

A court faces various audiences, including the public, the government, lawyers, the legal academy, and the business sector. Not every audience's perception contributes equally to the legitimacy of a court. For instance, in polities with outspoken academics whose opinions can sway public opinion, academia becomes an audience that the court ought to be sensitive to if judges want their decisions to penetrate society. In highly internationalized jurisdictions or states under the support of international aid, courts may also need to consider the opinions of foreign states and the international community, as thc functioning of the judiciary in these states are directly or indirectly shaped by foreign actors.

Audiences that matter to courts may react to its decisions differently. Their propensity to react in ways that might support or undermine the institutional health of the court is another point of consideration. Hence, it is important to understand the motivations, ideology, and institutional characteristics of critical audiences. For instance, a legitimate court's decision will be respected by its citizens even if some disagree with it. As a court loses the general public's support, their tolerance for further unpopular decisions wanes, and they may begin protesting against the court. To take another example: foreign businesses that view a court as legitimate support its reputation by pushing the legal system higher up rule-of-law rankings and free-economy indices. Such a court's decisions might be celebrated as reflective of the polity's commitment to rule-of-law values. As the court loses the trust of these audiences, though, we might also see companies retreating from the jurisdiction and diminishing their investment in the polity, potentially affecting the budget and composition of the judiciary. In more extreme circumstances, the home countries of foreign investors might even call out on the judges if the court is behaving in an allegedly biased manner. In short, some audiences and their relationships with the court matter more than others.

The relative salience of audiences is determined by the political configuration of the polity, and courts do not get to choose their audiences. Judges can play to different audiences for their own benefit, but the kinds of audiences faced by a court and how they matter is largely given by the institutional environment. Accordingly, applying the audience-based framework in a way that is sensitive to regime-type politics may help us better understand the political foundation of perceived legitimacy. Regime-type has a major role to play in determining which audiences matter. Let us apply the audience-based framework to compare the political foundations of perceived legitimacy in democracies and pure authoritarian regimes. The utility of the framework is further illustrated when it is extended to a hybrid regime later.

In democracies, electoral pressure is a key reason why the public's opinion of a court matters. As explained previously, public support, through electoral pressure, acts as a buffer between courts and the elected branches. A court that enjoys public support can induce the elected branches to comply with its decisions even when the elected representatives find the decisions repugnant. Politicians will exercise restraint in sanctioning a popular court if they or their parties desire reelection. The conventional view of perceived legitimacy outlined builds on the electoral logic in democracies. Using the audience-based framework, the public is *the* key audience in a democracy because a democracy is designed to align the views of the representatives with their constituencies. Public support for the court is crucial because it can be effectively translated into electoral pressure to threaten the government. Democratic representatives can, of course, try to mold the opinion of their constituencies, but it is risky to deviate too far from the people's will given electoral accountability. The independent views of the representatives matter to a much lesser extent when they are normatively bound by the preferences and interests of the people.

On the other hand, political power is centralized in a pure authoritarian regime. The general public's view of the court is of no direct relevance, not because public opinion is morally insignificant, but because the incumbent and its allies are the main audiences under this political configuration. Perceived legitimacy is mainly measured from the authoritarian leadership's angle. The extent to which courts are legitimate depends on how successful and faithful courts are in implementing the authoritarian will. An important, if not principal, aim of authoritarians is to maintain political control, and courts are expected to help realize this aim.[42] Courts help authoritarians establish social control, legitimize controversial decisions, and manage lower-level administrative agents.[43] Rule-of-law principles such as procedural justice are barriers to achieving authoritarian goals expediently. Incompetent, disobedient, or overreaching courts are illegitimate and put

[42] Philippe Nonet and Philip Selznick, *Law and Society in Transition: Toward Responsive Law* (Transaction Publishers 2001) 29–52.

[43] Tamir Moustafa and Tom Ginsburg, 'Introduction: The Functions of Courts in Authoritarian Politics' in Tom Ginsburg and Tamir Moustafa (eds), *Rule by Law: The Politics of Courts in Authoritarian Regimes* (CUP 2008) 4–11.

themselves at risk. The interests of other audiences, such as the general public or the international community, matter only if there are instrumental reasons for the authoritarian to consider them. Authoritarian regimes committed to economic development, for example, may care about what the business sector has to say. Public mobilizations that can potentially destabilize the regime can also give reason to comply with an unfavorable decision. The interests of audiences besides the authoritarian leadership may sometimes be given consideration, but their interests will always remain secondary to the authoritarian's.

The audience-based framework can be developed and applied in ways that are more sensitive to the peculiarities of a specific polity.[44] The brief illustration given in this section shows how an audience-based framework can help us understand how regime-type impacts our understanding of perceived legitimacy in different contexts. The relational aspect of perceived legitimacy becomes especially apparent in divided societies such as a hybrid regime, as deeply embedded ideological differences accentuate the tensions generated by the contrary expectations of the key audiences in such regimes.

5.3.2 The Paradox: Rival Stories of Judicial Legitimacy

The key to understanding the nature of perceived legitimacy in hybrid regimes is to first identify two stories of judicial legitimacy that are necessarily present in a hybrid regime. As discussed in Chapter 2, a hybrid regime is defined by two incompatible constitutional ideologies – democracy and guardianship. We also saw how this ideological conflict manifests in many aspects of a hybrid regime, from the structure of its legal system to its political dynamics. From these two incompatible ideologies emerge rival stories of judicial legitimacy, which describe what is expected of courts in hybrid regimes.

On the one hand, we have the democratic story, which views a constitutional court as the "necessary completion of constitutionalism."[45] This is essentially the liberal democratic story of courts many of us are accustomed to. Supporters of this story "appreciate the benefit of checks and balances in a system of government."[46] According to this view, courts should

44 The audience-based framework will be further developed in Chapter 7 to understand the potential of the social role of judges.

45 Dieter Grimm, 'Constitutional Adjudication and Constitutional Interpretation: Between Law and Politics' (2011) 4 *NUJS Law Review* 15, 17.

46 Carrubba (n 6) 65.

be independent and principled arbiters, guardians of constitutional rights, the bulwark against authoritarian encroachment, and sometimes even the engine of constitutional change.[47] Judges are the personification of justice. A "good" constitutional court in a hybrid regime is held to be one that is committed to fighting against authoritarianism and upholding rule-of-law and liberal democratic values. A more progressive version of the liberal democratic story might even expect an activist court to abandon its fidelity to the law and decide cases in ways that transcend the four corners of the law when the legal context is an unjust one.[48]

On the other hand, we have the authoritarian story, which we already touched on when explaining how the audience-based framework applies to a pure authoritarian regime. According to this view, a constitutional court is subordinate to, and simply an extension of, the ruler. It is one of many channels for the authoritarian to exercise power. President Museveni's famous rhetorical assault against the Ugandan courts captures the authoritarian vision of the role of courts: "the major work for the Judges is to settle chicken and goat theft cases but not determining the country's destiny."[49] The extent to which a court is legitimate depends on the court's ability to fulfil the mission set by the ruler.[50] This story suggests that a constitutional court needs to be loyal and effective in bringing about the incumbent's objectives. It is a constitutional court's task to be as puppet-like as possible and to adapt the law to the preferences of the authoritarian.

The previous paragraphs present stylized, rivalling accounts of judicial legitimacy in a hybrid regime. The democratic story sees the court as a constraint on arbitrary power and crucial for the protection of rights, while the authoritarian story sees the court as merely a tool of the ruler. These stories are also archetypal: how they are told in practice depends on sociopolitical context and culture. Authoritarians have, for instance, asserted their authority over judges in the name of populism (e.g. Hungary), nationalism (e.g. Mainland China and Hong Kong), and the divine right to rule (e.g. Thailand). Similarly, the democratic story can be justified by specific constitutional texts as well as the historical struggles experienced by a country. Because these stories are social claims, any

[47] See Tom G. Daly, *The Alchemists: Questioning our Faith in Courts as Democracy-builders* (CUP 2017).

[48] Jeffrey Brand-Ballard, *Limits of Legality: The Ethics of Lawless Judging* (OUP 2010).

[49] As quoted in Rachel Ellett, *Pathways to Judicial Power in Transitional States: Perspectives from African Courts* (Routledge 2013) 147.

[50] Nonet and Selznick (n 42) 29–52.

flaws or incoherence are largely irrelevant for our purposes, so long as the stories resonate with the political communities in a hybrid regime. Common to the stories told across hybrid regimes is the existence of these two strands of narratives about what courts should and should not do, with one narrative corresponding to democratic values, and the other to guardianship principles.

From a philosophical perspective, there is no way for the two stories to be reconciled, as they derive from fundamentally incompatible political ideologies. Many of the judicial qualities that flow from the two stories are contradictory. For example: independent versus subservient, principle-based versus outcome-oriented, and constitutionalism versus arbitrariness. For this reason, the legitimacy challenge faced by courts in hybrid regimes is best described as a paradox. The fact that a court is the subject of a legitimacy paradox should not come as a surprise: this is another manifestation of the hybridity of a hybrid regime.

5.3.3 The Democratic and Authoritarian Constituencies

The ideological conflict underlying the legitimacy foundation of courts in hybrid regimes is not only philosophically interesting, but also affects how a court should position itself. What distinguishes a hybrid regime from a democracy and a pure authoritarian regime here is the existence of two audiences espousing conflicting stories of legitimacy in a hybrid regime, *and* the critical importance of both audiences to the legitimacy of a constitutional court. Let us call the audience that subscribes to the democratic story the democratic constituency, and the other the authoritarian constituency.

In a pure authoritarian regime, a democratic constituency might exist, but, as previously explained, it is impotent given that the public or the opposition cannot effectively discipline the incumbent. In a democracy, even if there is an authoritarian constituency, their stories would have negligible impact on constitutional discourse because democratic norms are deeply entrenched.

In a hybrid regime, the voice of the authoritarian constituency needs to be heard because of their political dominance. The incumbent and the elites take most key political decisions and, ultimately, can determine the institutional structure of its judiciary. When dissatisfied with a constitutional court's performance, the authoritarian constituency could reverse the judges' decisions or even pack the court. The constitutional court's survival depends largely on the regard of the authoritarian constituency, given the disproportionate amount of political power that constituency enjoys.

The authoritarian constituency and the democratic constituency are not on equal footing: the former enjoys the upper hand due to the systematic inequalities within the system. Unlike a pure authoritarian regime, however, the democratic constituency in a hybrid regime remains of critical importance as it can provide a power base for the court and public confidence in the court is valued by the regime. The two reasons for this go back to the defining characteristics of a hybrid regime. First, a hybrid regime needs to preserve its democratic appearance by ostensibly respecting democratic norms. The incumbent relies on the existence of the democratic constituency to ensure that a hybrid regime looks like a democracy. The incumbent must, to a certain extent, play along with the views of the democratic constituency. Otherwise, an image of democratic pluralism would not be credible. Relatedly, a hybrid regime wants the court to have public legitimacy as this bolsters the overall credibility of the government.

Second, the democratic constituency in a hybrid regime is not entirely incapacitated. Peaceful change of powers are unlikely but still possible in a hybrid regime, as took place in Pakistan and the Gambia. As previously argued, the uncertainty that comes with a semi-competitive election is sufficient to constrain an incumbent, who is forced to take seriously the democratic constituency's demands in order to maintain stability.[51] Voting is also not the only way for the democratic constituency to threaten the incumbent. The democratic constituency can organize protests and resort to mass mobilization to counter the authoritarian constituency. The costs of interfering with a court that enjoys the support of a democratic constituency is much higher in a hybrid regime than an authoritarian one. In turn, a court that is backed by the democratic constituency enjoys greater latitude to challenge the incumbent, and its decisions are more likely to be respected by the authoritarian constituency.

The account given in the previous paragraphs explains why and how the perceptions of these two constituencies matter to a court in a hybrid regime. A hybrid regime's authoritarian core suggests that the expectations of the authoritarian constituency cannot be ignored because of its fundamental control over the judiciary. The democratic constituency can potentially counteract the authoritarian constituency's pressure on the

[51] See Epperly (n 32).

courts. Like the public's role under the conventional view, the democratic constituency can provide institutional cover for a hybrid regime's constitutional court by threatening to undermine the stability and power of the incumbent.

What does this tell us about institution-building and judicial empowerment? Given the importance of the democratic constituency, it becomes particularly useful for a court to enlist the help of the democratic constituency in a hybrid regime. A common feature of the successful hybrid regime courts discussed in this book is their enjoyment of a democratic constituency's support. While the opposition has never won a majority in the Hong Kong legislature, it had obtained a majority of votes, and had effectively vetoed government policies through filibustering and street protest. With its impartial image and many liberal rulings, the judiciary is consistently rated the most trusted public institution in Hong Kong.[52] Even under pressure from the largest authoritarian force in the world, virtually all Hong Kong courts' decisions, including those that rule against the government, have been respected. The support of the democratic constituency has made attacks on courts politically costly.[53]

The Chaudhry court in Pakistan has gone a step further by actively mobilizing the democratic constituency. The Chaudhry court garnered public support in its first few years of tenure through a progressive use of *suo moto* actions and its direct confrontation with the Musharraf regime.[54] In 2007, the suspension and dismissal of the Supreme Court by Musharraf sparked nationwide antigovernment protests. Dubbed the Lawyers' Movement, the protests were led by a democratic constituency consisting of the opposition, lawyers, retired judges, and civil society organizations. Fully aware of the support it commanded, the judiciary refused to take a new oath under the emergency law and continued to defy the incumbent. Musharraf ultimately lost power in 2008, a result of the backlash from his attempt to undermine a popular court, which was eventually reinstated after the election.

[52] See Julius Yam, 'Approaching the Legitimacy Paradox in Hong Kong: Lessons for Hybrid Regime Courts' (2021) 46 *Law & Social Inquiry* 153. The political developments since 2019 have, however, taken a toll on the judiciary's reputation.

[53] See Eric C. Ip, *Hybrid Constitutionalism: The Politics of Constitutional Review in the Chinese Special Administrative Regions* (CUP 2019).

[54] Asher A. Qazi, 'Suo Motu: Choosing Not to Legislate Chief Justice Chaudhry's Strategic Agenda' in Moeen H. Cheema and Ijaz S. Gilani (eds), *The Politics and Jurisprudence of the Chaudhry Court 2005–2013* (OUP 2015).

The position of the Ugandan courts is arguably more tenuous, as Ugandan dictators have a history of attacking the institution and even killing judges. The most notable and gruesome instance is then-President Idi Amina's abduction of Chief Justice Benedicto Kiwanuka from his judicial chambers in 1972, who was reportedly tortured and murdered afterwards. Perhaps realizing the fragility of its institutional position, the Ugandan courts over subsequent decades have labored to enhance their reputation among the democratic constituency. The courts have kept a close relationship with the bar, relying on the Ugandan Law Society and other lawyers to fend off attacks against the judiciary.[55] Most interestingly, Ugandan judges have, over the years, cleverly leveraged this tragic past, playing the "narrative of victimisation" card to win the support of the public and elites.[56]

The examples of Hong Kong, Pakistan, and Uganda demonstrate the importance of a democratic constituency in a hybrid regime in maintaining judicial power. While a democratic constituency cannot always immunize a constitutional court, it provides an invaluable bulwark against authoritarian attacks by acting as a buffer between the authoritarian constituency and the court. In all three examples, the constitutional courts established a close relationship with the democratic constituency by deciding in ways and creating political conditions that protected the democratic constituency and helped further the democratic cause. In turn, the active support of the democratic constituency (through, for instance, public pressure, boycotts, and mass protests) gave the constitutional courts greater room to support democratic ideals without fear of political backlash. The next two chapters discuss the ways in which judges can build support among institutions that can protect the court, as well as how judges can potentially expand the size of the democratic constituency.

However, what was just described forms only half the story. The support of the democratic constituency protects a constitutional court, but that support can sometimes be a curse. A court that is too popular among the democratic constituency risks arousing the suspicion of the authoritarian constituency. It must be remembered that the two constituencies tell rivalling stories of legitimacy. In many politically salient questions, a democratic constituency's "right" is an authoritarian constituency's "wrong," and vice versa. The protection of democratic rights,

[55] Ellett (n 49) 193.
[56] *ibid* 206.

for example, implies curtailing the powers of the authoritarian constituency, while promoting authoritarian aggrandizement encroaches upon the interests of the democratic constituency. A democratic constituency is able to provide temporary cover for a court by increasing the political costs of court-curbing actions. A change of political dynamics, however, may present opportunities for the authoritarian to act out on the hostility accumulated throughout the years.

The Hungarian experience of the 1990s, recounted in Chapter 3, reminds us of the long-term dangers of overplaying a court's hands in the face of an authoritarian constituency. The Hungarian constitutional court was widely championed as the most democratic institution in Hungary during the early years of the country's transitional days. Authoritarian populist Viktor Orbán's assumption of office in 1998 was a game-changer in Hungary's judicial political dynamics. Pre-1998, the court's activist role created a long list of political enemies who "never forgave" the court.[57] Learning from the mistakes of the past, the newly elected government coalition decided not to renew the terms of all sitting judges, and the constitution was swiftly amended to limit the court's jurisdiction. The Hong Kong courts are also beginning to suffer the side-effects of the liberal democratic approach it adopted in the first two decades after the handover. The passing of the national security law has essentially eliminated the space for meaningful opposition in Hong Kong. The COVID-19 pandemic also made mass protest challenging, if not impossible. With semi-competitive elections eliminated and a crackdown on civil society, Hong Kong judges have lost the protection once offered by the democratic constituency. State-controlled media have orchestrated waves of attacks against some of the courts' decisions, and national security laws are immune from constitutional review. There has also been increasing debate about appointing loyalist judges onto the bench and removing those believed to be associated with the democratic constituency. The authorities have taken a renewed "interest" in some of the courts' older judgments, arguing that the courts in the past failed to give effect to the true meaning of the city's mini constitution.[58]

[57] Kim Lane Scheppele, 'Democracy by Judiciary. Or, Why Courts Can Be More Democratic than Parliaments' in Adam Czarnota, Martin Krygier, and Wojciech Sadurski (eds), *Rethinking The Rule Of Law After Communism* (Central European University Press 2005) 53.

[58] Hong Kong has arguably shifted to a pure authoritarian regime, and the political backlash it is suffering now does not necessarily undermine the approach it had adopted during

Both examples demonstrate the risks of only attending to the democratic constituency in a hybrid regime. The court must also address the authoritarian constituency. In more concrete terms, this involves deferring to the government and avoiding political controversies. A "particularly appealing" way to address the legitimacy paradox, as Shapiro notes, might be for courts to "stay out of politics" or to "wait and fight another day."[59] Deferential and avoidance tactics are attractive because comparative experiences have shown how vulnerable a court can be in the face of an authoritarian.

The authoritarian-leaning approach helps reduce the friction between a court and the authoritarian constituency, but a democratically committed court cannot rely solely on this strategy. Avoiding backlash is not an end in and of itself; its ultimate aim is to *preserve* the institutional strength of a court. A court maintains and capitalizes on the mutually dependent relationship between the authoritarian and the court by occasionally ceding to the authoritarian's preferences. A court that only submits to the authoritarian is self-defeating. Leaning too close to the authoritarian is also potentially counterproductive. Legitimacy, as previously indicated, is hard to replenish. Giving in to the authoritarian risks losing the support of the democratic constituency. Once a court loses the backing of its allies, it becomes even more vulnerable to direct control from the authoritarian camp.

A conundrum begins to reveal itself: the two constituencies are crucial to the perceived legitimacy of a court, but it is unclear how a court should proceed given how the two constituencies hold opposing beliefs. The court is responsible for implementing the constitution and at the forefront of patrolling the ideological boundaries between the two constituencies. The clash in ideologies creates many zero-sum problems for the constitutional court to resolve. The practical implications of the legitimacy paradox are most obvious when the cases confronting the court touch on issues that deeply matter to both constituencies. To establish a "lowest common denominator of agreement"[60] under these circumstances is challenging, to say the least. Describing the challenges divided societies present to a constitution, Tarun Khaitan writes, "straightforward accommodation in the face of deep disagreement creates a new problem as it solves another, because accommodation of one group is likely to anger

Hong Kong's hybrid regime era. Nevertheless, developments in Hong Kong illustrate how weak courts can be once the democratic constituency is disabled.

59 Shapiro (n 1) 334.

60 Radmilovic (n 20) 859.

another. Taking everyone along requires a fine balancing act, one that offers enough sops to the dissenters, but not so many that their detractors in turn feel tempted to jump ship."[61] This is analogous to the classic dual agency scenario, where an agent is accountable to two principals with conflicting interests. The court is an agent of the democratic and authoritarian constituencies, with responsibilities to both. In private law, an agent can and should withdraw when there is a conflict of interest. Withdrawal is not always available to a court; even if it is, it is not necessarily a "neutral" option that satisfies both constituencies. Withdrawal can also be interpreted as retreat by those wanting a court to take action.

Another way to express the challenges posed by the legitimacy paradox is to use Lee Epstein, Jack Knight, and Olga Shvetsova's model of "tolerance interval."[62] We have here two sets of actors – the democratic constituency and the authoritarian constituency – subscribing to opposing ideologies. Each set has its own expectations of courts, and in each case presented to the court, each has its own preferred outcome. The space of the preferred position is called the "tolerance interval." Each set of actors' regard toward the court depends on the extent to which the court's judicial decision-making patterns fall within its zone of tolerance. The judicial political dynamic described under this model is not one-off, but involves sequential interactions. Deviating from the tolerance interval increases the chances of a hostile reaction from the group; repeatedly staying within the interval helps expand the zone. Accordingly, the decision-making patterns of a court have cumulative effects on its legitimacy.[63]

A court should ideally stay within the overlapping tolerance intervals of the democratic and authoritarian constituencies. This is possible if the tolerance intervals of the two constituencies intersect. For example, it might be in the interest of both constituencies to tackle corruption, under the assumption that the destabilization of patronage networks does not fundamentally undermine the incumbent's control and might even improve its governance. Because these two groups tell rivalling stories of judicial legitimacy, their tolerance intervals are more likely to be

[61] Tarunabh Khaitan, 'Directive Principles and the Expressive Accommodation of Ideological Dissenters' (2018) 16 *International Journal of Constitutional Law* 389, 408.

[62] Lee Epstein, Jack Knight, and Olga Shvetsova, 'The Role of Constitutional Courts in the Establishment and Maintenance of Democratic Systems of Government' (2001) 35 *Law and Society Review* 117.

[63] *ibid* 131.

mutually exclusive in politically salient decisions. Halfway-house decisions in these instances please no one. As I explained, the consequences of deviating from the two constituencies' tolerance intervals are different. The authoritarian might pack the court, while the democratic constituency will gradually withdraw its support. The consistent absence of overlapping tolerance intervals and the absence of a dominant strategy present grave risks to the legitimacy of a court.

5.4 Conclusion

Using an audience-based framework to conceptualize judicial legitimacy, this chapter describes a legitimacy problem faced by hybrid regime courts. The hybridity of a hybrid regime requires a constitutional court to be sensitive to the views of both the democratic constituency and the authoritarian constituency. Courts in hybrid regimes have an advantage over those in pure authoritarian contexts, insofar as political elites in hybrid regimes must pay at least some attention to public opinion. Given the nature of the paradox, a constitutional court needs to marshal the support of the democratic constituency *and* avoid triggering the authoritarian constituency. The challenge lies in the fact that the two constituencies subscribe to fundamentally opposing ideologies and tell rivalling stories of judicial legitimacy. Failure to accommodate either or both constituencies destabilizes a court's constitutional position.

Two things need to be emphasized before concluding the chapter. First, while the paradox is a serious problem confronting a court in a hybrid regime and deserves greater attention, we should not forget that there are instances where the perspectives of the two constituencies can align. There are advantages to the regime when the people have confidence in the court, and not every case presented to the court touches on issues that are of fundamental importance to the regime. These instances may lie outside the paradox, but are nonetheless useful opportunities for the court to develop its institutional capacity and doctrines that promote liberal-democratic values.

Second, the legitimacy paradox is only really relevant to a court which is committed to liberal democratic values, as judges who are determined to serve the authoritarian incumbent have no reason to consider the views of the democratic constituency. However, should a court decide to take up a democratic role, as suggested in the previous chapter, it must figure out how to navigate the political minefield presented by the paradox. Also, the chapter leaves open the possibility that the legitimacy paradox, or traces of it, can be found outside hybrid regimes, especially in democracies with polarized political communities and pure authoritarian regimes that have recently transitioned from a hybrid regime. Regardless, this chapter shows that the legitimacy paradox is a central feature of a hybrid regime and must be addressed by a constitutional court.

This leaves us with the question of how a democratically committed court should approach the legitimacy paradox. There is no easy answer to this question. "A fine balancing" is required, as Khaitan rightly pointed out. However, is it possible to provide more guidelines to the court? There is a glimmer of hope: Comparative experiences around the world provide insights regarding how to address some of the challenges described in this chapter. The next two chapters offer theoretical and practical solutions that would enable hybrid regime courts to undertake those democratic roles identified in Chapter 4 in a sustainable manner.

6

Democratic Judging under Authoritarianism

6.1 Introduction

Five democracy-enhancing roles that courts in hybrid regimes can and should assume were outlined in Chapter 4. A problem generated from those roles is that they will result in confrontations with the authoritarian constituency. So in Chapter 5, we saw that courts in hybrid regimes face a legitimacy paradox, and failing to satisfy the authoritarian to some degree will destabilize the court.

Regime politics is not the only determinant of the fate of the judiciary, however. Judges are also in a position to create conditions favorable to the development of their roles. For judges to navigate the number of complexities that arise in trying to enhance democracy in the face of the legitimacy paradox, they have to take the political context of a hybrid regime seriously. How should judges committed to democracy conduct themselves when they are under authoritarian pressure? This question will be addressed in this chapter and the next. The tools to be offered in these two chapters are divided into what judges can and should do inside *and* outside the courtroom. This chapter proposes an adjudicative framework (which can be referred to as "Sustainable Democratic Adjudication") that allows judges to systematically incorporate both constitutional legal principles and judicial strategies, while Chapter 7 moves beyond the adjudicative context and considers how judges can create allies and defuse enemies using non-adjudicative strategies. These two chapters argue that judges who hope to give effect to their democracy-enhancing roles have no choice but to find creative ways to accommodate authoritarian pressures. Turning a blind eye to threats to the judicial institution will inevitably lead to its demise. The salient question, then, is not whether judges in authoritarian contexts *should* be sensitive to their political environment (as I will argue, the answer is that they must), but rather *how* they should account for authoritarian pressures if they aim to fulfil their democratic roles sustainably.

The framework proposed in this chapter is designed for hybrid regimes in which judges *have a role* in imposing meaningful constraints on authoritarian rulers. In particular, this chapter focuses on judges with constitutional jurisdiction who see themselves as constitutional guardians. These judges are most proximate to matters of political significance, and, consequently, are most likely to clash with the incumbent regime. The law in some authoritarian regimes leaves little or no space for judges to play such a role. In these cases, the proposed framework will be irrelevant (or of limited relevance). However, as we have seen in previous chapters, judges in hybrid regimes are not necessarily puppets,[1] and some actively defend the constitution and constrain authoritarian action. This chapter offers practical guidance to judges who seek to embody this role, and advises them on how to evaluate and decide between their options given the challenges raised by authoritarianism.[2]

While focused on hybrid regimes, the following discussion might also benefit judges in democracies, some of whom sit on judicial panels in nondemocratic jurisdictions as foreign judges, and are occasionally asked to decide on constitutionally salient issues.[3] More importantly, institutional resilience is a concern of judges regardless of regime-type.[4] Democracies are not immune to authoritarian forces and their judges can be subjected to political capture and executive attacks. The threats to judges in democracies might differ in degree and kind from those in authoritarian regimes, but some of the institutional challenges those judges face may be similar in nature to those identified later in this

1 See e.g. Steven D. Schaaf, 'When Do Courts Constrain the Authoritarian State? Judicial Decision-Making in Jordan and Palestine' (2022) 54 *Comparative Politics* 375; Alexei Trochev and Peter H. Solomon, 'Authoritarian Constitutionalism in Putin's Russia: A Pragmatic Constitutional Court in a Dual State' (2018) 51 *Communist and Post-Communist Studies* 201; Tamir Moustafa, *The Struggle for Constitutional Power: Law, Politics, and Economic Development in Egypt* (CUP 2007).

2 Readers might object that committed judges should resign in protest, as remaining on the bench legitimizes an authoritarian regime. This chapter leaves aside the question of whether or when judges should resign, and focuses on what judges should do *if* they are able and intend to constrain authoritarianism. Moreover, resigning can be counterproductive: Vacant offices will likely be filled by regime-loyalists, thereby accelerating the pace of constitutional deterioration. See Hans Petter Graver, *Judges Against Justice: On Judges When the Rule of Law Is Under Attack* (Springer 2016) 267–70.

3 For example, judges from the United Kingdom and South Africa have sat on courts in Hong Kong and Brunei, and Eswatini respectively. See Anna Dziedzic and Simon Young (eds), *The Cambridge Handbook of Foreign Judges on Domestic Courts* (CUP 2023).

4 See Rosalind Dixon, 'Strong Courts: Judicial Statecraft in Aid of Constitutional Change' (2020) 59 *Columbia Journal of Transnational Law* 298; Theunis Roux, *The Politics of Principle: The First South African Constitutional Court, 1995–2005* (CUP 2013).

chapter. The adjudicative framework I propose can potentially be adapted to a democratic political context, and hopefully shape the conduct of judges in democratic states as well.

The rest of the chapter proceeds in three parts. Section 6.2 outlines the two steps involved in the Sustainable Democratic Adjudication framework, the goal of which is the long-term, sustainable realization of the democracy-enhancing roles of judges in the face of authoritarian pressure. First, judges need to form an initial view on what the law requires under the democracy-orienting approach proposed in Chapter 4. During this step, they must apply a presumption of "institutional blindfold,"[5] ignoring the possible influence of prudential considerations such as political pushbacks and backlashes, and considering only the relevant law and facts of the case as informed by constitutional democratic principles. I term the tentative conclusion reached at this stage the "formal legal position." The term "formal" here is not used to denote "legal formalism" or a formalistic account of constitutional adjudication, but instead to describe the position that results from the court's application of the law without factoring in prudential considerations. The second step involves judges lifting the blindfold to check whether, and if so how, the formal legal position should be supplemented with or adjusted by strategic considerations. These are questions determined by the level of risk incurred by maintaining the formal legal position.

The level of risk is a function of the severity of the anticipated adverse consequence of maintaining the formal legal position and its likelihood of eventuating. I identify four scenarios: If the risk level is (1) *negligible or nonexistent*, judges should consider how judicial strategy can enhance the impact of their decision or bolster the institutional position of the court without fundamentally altering the formal legal position and increasing the level of risk. If the risk level is (2) *high*, judges will need to examine how much strategic deviation from the formal legal position is necessary to accommodate authoritarian pressure. There might be instances where such pressure cannot be accommodated, because the required level of accommodation either (3) *crosses a moral baseline*, or the risk level is so high that the threat is (4) *unavoidable*. The last two scenarios, I suggest, justify maintaining the formal legal position. While the first two scenarios encompass a spectrum of risk and should not be treated as

[5] This term is borrowed from Roni Mann's "non-ideal theory." See Roni Mann, 'Non-ideal Theory of Constitutional Adjudication' (2018) 7 *Global Constitutionalism* 14.

determinate categories, the latter two should be treated as different in kind, as they are subsets of the high-risk scenario.

Drawing on insights from interdisciplinary studies and illustrating with comparative examples, Section 6.3 of this chapter examines the strategies that judges can deploy during the adjudicative process. These are organized into four groups based on different dimensions of the adjudicative process: Outcome, reasoning, language, and timing. These strategies can be used not only to accommodate prudential considerations, but also to build support for the judiciary and to enhance the effectiveness of the formal legal position. The social effects of these strategies and how they might be relevant to the four contexts described will be explored. Concluding remarks are offered in Section 6.4.

6.2 Sustainable Democratic Adjudication

The challenges posed by the legitimacy paradox beg the question of how judges ought to exercise their authority if they wish to promote constitutional democratic norms sustainably. This part proposes a two-step adjudicative framework to address this question. The first step of the framework requires judges to form an initial view of what the law requires under the democracy-orienting approach proposed in Chapter 4, and without regard for the possible adverse consequences they might face as a result of maintaining their fidelity to constitutional democratic norms. During the second step, judges need to carefully anticipate the potential ramifications of their democratically informed interpretation of the law, and address those prudential concerns using judicial strategies. The first step is based on the legal merits of a case and guided by constitutional democratic principles, but reasons at the first step may be defeated at the second step after an evaluation of the broader implications of their verdict. In other words, the second step may require judges to deviate from the democracy-enhancing roles. Such deviations, I argue, are justified when they enable judges to conserve their institutional strength. Exceptions to this will also be explored.

The approach outlined in this chapter will involve occasionally compromising on constitutional democratic norms, which may at first sight appear to go against the arguments in Chapter 4. Counterintuitively, at least under authoritarian regimes including hybrid regimes, such norms may sometimes have to give way to prudential considerations in the short term if we are serious about the *long-term promotion* of these norms. As Jeff Goldsworthy points out, "just as a violation of one human right might enhance the protection of human rights overall ... so too a one-off violation of the rule of law might advance the cause of justice or good government, or even strengthen the rule of law in other respects and overall."[6] That is, of course, not to suggest that judges should always bow to the pressures levied by incumbent authoritarians, but we must be realistic about what they can achieve. Given that it is virtually impossible for judges in hybrid regimes to consistently give the fullest effect to their democracy-enhancing roles, the second-best option that judges should aim for is *approximating constitutional democratic norms as much as is practically possible.*

The approach adopted here requires the judicial consideration of prudential reasons, and some might rightly notice a tension with the individual interests of some litigants. Courts are tasked to settle legal disputes between parties through an impartial application of the law. The adjudicative framework proposed in the chapter appears to create injustice, as parties to litigation may sometimes win or lose for reasons that have nothing to do with the law. There is, however, no guarantee that a legally sound but politically insensitive judicial decision will be enforced by an authoritarian government, especially one that runs contrary to its interests. Furthermore, committed but tactless judges will probably eventually be replaced by those loyal to the regime, who lack the motivation to defend the constitution. The legalistic approach, which initially appears more morally sound, may inadvertently promote the further consolidation of authoritarian power to the detriment of constitutional democratic norms. However, the framework proposed does acknowledge that there are some kinds of individual interests that simply cannot be surrendered. These situations will be discussed in detail later in this chapter.

Another possible set of objections to judicial consideration of prudential reasons is that judges lack political acumen. This presumption can be challenged on several fronts. First, most judges share a social and cultural context with their fellow citizens, and are therefore likely to have a good grasp of political culture, contemporary social issues and cleavages, as well as the significance of past events.[7] Any gaps in their understanding of the motivations of different audiences and/or the potential consequences of their decision(s) can be filled via independent research, possibly

[6] Jeffrey Goldsworthy, 'The Limits of Judicial Fidelity to Law: The Coxford Lecture' (2011) 24 *Canadian Journal of Law & Jurisprudence* 305, 306.

[7] Anna Dziedzic, *Foreign Judges in the Pacific* (Hart Publishing 2021) chapter 5.

supported by their clerks in certain jurisdictions. The submissions made and evidence produced in the courtroom can also be instructive, as courtroom interactions sometimes reflect power dynamics outside the courtroom. Most importantly, judges might be privy to certain channels of information. Judges are government officials, and the judicial appointment process directly or indirectly involves political actors. Their proximity to certain political networks means that they might be particularly attuned to the potential reactions of groups close to the incumbent.[8]

For those who remain skeptical of strategic approaches, my ultimate response is that, at least in authoritarian contexts, judges often have *no choice but to make political and strategic calculations*. They have to play the hand that they are dealt. A politically insensitive court is doomed to fail in a hybrid regime; its demise accelerates autocratization. Tackling authoritarianism requires taking authoritarian realities seriously. A dose of pragmatism that properly accounts for the institutional position of a court, or a "combination of principle and pragmatism,"[9] becomes necessary when existential threats to the judiciary are unexceptional occurrences.

Not only does the adjudicative framework help constrained judges systematically evaluate the options presented to them, it also highlights the importance of judicial agency. Much of the pessimism about the potential of judges in authoritarian regimes is rooted in the assumption that judicial politics is conditioned and limited by regime-type politics.[10] This assumption is so widely held that we tend to overlook the *choices* that judges can make even under authoritarian pressure.[11] These choices reflect judges' potential to instigate meaningful change. Raymond Wacks and Ronald Dworkin have argued that judges in apartheid South Africa and Nazi Germany could have instilled legality to oppressive laws, exercised discretion in ways that were friendlier to human rights, or lied about or bent the law.[12] Or, as Hans Petter Graver suggests, "there was judicial scope for the protection of fundamental rights" even under the

[8] See Björn Dressel, Raul Sanchez-Urribarri, and Alexander Stroh, 'The Informal Dimension of Judicial Politics: A Relational Perspective' (2017) 13 *Annual Review of Law and Social Science* 413.

[9] Theunis Roux, 'Principle and Pragmatism on the Constitutional Court of South Africa' (2009) 7 *International Journal of Constitutional Law* 106, 108.

[10] See Donald W. Jackson and C. Neal Tate (eds), *Comparative Judicial Review and Public Policy* (Greenwood Publishing Group 1992); C. Neal Tate and Torbjörn Vallinder (eds), *The Global Expansion of Judicial Power* (NYU Press 1995).

[11] See also Dixon (n 4) 302; Roux (n 4) 93–104.

[12] See Raymond Wacks, 'Judges and Injustice' (1984) 101 *South African Law Journal* 266; Ronald Dworkin. *Law's Empire* (HUP 1986) 105.

Third Reich.[13] The choices judges make may have significant implications for the constitutional order and their institutional position, so we ought to consider how these choices should be made.[14]

6.2.1 *Step 1: Ascertaining the Formal Legal Position with the Blindfold On*

The first step of the adjudicative framework entails ascertaining what the law requires if the judges were to assume the democracy-enhancing roles suggested in Chapter 4, while blindfolded from prudential factors such as potential pushbacks and backlash from the public and political elites. It is often argued that the integrity of the law depends on judges' ability to uphold the law. Allowing prudential factors to influence the adjudicative process is inconsistent with the demands of justice and blurs the distinction between law and politics, thus threatening to undermine the rule of law. The first step of the framework flows naturally from our common understanding of the judicial role. The formal legal position of a case can only be revealed if judges interpret the law and facts in accordance with established constitutional legal principles, independently of the potential social and political consequences that the legal position might attract.

The framework does not prescribe what the law should be in each case and accommodates a range of adjudicative theories. While the chapter fills the framework with the democracy-enhancing roles developed earlier, any normatively sound theory of adjudication that takes constitutionalism seriously – from the conventional common-law model to more demanding and democratically oriented approaches such as Dworkin or Ely's interpretative theories – is sufficient to activate the first step and provide the content for this framework. There can be disagreements under this step, so long as those disagreements are reasonable, informed by constitutional democratic principles, and arise from questions of law and legal or constitutional interpretation.

13 Graver (n 2) 269–70.

14 The adjudicative framework proposed in this chapter arguably resembles rational choice models, as both are agent-focused and concerned with utility maximization, broadly defined. See Lee Epstein, Jack Knight, and Olga Shvetsova, 'The Role of Constitutional Courts in the Establishment and Maintenance of Democratic Systems of Government' (2001) 35 *Law and Society Review* 117. However, my approach takes the role of law seriously. It assumes that getting the law right and the promotion of constitutionalism are among the most important goals judges seek to realize, and that judges are bound by legal norms in their reasoning.

It should also be emphasized that the framework does not apply when the legal position arrived at during the first step is *anti*constitutionalist, such as when the conclusion legitimizes the arbitrary application of discretionary power or leads to a reduction or elimination of checks on the authoritarian ruler.[15] This flows from the assumption stated earlier: that the arguments proposed only apply when judges have a role in promoting constitutionalism and constraining authoritarian abuses of power. Situations where room for meaningful judicial enforcement of the constitution has been completely eliminated are less common than one might think, however, especially if one adopts the widely shared view that legal texts alone do not determine a legal outcome. Even under authoritarian regimes, the constitution will, in many cases, leave sufficient room for judges to interpret the law and facts in ways that correspond with constitutional norms. In any event, even when the framework is inapplicable, judges may have alternatives other than simply endorsing an unattractive legal position. For example, they can lie about the law or resign in protest. The normativity of these options is beyond the scope of this chapter, but the judicial strategies outlined in the next part are of general relevance to adjudicative courses of action.

The blindfold confers several advantages on judges operating in hybrid regimes. Modern authoritarians, as Erin Jenne and Cas Mudde observe, "bend or break" the law because they are able "to get away with it."[16] This step maximizes the number of opportunities to hold authoritarians accountable to the constitutional democratic norms. In the face of constant pressure, judges in authoritarian regimes are often conditioned to "respond with anticipatory obedience."[17] Critical thinking is easily abandoned as a result. This habit leads judges to surrender to political pressure *more than they should*, causing them to miss opportunities to work toward a more constitutionally compliant and democratic state. This step reminds us of the basic tenets of being a judge: to arrive at fair and just outcomes based on legal and constitutional principles, and of the distinct moral responsibilities that comes with being a judge in a hybrid

[15] Aside from "constitutionalist" and "anti-constitutionalist," a formal legal position can also be constitutionally neutral, for instance, when the nature of the legal dispute does not involve constitutional norms. The framework will apply not only to a constitutionalist legal position, but also to a constitutionally neutral one, as even such a position can antagonize the authoritarian.

[16] Erin K. Jenne and Cas Mudde, 'Hungary's Illiberal Turn: Can Outsiders Help?' (2012) 23 *Journal of Democracy* 147, 148.

[17] Jens Meierhenrich, *The Remnants of the Rechtsstaat: An Ethnography of Nazi Law* (OUP 2018) 184.

regime. Because opportunities to promote constitutional democratic norms can sometimes be subtle and occur at unexpected times, judges should strive to inspect each case with the blindfold on first. Whether the formal legal position will be eventually compromised is a separate matter, but the blindfold reveals the normative potential of every opportunity presented to a judge.

6.2.2 *Step 2: Supplementing and/or Adjusting the Formal Legal Position*

Step two requires lifting the blindfold to check whether, and if so how, the formal legal position should be supplemented with and/or adjusted by judicial strategies. Maintaining the formal legal position can attract a variety of adverse reactions that may justify a strategic response. The framework proposed here recommends that judges always lift the blindfold and be prepared to act strategically, but does not require that they depart from their initial position in every instance.

One might question the importance of the first step, given the eventual lifting of the blindfold. The benefits of the first step exist independently of the second step. Without going through step one, judges would remain unaware of the sacrifices made by accommodating strategic concerns. Furthermore, lifting the blindfold does not always result in a departure from the formal legal position. It requires judges to consider the pragmatic implications of their rulings, but does not mandate that judges should always act on those considerations and modify the formal legal position. Later, we will review scenarios that would justify retaining the formal legal position after a careful assessment of the risks involved. Moreover, strategizing sometimes produces only cosmetic changes to a decision without fundamentally altering the formal legal position. In these circumstances, strategies leave the core of the formal legal position intact.

To act strategically does not mean abdicating the constitutional responsibilities of being a judge. Instead, it highlights judges' capacity to devise solutions beyond the law to address prudential concerns. This is imperative in hybrid regimes where judicial authority tends to be weak and judicial-political dynamics are volatile. The social authority and institutional health of a court are *not* ends in and of themselves. Rather, these qualities are necessary in order to sustainably give effect to constitutional democratic norms. Moreover, as mentioned, hybrid regimes today are relatively durable; resisting authoritarian encroachment is a long-term battle. Precisely because judges are in for the long haul, it is necessary to adopt a strategic approach that accounts for the importance of the judiciary's institutional health.

The second step involves evaluating the institutional position of the court and the potential consequences of maintaining the formal legal position. When deciding whether to supplement and/or adjust the formal position with judicial strategy, judges should consider three factors: (1) The nature and extent of any negative outcome if the formal legal position is maintained; (2) the likelihood that a negative outcome will eventuate; and (3) the amount of deviation from the formal legal position required to remove or mitigate the expected risk. The first two factors define the expected level of risk associated with the formal legal position. As explained later, this approach is more sympathetic toward the circumstances faced by judges in hybrid regimes, and leaves judges the room to tailor their solutions to a wide range of often unexpected situations.

6.2.3 Risk Assessment

Before deciding whether, and if so how, the formal legal position needs to be supplemented by judicial strategies, judges must first assess the risks of maintaining the formal legal position. This, as mentioned, involves two factors: (1) The nature and severity of a negative reaction, and (2) the likelihood of such a negative reaction materializing.

In thinking about possible negative reactions to maintaining the formal legal position, it is helpful to first identify their likely *form*. Domestic courts commonly encounter four types of unfavorable responses: Negative publicity, noncompliance or reversal, institutional reform, and actual violence.[18] These four categories are arranged in ascending order of severity: Negative public discourse often has no real bite, but might at times portend future problems; noncompliance or reversal directly undermines the efficacy of a court; institutional reform is a severe kind of counterattack, which reverses a court's institution-building efforts; and outright violence, which endangers judges' lives.

[18] My typology draws on the work of Mikael Rask Madsen, Pola Cebulak, and Micha Wiebusch, 'Backlash Against International Courts: Explaining the Forms and Patterns of Resistance to International Courts' (2018) 14 *International Journal of Law in Context* 197.

6.2.3.1 Negative Publicity

High-profile judgments draw media attention and are likely to attract criticism from a range of social groups. Detractors are not always politically motivated; some may have constructive and legitimate comments. Even unfair criticism is sometimes valuable, as it spotlights subtler issues relating to the judiciary or legal system that may merit closer scrutiny.[19] The legitimacy of these critiques aside, the impact of negative publicity on a court's social authority depends on where the critique originates from and what it signifies. In this instance, it is useful to distinguish between different kinds of critics, including government officials, political elites, the legal community, academia, civil society organizations, the business community, international organizations, and sometimes even foreign officials. How much weight a court should give to these responses depends on the relative standing of the critic.

While negative publicity may at first seem rather harmless, there are two reasons why it deserves closer attention. First, it may be an early signal of possible retaliatory action. If the critic is one with substantial power over the court, their reaction may foreshadow court-curbing actions. Second, negative public discourse may mobilize other constituencies, creating more leverage for those who plan to attack the court. State officials' public denouncements, for example, not only directly pressurize judges, but also reflect the state's attempt to manipulate the public's perception of the judiciary. Similarly, the legal and/or academic community's publicly expressed disappointment in a decision may weaken the public's and other constituencies' confidence in the judiciary. Thus, although the immediate effects of negative public discourse may seem negligible, persistent negative publicity can lead to a loss of public support, weaken the court's authority, and trigger other more severe responses.

6.2.3.2 Noncompliance or Reversal

Enforcing judicial decisions relies on the cooperation of the political branches and ordinary citizens, both of whom may elect to disobey the court's decision(s). Those with political power may respond with laws or constitutional amendments that effectively annul a decision. Defiance (including noncompliance and reversal) limits the efficacy of the court, and can have long-term effects on the court's reputation and its judicial

[19] See Scott Stephenson, 'Are Political "Attacks" on the Judiciary Ever Justifiable? The Relationship between Unfair Criticism and Public Accountability' (2023) 71 *American Journal of Comparative Law* 748.

authority. As Jeffrey Staton and Georg Vanberg argue, defiance, especially by the government and other visible actors, has "corrosive effects": "noncompliance by a policy maker today may begin to undermine the general perception that court decisions must be respected, and thus induce more and more noncompliance as citizens and political elites become less likely to react when policy makers fail to adhere to judicial rulings."[20]

One-off instances of defiance may, over time, become habitual, gradually eroding the social legitimacy of the court. Ultimately, it can become an existential threat by contributing to a culture of cynicism and giving enemies of the court the political ammunition to take down the judges.

6.2.3.3 Institutional Reform

Institutional reform, which includes court-curbing actions and court-packing, is usually the worst kind of institutional response that a court can attract, for it tends to cause long-term damage to the judiciary as an institution. It diminishes the power of a court in a way that is often irreversible (at least in the near term) and makes judicial maneuvering much harder. Institutional reform changes the rules of the game of judicial politics and fundamentally disrupts the calculus of judges. It includes appointing loyal judges or removing defiant judges; impeachment; redesigning the structure of the court, such as its size; amending court procedures, such as access rules or the number of votes required to render a decision; changing the formal powers of the court, such as carving out the court's jurisdiction or disabling judicial review; and diminishing the court's budget.

6.2.3.4 Actual Violence

Once in a while, a decision may result in the assassination of judges, physical damage of the court building, and other kinds of violent responses. This happens more often in authoritarian regimes with a strong military presence and in states experiencing intense, violent conflict. The *threat* of physical violence has similarly coercive and chilling effects.

6.2.4 A Holistic Assessment

The typology set out in the previous paragraphs captures most kinds of adverse reactions faced by domestic courts. By pinpointing the kind(s) of

[20] Jeffrey Staton and Georg Vanberg, 'The Value of Vagueness: Delegation, Defiance, and Judicial Opinions' (2008) 52 *American Journal of Political Science* 504, 507.

resistance that can emerge, judges should be in a better position to anticipate the severity of the negative political outcome(s) of maintaining the formal legal position. It should be emphasized, though, that these categories are only heuristics for thinking about the question of severity. While, for example, institutional reform tends to be more drastic than reversal, some kinds of institutional reforms are relatively mild, such as reducing the retirement age of judges by one year. Judges might also reasonably expect resistance from multiple sources, which may have a cumulative effect when combined.

After estimating the severity of the negative outcome, judges need to have a sense of the likelihood of it occurring. This is not a scientific exercise, and uncertainty around any kind of political forecasting is unavoidable. Even the savviest judges can get it wrong. Case studies of authoritarian judicial politics offer several generalizable lessons to help judges in this regard. First, the likelihood (and severity) of a negative reaction is often correlated with the salience of the issue confronting the court. Antiregime decisions that touch on matters fundamental to the incumbent's survival will most probably trigger an immediate and negative reaction.[21] Second, macropolitical events outside the courtroom might explain variation in the likelihood of political attacks occurring. The regime's tolerance of an uncooperative judiciary will naturally be at its lowest when the incumbent perceives that political circumstances threaten its own existence.[22] Third and relatedly, court-curbing threats or actions cannot always be traced back to a specific judicial decision. They might sometimes be the result of accumulated past incidents. The second and third lessons imply that a holistic and longitudinal assessment of relevant judicial political dynamics helps to predict the likelihood and severity of political attacks more accurately.

In sum, the risk assessment considers factors relating to severity and likelihood. Again, the "formula" proposed is not a mathematical equation. Rather, it is an analytical tool to help judges under authoritarian regimes carefully consider the political consequences of maintaining a formal legal position by distilling the factors they ought to be paying attention to. Judges are not asked to produce an exact estimate, but

[21] See Yasser Kureshi, 'Selective Assertiveness and Strategic Deference: Explaining Judicial Contestation of Military Prerogatives in Pakistan' (2021) 28 *Democratization* 604; Julius Yam, 'Approaching the Legitimacy Paradox in Hong Kong: Lessons for Hybrid Regime Courts' (2021) 46 *Law & Social Inquiry* 153.

[22] Epstein, Knight, and Shvetsova (n 14).

instead ascertain whether the risks of pushbacks and backlash are *sufficiently high* to warrant strategic considerations.

6.2.5 *Deciding Whether and How to Supplement the Formal Legal Position*

After gauging the level of risk exposed to a court, judges will need to determine the amount of deviation from the formal legal position required, if any, to address the expected risk. Different risk exposure levels warrant different kinds of strategic responses. The low-risk and high-risk scenarios discussed in this section are not hard categories, while the baseline and unavoidable scenarios differ in kind and overlap with the high-risk scenario.

6.2.5.1 Low-Risk Scenario

In some situations, the risk level might be so low that there is no need to deviate from the formal legal position ("the low-risk scenario") because, for example, the likelihood of any backlash is very remote. Even in these situations, judicial strategy may still be relevant. As I will explain, some strategies are cosmetic, by which I mean that whatever changes they result in leave the core of the decision (or the formal legal position) untouched. For example, judges can consider deploying strategies to improve the social impact of the decision or the social authority of the court. Strategies may also be applied to run-of-the-mill cases to entrench constitutional legal principles, which over time can be used to justify far more consequential decisions. Such approaches to a low-risk context are acceptable, so long as they do not materially increase the risk level (and keep the formal legal position intact).

6.2.5.2 High-Risk Scenario

There are also instances where the risk is serious enough to justify a departure from the formal legal position ("the high-risk scenario"). Judicial strategies here primarily function to protect the institutional integrity of the court while approximating the formal legal position as much as is practically possible. When deciding between different strategic routes, there are three principles judges should bear in mind.

First, the priority is to whittle the available options down to those with manageable levels of risk. It may be impossible or excessively costly to completely neutralize all risk. Self-preservation, again, is not the goal, but a court needs to be sufficiently confident of its institutional survival if it wants to realize its constitutional role sustainably. Second, among the options that present tolerable levels of risk, judges should select a path that preserves as much of the normative content of the formal legal position as is practically possible.

It may be that the deviation from the formal legal position required does not allow any constitutional substance to be salvaged. If so, the third principle requires judges to choose an option that minimizes the authoritarian effects of deviating from the formal legal position. This is particularly important because a court can entrench authoritarian norms as easily as it can embed constitutional legal norms. This is the flip side of a court's rule-of-law potential.

6.2.5.3 Baseline Scenario

There are two scenarios in which maintaining the formal legal position is justified *despite* risk levels being high. The first exception to the high-risk scenario is when a departure from the formal legal position crosses a moral baseline ("the baseline scenario"). As suggested, attempts to avoid political backlash might sometimes lead to the adoption of a position with authoritarian effects. While one of the principles proposed just now requires minimizing such effects as much as practically possible, there are times when *any* deviation from the formal legal position would lead to an evil or profoundly immoral outcome. The moral costs might in these cases be too high to justify any kind of strategic deviation. For example, questions about whether slavery or genocide are constitutional are undisputable. I confine this exception to moral evils such as when what is at risk is people's lives or security. Strategic deviation is morally impermissible here, as the individual interests at stake are too important. In these cases, if a judge can temper an evil system, he or she should do so, and strategies should be used for ends other than mere institutional preservation, such as increasing the reach and impact of the decision.[23]

6.2.5.4 Unavoidable Scenario

A second exception is when the likelihood of a severe political backlash is so high that no practical amount of strategizing is able to mitigate the risk ("the unavoidable scenario"). In other words, an existential threat to the judicial institution is inescapable and judicial strategy is immaterial. "Living to fight another day"[24] only makes sense if "another day" exists.

[23] Another option judges may consider is resigning in protest when there are outcomes that none can in good conscience reach.

[24] Rosalind Dixon and Samuel Issacharoff, 'Living to Fight Another Day: Judicial Deferral in Defense of Democracy' (2016) 4 *Wisconsin Law Review* 683.

Our assumption about courts adopting a long-term horizon does not hold here, as the court itself will soon cease to exist. Judges facing such dire circumstances should stand firm and execute their democracy-enhancing roles to the best of their abilities until the court is dissolved. Not only is this the right thing to do, but the court's refusal to admit defeat may mobilize domestic and international support by highlighting abuses of authoritarian power. Strategic deviation in this instance will not save the court, but strategies can nonetheless be used to undermine the authoritarian's plans.

Figure 6.1 summarizes the Sustainable Democratic Adjudication framework in the form of a flowchart.

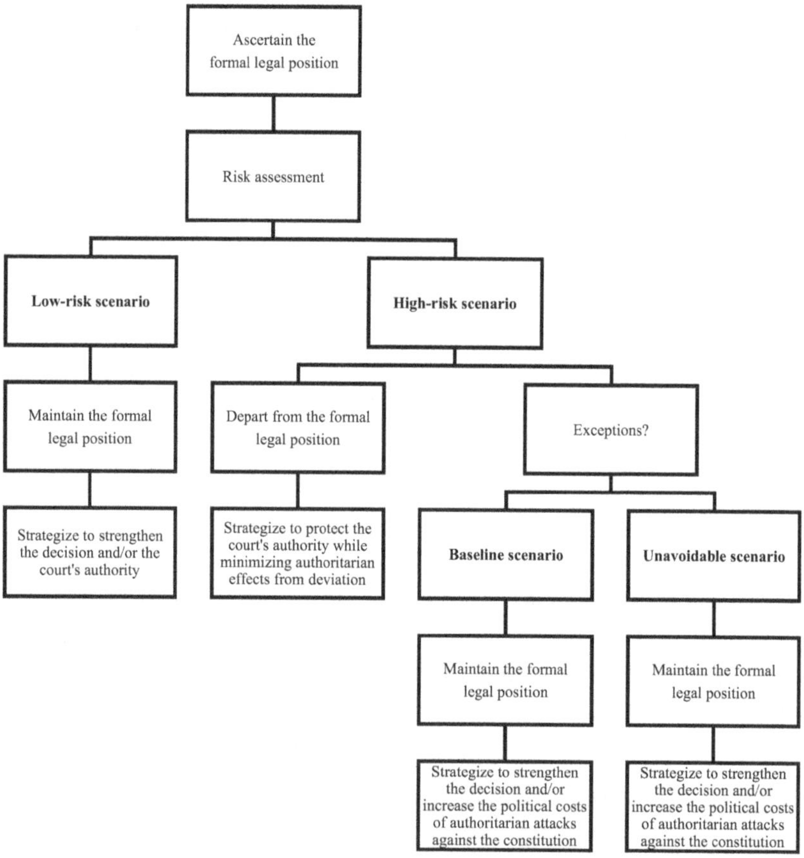

Figure 6.1 Sustainable Democratic Adjudication flowchart.

6.3 A Menu of Strategies

We have discussed *when* judges should consider judicial strategies, and *how* judges should integrate judicial strategies into the adjudicative process to accommodate authoritarian pressures. Two important questions remain: *What* kinds of judicial strategies are available, and what are their functions?

Effective strategizing relies on a judge's ability to make legally and politically sensible assessments suitable to the environment they operate in. Simply highlighting the importance of strategizing would be "anti-theory," as it leaves everything to judicial statesmanship.[25] To balance judicial agency with insights from the judicial strategy literature, I focus on the aspects of the adjudicative process with potential consequences for the institutional status of judges and identify the conditions under which each technique may be salient. The virtue of this approach is that it shows judges when and where strategic opportunities may arise, and their practical implications, while leaving room for judges to select strategies most appropriate to the specific contexts they face. After all, based on different judges' reading of the situation, there can be multiple ways to address their strategic needs.

Drawing on international and comparative examples from various regime types, this part presents a catalogue of the strategic opportunities relevant to a domestic court. The strategies introduced in this section are by no means exhaustive. As will become clear, some strategies may be more effective in certain kinds of hybrid regimes, depending on, for instance, the extent to which the regime grounds its legitimacy in legality, or whether it cares about the regard of international audiences. The judicial-legal culture within which judges operate will inevitably influence the range of options available to them. The objective here is to highlight strategies that are generally relevant to judges in hybrid regimes facing authoritarian pressure. The effects of these strategies will vary depending on which of the four scenarios judges face. In a low-risk scenario, judicial strategies may further entrench constitutional democratic norms and enhance a decision's social impact. In a high-risk scenario, judicial strategies are needed to mitigate the risks generated as a result of the formal legal position, and may involve departing from the formal legal position. Even in the baseline and unavoidable scenarios,

[25] Mann (n 5) 32.

strategies may help consolidate the formal legal position and increase the political costs of pushback by the authoritarian.

For our purposes, there are four dimensions of judicial decision-making along which judges can factor in strategic considerations: (1) Outcome, (2) reasoning, (3) language, and (4) timing.[26] How the strategic opportunities arising from each dimension may become relevant in each of the four scenarios will also be discussed.

6.3.1 Outcome

Given that the final outcome of a case can have profound, immediate effects on the litigants and those related to the decision, it is often the most strategically significant aspect of the adjudicative process. For similar reasons, altering the outcome is arguably the most contentious strategic response among the options discussed here. However, as suggested, it may be necessary to let the authoritarian win at least parts of the judgment in order to defuse an institutional crisis, especially in a high-risk context. Furthermore, in what follows, I argue that outcomes can be adjusted in nuanced ways to preserve certain normative aspects of a formal legal position while mitigating the more pressing authoritarian risks.

6.3.1.1 Binary and Multitiered Outcomes

A judicial decision is often thought to involve a binary outcome: Someone wins, and someone loses. Judges need to be aware of the expectations of different and potentially conflicting judicial audiences, as well as how their judgments might impact these stakeholders.

While outcomes often look binary, judges can sometimes create multitiered outcomes by disaggregating the issue at stake. One side, for instance, can win on the first and third grounds, while the other may take the second and fourth grounds. These are what might be called halfway-house or "win–win" decisions, whereby an outcome is split into several parts in order to try and satisfy the expectations of various social groups.[27] These decisions may also help preserve parts of the formal legal

[26] Rosalind Dixon and Yvonne Tew have also written about the different techniques of judicial statecraft that would enhance the perceived legitimacy and judicial power of a constitutional court. While substantively different to the proposals here, the dimensions they focus on are similar. See Dixon (n 4); Yvonne Tew, 'Strategic Judicial Empowerment' (2024) 72 *American Journal of Comparative Law* 170.

[27] Yam (n 21) 170.

position while lowering the risk of authoritarian backlash to manageable levels. To illustrate this technique, Wen-Chen Chang uses the examples of constitutional courts in South Korea and Taiwan, whose judgments allowed "everyone [to] obtain . . . some portion of what he or she desires, just not all of it."[28]

The feasibility of this technique depends on the nature of a case. It might be impractical in cases that are too preoccupied with a single, narrow issue that cannot be carved up further. In some instances, any attempt to draw finer distinctions will have minimal or even counterproductive social effects, even if these distinctions are legally significant. For example, the Hong Kong Court of Final Appeal's attempt to please the prodemocracy and pro-China camps by imposing a lenient sentence on a democracy leader while issuing harsher sentencing guidelines for future cases in *HKSAR v. Wong Chi Fung* triggered pushbacks from both sides, as each perceived the other half of the outcome to be unfair or biased.[29]

6.3.1.2 Remedies

Judicial remedies introduce additional subtleties to the notion of outcomes. Traditionally, courts with constitutional jurisdiction are vested with the power to strike down laws and executive actions that are inconsistent with the constitution. The same courts, however, have begun to develop an extensive array of remedies. These remedies might be considered novel because they push the constitutional boundaries of a court and sometimes lack constitutional and/or statutory authorization.[30] Some examples include constitutional damages, engagement orders that oblige the government to engage with victims of constitutional violations, suspension orders coupled with read-in provisos that automatically take place if the government does not respond in time, and remedial interpretations.[31]

Aside from their ability to address complex legal questions, these remedies also have strategic effects and give judges the tools to express themselves in nuanced ways. Engagement orders, for instance, can soften the blow of a judgment on the government. They position the court as deferring to the incumbent regime, even as its ruling admonishes the incumbent's actions, by engaging them in a collaborative partnership. A clever use of remedial interpretation may also appear to superficially

[28] Wen-Chen Chang, 'Strategic Judicial Responses in Politically Charged Cases: East Asian Experiences' (2010) 8 *International Journal of Constitutional Law* 885, 900.

[29] [2018] 2 HKLRD 657.

[30] See Po Jen Yap (ed), *Constitutional Remedies in Asia* (Routledge 2019).

[31] See Po Jen Yap, 'New Democracies and Novel Remedies' (2017) 1 *Public Law* 30.

preserve the constitutional authority of the government while injecting constitutional legal substance into unattractive laws.

6.3.2 *Reasoning*

The reasoning is the flesh of a decision, and varying aspects of judicial reasoning can have strategic implications. Reasoning is salient in all four scenarios. It may help address the political dangers in a high-risk scenario, fortify a formal legal position adopted in a low-risk or baseline scenario by amplifying certain parts of the judgment, or increase a decision's symbolic effects in the unavoidable scenario. Some of the techniques outlined in the following paragraphs may result in a departure from the formal legal position; others are cosmetic, and are used to communicate and develop relationships with the court's audiences.

6.3.2.1 Depth and Breadth of Reasoning

Not only are judges in control of how to divide the issues at hand, but they exercise discretion over which issues to address and the amount of coverage given to each issue. A shallow ruling that leaves foundational questions undecided may be appropriate in a high-risk scenario.[32] This approach would draw conclusions based on rationales that already command wide support, or build consensus by avoiding matters that are likely to provoke disputes. A court that seeks to limit the precedential value of its decision (perhaps because of the authoritarian effects arising from strategic deviation) may also consider particularizing a decision based on the facts of the case.

A minimalist approach is not always successful in defusing political risks, though. Tensions are sometimes so high that common ground cannot be feasibly established. Or, both sides might demand that judges engage with deeper constitutional questions; in these circumstances, failing to do so would impair the court's legitimacy and prolong social tensions. In such situations, judges might have to consider a more maximalist approach by giving their opinions on the core issues involved. This may seem strategically counterintuitive, as deeper rulings can create more points of contention. However, a more thoroughly reasoned judgment also allows judges to clarify their positions, which reduces the room

[32] Cass R. Sunstein, *One Case at a Time: Judicial Minimalism on the Supreme Court* (HUP 2001).

for misinterpretation, distortion, and the uncertainty that might otherwise follow.

The depth and breadth of reasoning can also be adjusted to increase the court's social impact. When a risk is reduced to a tolerable level, judges may engage in deeper reasoning to lay the foundations for future decisions that are conducive to the advancement of constitutionalism. Similarly, in a low-risk context, it may be preferable to issue broad decisions in order to capitalize on favorable political conditions and develop meaningful principles. This may include, for instance, adopting an expansive reading of a constitutional right. The baseline and unavoidable scenarios are also relevant in this regard. When there is only one morally acceptable answer, or when the inevitable is near, judges should seize the opportunity to point out and explicate unconstitutional and unjust developments. The aim is to undermine the legitimacy of the incumbent regime and increase the political costs of authoritarian attacks against the constitution.

6.3.2.2 Legal Methodology

Deciding how to justify an outcome affects the persuasiveness of a decision. A court may need to adopt a kind of reasoning that resonates with its intended audience. Judges may, for instance, ground a decision in guardianship or "Schmittian" logic if they want to convince their authoritarian readers. They may also adopt a legal methodology that is favored by their audiences, just as how conservative groups in the United States might prefer originalism. To use Robert Hume's words, the objective here is to "choose a legal grounding that will advance their relationship with the audience that they are most interested in targeting based on the conditions presented in each case."[33]

The distinction between procedural review and substantive review is illuminating, as, beyond their technical differences, they broadly reflect two different ways of grounding a decision. Substantive review involves deeper scrutiny of the merits of the case and the validity of the arguments put forth by the parties. Procedural review involves checking whether the parties have complied with established rules and procedures during legal proceedings. Procedural review appears to leave less space for judicial discretion, given that rules and procedures are usually drafted in more

[33] Robert J. Hume, 'Courting Multiple Audiences: The Strategic Selection of Legal Groundings by Judges on the US Courts of Appeals' (2009) 30 *Justice System Journal* 14, 17.

unequivocal terms. I say "appears to" because interpretative room is a matter of degree, and judges can sometimes still find the space to creatively construe procedural provisions.

Relying on procedural grounds to dispose of a case may help preserve a court's neutral appearance. There is a shared belief that the administration and interpretation of procedural rules is part and parcel of a judge's duty.[34] A commitment to procedural justice through an impartial use of procedural review not only lowers the political risk of a supposedly controversial position, but can also help bolster judges' professional image.[35] Hume makes a similar argument, finding that American appeal courts in the administrative law context can more effectively deflect scrutiny from higher court judges and other political actors by confining their analyses to the facts of the case and avoiding engagement with the substantive points raised by the litigants.[36] Nevertheless, it should be noted that when the underlying procedures are widely perceived as unfair, an unwavering commitment to a formalistic vision of proceduralism is likely to damage a court's legitimacy. In other words, it may sometimes be impossible for judges to appear neutral when the very rules that they are asked to interpret lack social authority. Hence, the procedural approach is not necessarily foolproof.

6.3.2.3 Strategic Citation

Citations in a judgment affect how judges are perceived. To use legal precedents to justify an argument is the essence of common-law reasoning and an accepted practice in many civil-law jurisdictions. Studies have found that when judges anticipate pushbacks when laying down a new doctrine, they tend to argue more carefully and cite more extensively.[37] This increases the chances of acceptance by the legal community. Not only are judicial citations used to convince legal actors, their strategic effects can reach those outside the legal field as well. Olof Larsson and his colleagues, for example, find that the Court of Justice of the European

[34] Philippe Nonet and Philip Selznick, *Law and Society in Transition: Toward Responsive Law* (Transaction Publishers 2005) 58, 66.

[35] Tom Tyler, 'Psychological Perspectives on Legitimacy and Legitimation' (2006) 57 *Annual Review of Psychology* 375.

[36] Hume (n 33).

[37] David Walsh, 'On the Meaning and Pattern of Legal Citations: Evidence from State Wrongful Discharge Precedent Cases' (1997) 31 *Law & Society Review* 337; Yonatan Lupu and Erik Voeten, 'Precedent in International Courts: A Network Analysis of Case Citations by the European Court of Human Rights' (2012) 42 *British Journal of Political Science* 413.

Union tends to embed its decisions in caselaw when ruling against European governments in order to persuade them of the legal quality of its decisions.[38] The fact that these governmental actors are, strictly speaking, neither lawyers nor jurists is irrelevant, as they have legal experts who can help policymakers appreciate the significance of the legal justifications.

The selective use of precedents can liberate judges from tight spaces. This is especially so for apex-level courts that are not bound by precedents. This point is best illustrated by the strategic use of comparative jurisprudence, which includes foreign and international law. The extent to which comparative citation is available to judges as a strategic tool depends on preexisting institutional rules and legal norms, for example, whether the law explicitly sanctions this practice, or whether there is a history of doing so.[39] Even without explicit authority, however, there are many constitutional courts that cite comparative law "voluntarily."[40] Some judges have been candid about how selective their approach is when it comes to the use of comparative citation.[41]

The kinds of comparative jurisprudence cited reflect the image that a court wants to project. Just as authoritarian regimes may attempt to pass themselves off as democratic, courts under pressure from authoritarian rulers may wish to "defer" to foreign practice by citing precedents decided by the more "canonical" group of courts.[42] This technique may help establish links with reputable overseas courts. For instance, the Ugandan courts do not enjoy explicit constitutional authority to refer to foreign and international jurisprudence, but foreign and international laws have played an important role in the country's constitutional legal developments. Johanna Kalb argues that comparative citations have been used to strengthen the authority of antiregime decisions and to improve the judiciary's reputation in the eyes of domestic and international NGOs and donors.[43] Furthermore, citing foreign and international jurisprudence is

[38] Olof Larsson and others, 'Speaking Law to Power: The Strategic Use of Precedent of the Court of Justice of the European Union' (2017) 50 *Comparative Political Studies* 879.

[39] Yam (n 21) 171–2.

[40] Ran Hirschl, 'In Search of an Identity: Voluntary Foreign Citations in Discordant Constitutional Settings' (2014) 62 *American Journal of Comparative Law* 547.

[41] Anthony Mason, 'The Place of Comparative Law in Developing the Jurisprudence on the Rule of Law and Human Rights in Hong Kong' (2007) 37 *Hong Kong Law Journal* 299, 306.

[42] Hirschl (n 40) 564.

[43] Johanna Kalb, 'The Judicial Role in New Democracies: A Strategic Account of Comparative Citation' (2013) 38 *The Yale Journal of International Law* 423, 446–8.

a way of signaling respect to allies abroad. A court can also refrain from referring to "unattractive" jurisdictions or lines of jurisprudence, even if these might be legally relevant, in order to avoid associating itself with "the wrong crowd." Given the plethora of comparative jurisprudence in existence, selective use of comparative citation is a technique that serves ideologically diverse outcomes.

Aside from domestic and comparative precedents, judges may cite nonbinding secondary materials in their judgments to persuade nonlegal actors.[44] These materials may include legal dictionaries, works by prominent jurists and philosophers, statements by political figures, and treatises. This technique is based on a psychological phenomenon called priming, which describes how exposure to certain stimuli, such as the prestige or legitimacy of the cited materials, might unconsciously affect how a judgment and the court are perceived.[45] Unlike the citation of legal precedents, however, these materials lack legal authority and do not increase the legal persuasiveness of a decision. Still, this technique improves the standing of the court and enhances the persuasiveness of its decisions in the eyes of audiences who can appreciate the secondary materials being cited.

6.3.3 *Language*

The language used in a judgment is crucial for effectively communicating legal ideas. It can also shape the social authority of the decision and judicial audiences' attitudes toward the court. Language-related techniques tend to be more cosmetic, and there can be multiple ways to linguistically frame the same legal position. The techniques covered in the following paragraphs can be applied in all four scenarios, but how they should be applied depends on whom judges are trying to communicate with.

6.3.3.1 Natural Language or Legal Language?

There is an ongoing debate about what sort of language – natural language or legal language – judges should use in their opinions. These debates are, to some extent, conditioned by societal expectations. For those pushing for legal accessibility, using natural language may help

44 Robert J. Hume, 'The Use of Rhetorical Sources by the U.S. Supreme Court' (2006) 40 *Law & Society Review* 817.

45 *ibid* 821.

legitimize the court by "bringing the author down nearer to the human level of the litigants" and "humaniz[ing] . . . the judicial process."[46]

This choice has strategic implications. The traditional law and politics divide suggests that legal language is peculiar to the legal field, and its use purports to obscure the role of politics in law. Judges, it is argued, can conceal their intentions and the political substance of the case behind the "mask" of the law.[47] As Michael Blauberger and Dorte Martinsen put it, "politically unwelcome case law can only be challenged on its own legal terms."[48] Framing a judgment in technical legal terms creates a mythical aura that shields judges from attacks by laypersons. The decisions of the German Constitutional Court have been described as "dry" and "technical,"[49] but its self-presentation as a technocratic court has helped build its reputation for impartiality. This technique may be particularly useful in divided societies seeking reintegration, as it may help downplay the political saliency of contentious topics. Judges may also plant the seeds of progressive doctrinal development by inserting legal justifications into their decisions that require deciphering. These can be "unlocked" in the future when the conditions are right.

Natural language offers its own set of advantages. A more layperson-friendly approach allows ideas to travel to a wider range of audiences. Judges can only create attractive soundbites when the general population finds the judgment to be accessible. This technique is especially relevant when judges are trying to educate the public, or when they want to make a strong statement, as in the baseline and avoidable scenarios.

Judges hoping to reduce the likelihood of noncompliance – which, as suggested, is a common type of adverse response they face – should also consider using natural language. Those asked to comply with a judgment cannot use ignorance as an excuse for disobedience when that judgment is clearly and simply expressed. Judges may also deploy affective terminology or value-laden language to persuade lay actors to abide by their decisions. A study of World Trade Organization panels by Marc Busch and Krzysztof Pelc found that the extent to which the panels used "words

46 Patricia M. Wald, 'The Rhetoric of Results and the Results of Rhetoric: Judicial Writings' (1995) 62 *The University of Chicago Law Review* 1371, 1417.

47 Anne-Marie Burley and Walter Mattli, 'Europe Before the Court: A Political Theory of Legal Integration' (1993) 47 *International Organization* 41, 72.

48 Michael Blauberger and Dorte Sindbjerg Martinsen, 'The Court of Justice in Times of Politicisation: "Law as a Mask and Shield" Revisited' (2020) 27 *Journal of European Public Policy* 382, 384.

49 Michaela Hailbronner, 'Transformative Constitutionalism: Not Only in the Global South' (2017) 65 *The American Journal of Comparative Law* 527, 551.

denoting overt positive or negative sentiment" in their rulings depended on the political sensitivity of the issues involved.[50] Courts looking to have their rulings enforced and followed must be able to communicate effectively, and, as the authors argue, affect offers the necessary discursive resources to persuade public audiences.[51]

6.3.3.2 Strategic Vagueness

Another rhetorical resource that judges can utilize is specificity. Highly specific language aligns the outcome with the judges' intentions by making deviations from the law easier to detect.[52] Judges should be specific when asserting themselves and attempting to make their point clear. Conflict aversion or covert resistance, however, may necessitate toning down on the specificity of the decision's language.[53] For example, judges may establish a new constitutional principle but underspecify the context in which it applies. Points of contention can be suppressed by using fuzzy language. However, vagueness can be abused by judicial audiences, since judges rarely have the opportunity to correct a widespread misinterpretation of their writings. Any side-effects of strategic vagueness may be long-lasting as a result.

6.3.3.3 The Power of Narrative

Judges also control the narrative of the judgment. This relates to, but goes beyond, our previous discussion on the choice of language. A distinction here needs to be made between narration, which appeals to emotion, and argumentation, which appeals to logic.[54] Argumentation relies on accepted modes of reasoning with the help of evidence to justify legal claims, whereas narration involves framing the flow of events and the relevant characters. Narration helps audiences create experiences. Legal scholars and lawyers typically focus on the argumentative elements of a judgment, such as the admissibility of the evidence, the appropriateness of the adopted mode of interpretation, and the relevance and authority of

[50] Marc L. Busch and Krzysztof J. Pelc, 'Words Matter: How WTO Rulings Handle Controversy' (2019) 63 *International Studies Quarterly* 464.

[51] It is worth mentioning that World Trade Organization panels aim to persuade national governments rather than domestic audiences directly. The authors originally argue that the discursive resources are offered to governmental actors in order to persuade their citizens.

[52] Lee Epstein and Tonja Jacobi, 'The Strategic Analysis of Judicial Decisions' (2010) 6 *Annual Review of Law and Social Science* 341, 354.

[53] Staton and Vanberg (n 20).

[54] This distinction can be traced back to Aristotle's work *Rhetoric*.

the cited precedents. The strategic importance of argumentation has already been highlighted in the earlier discussion on reasoning.

Which narrative the court adopts can significantly influence the attitude of certain audiences toward the court and determine the social impact of a decision. Courtrooms are often described as battlegrounds for litigants to assert their preferred narratives. A judge imparts a narrative by adopting a particular vocabulary, portraying certain actors as protagonists and antagonists, recounting events in a particular sequence, and selectively foregrounding particular principles or factual elements. The choices made by judges in telling the "story" of the case can construct and reconstruct historical events as well as create new frames for interpretation. The power of narrative is perhaps best displayed by the Indian and Pakistani courts, both of which are famous for their populist rhetoric.[55] Their strategies involve using natural language, but they go further by actively attempting to connect with "the people" through appeals to public sentiment and appropriating the vocabulary of politicians. The Indian Supreme Court has even quoted poetry in its judgments.[56] Courts in these countries are sometimes denounced as populist and politicized, but their ability to mobilize the public by deploying narratives cannot be understated.

6.3.4 *Timing*

A consensus among students of judicial strategy is that timing is always a factor at play. This chapter assumes that interactions between the court and political actors persist over an extended period. The importance of being sensitive to timing is built into the two-step framework and is relevant in all four scenarios, as judges are required to evaluate their current and future political circumstances, drawing partially on past experience. However, what does "good timing" mean?

Timing is "right" in the sense that a case is decided at a moment with optimal effects for judicial empowerment and/or the legal position they wish to advance.[57] For instance, the *Obergefell v. Hodges* decision in the

[55] Anuj Bhuwania, 'Courting the People: The Rise of Public Interest Litigation in Post-emergency India' (2014) 34 *Comparative Studies of South Asia, Africa and the Middle East* 314; Yasser Kureshi, 'What Is Judicial Populism and How Does It Work in Pakistan?' Dawn, February 1, 2019, available at www.dawn.com/news/1461194 [https://perma.cc/389V-6AMH], last visited January 10, 2026.

[56] Hailbronner (n 49) 552.

[57] David Fontana, 'Docket Control and the Success of Constitutional Courts' in Tom Ginsburg and Rosalind Dixon (eds), *Comparative Constitutional Law* (Edward Elgar Publishing 2011).

United States to recognize the right to same-sex marriage is considered well-timed because it coincided with increasingly liberal attitudes toward gender issues.[58] The landmark *Ng Ka Ling & Ors v. Director of Immigration* case decided by the Hong Kong Court of Final Appeal to establish its power of judicial review in the early days of the handover was also well-timed from an *institutional* perspective as the court found and exploited the political opportunities present during the early post-handover period to effectively entrench its powers, when China was still under close international scrutiny.[59] From a *policy* or *legal* perspective, however, the decision was badly timed, as the decision to broaden the right of abode in the same case was eventually "overruled" by the Chinese authorities. The judges did not anticipate how unpopular their decision would be, considering immigration was a hugely controversial topic at the time.[60]

6.3.4.1 Timing in Three Stages

Timing is important. But, more crucially, judges have opportunities to control issues relating to timing. These opportunities are best understood through "the life cycle of a case"[61] – the ex-ante stage of deciding whether to hear a case, the in-medio stage of hearing a case, and the ex-post stage of the release of the judgment. Each stage presents different opportunities for judges to exercise their agenda-setting powers. Judges have three options when it comes to time-related opportunities: To delay, to avoid, or to engage. Judges may want to delay or avoid politically risky cases when the conditions are not ripe, and engage with those cases when conditions are favorable. The opportunities described in subsequent paragraphs draw attention to how judges can adapt the timing of their decisions to take advantage of their surrounding circumstances.

Crucial to a court during the ex-ante stage is its docket control power, that is, its power to decide whether to hear a case or not.[62] The docket control power of courts vary in practice. In some countries like India and Pakistan, judges enjoy *suo moto* powers to pursue an action of its own

[58] *Obergefell v. Hodges* 576 U.S. 644 (2015).

[59] *Ng Ka Ling & Ors v. Director of Immigration* [1999] 1 HKLRD 315.

[60] See Eric C. Ip, 'Constitutional Competition between the Hong Kong Court of Final Appeal and the Chinese National People's Congress Standing Committee: A Game Theory Perspective' (2014) 39 *Law & Social Inquiry* 824, 832–3.

[61] This framework is borrowed from Erin F. Delaney, 'Analyzing Avoidance: Judicial Strategy in Comparative Perspective' (2016) 66 *Duke Law Journal* 1, 5.

[62] Fontana (n 57) 625.

accord, and can actively control their own agenda and the pace of the judicial process. Most courts lack such powers, though. For them, the docket control power depends to a large extent on the supply of cases. Some, such as the United States Supreme Court, have complete discretion as to whether to hear a case brought by applicants. More intricately, as Theunis Roux observes, the South African Constitutional Court's expansive jurisdiction over public law matters coincided with its strict approach to determining which cases it hears.[63] The strategy allows the court to "measure the political temperature" of cases directly brought by applicants before deciding whether to accept the petition.[64] In most systems, the discretionary power to decide whether to hear a case is subject to a number of legal principles and rules. In many common-law jurisdictions, an applicant must demonstrate that the case is of sufficient public importance or meets a merits test. Constitutional courts in civil-law jurisdictions are often mandated by the law to hear almost every case, though in practice they still enjoy considerable discretion. For instance, judges can interpret procedural and standing rules to control the flow of the cases, and allocate their time and effort efficiently through a more strategic allocation of judge panels.[65]

The strategic importance of docket control power is best illustrated by its absence. A passive court will be at the mercy of external actors when it comes to when and what kinds of cases are to be heard. This is particularly troublesome in judicialized polities, as a passive court will have no choice but to confront all sorts of highly controversial cases. Those looking to undermine judicial authority may even manipulate the agenda of defenseless judges by deliberately launching claims that are likely to lead to unpopular outcomes. Docket control power provides much-needed flexibility to the court to cope with shifting circumstances. Judges can exercise their discretion to pick attractive cases, delay others to the future when the political conditions are favorable, and avoid engaging in high-risk scenarios. Again, the extent to which a court can utilize its docket control power for strategic purposes is limited by preexisting rules that govern its behavior.

There is also room for strategic maneuvering in the next two stages. In particular, during the in-medio hearing and trial stage, judges first get to

63 Roux (n 4) 377–83.

64 *ibid* 366.

65 Christoph Engel, 'Does Efficiency Trump Legality? The Case of the German Constitutional Court' in Yun-chien Chang (ed), *Selection and Decision in Judicial Process around the World* (CUP 2019).

decide when to hear a case. Second, they have a say with regard to the amount of time dedicated to the trial. Third, and most importantly, judges can be selective about what issues to address. As discussed previously, a narrow focus enables the discussion of certain issues to be delayed, though this is impossible if the controversy the court is seeking to avoid forms the crux of the case.

The final stage is when the judgment is released. The social effect of the decision takes place once the judgment is published. Finding the right time to issue the decision is of great strategic importance, and judges can time the releasing of their decisions to shape their image and public discourse. This is an area limited by case management norms. Each jurisdiction has its own practice in this regard, but authoring judges usually retain some room for discretion. For example, a common reason to expedite a case is when it involves matters of significant public importance. Despite a huge backlog of pending cases, the Supreme Court in Pakistan has often prioritized such cases.

A more substantive temporal element regarding the final stage is remedies. We have discussed how choosing between different remedies allows for varying degrees of intrusiveness. Remedies can also be analyzed temporally. Some remedies take place immediately, such as the nullification of a provision, but other effects might be intentionally delayed. What a suspension order does, for instance, is to effectively suspend the declaration of unconstitutionality for a period in order to allow political actors the time to comply with the decision. Engagement orders have similar delaying effects, as they give political actors considerable discretion over how best to implement the aspirations specified in the decision. Normatively, delayed remedies are often justified on grounds of democratic legitimacy.[66] They are a humble judicial technique to engage the political branches of government in constructive dialogue. Strategically, delayed remedies may reduce the risk of immediate backlash by effectively pushing trickier questions of implementation to a later date, or by signaling respect for the incumbent regime by engaging its members in a collaborative relationship.

6.3.4.2 Incrementalism

A time-related theme that is worth highlighting is incrementalism. In some ways, strategy is by definition incremental – it is a plan, or steps in a plan, to realize a long-term, overarching goal. As mentioned, the

[66] See Delaney (n 61).

framework proposed here assumes a long-term horizon: the benefits of applying it are not always immediate, and the goals of building institutional strength and the advancement of constitutionalism are continuous. This is consistent with the understanding that regime change, or democratization, is a gradual and often uneven process.[67]

Incrementalism refers to the idea of achieving progress through small, successive steps. Incrementalism is best contrasted with a revolutionary approach that seeks to align reality with certain goals immediately through large-scale transformations. Incrementalism has been applauded by constitutional scholars for its normative benefits: It tends to reduce error cost as a result of competency limitations of a court, offers more possibilities for judges to adapt to changing and complex circumstances, and is more respectful of democracy because it leaves more room for judges to collaborate with the political branches.[68]

From a strategic perspective, judicial incrementalism is often a more sensible approach as well, for two reasons. First, the objective here is the entrenchment of constitutional norms, as evidenced by a change in how things are done politically and the attitudinal shifts in the public and within the government. All things being equal, it is unrealistic to expect these changes to happen overnight via revolutionary action. Second, courts are vulnerable institutions, and a backlash may cause irreparable damage. Losing the court means closing down one of the few avenues for positive constitutional change in a hybrid regime. A revolutionary approach might be warranted in the unavoidable and baseline scenarios. Outside those cases, incrementalism seems to be preferred. Finally, incrementalism may help hone judges' political intuitions. Through each successive step, a court is expected to incorporate and consider feedback from society. This dynamic process provides an opportunity for judges to gain a better understanding of their local context.

6.3.5 *Combining the Techniques*

It is important for judges to remember that these techniques can and should be combined. For example, the Ugandan courts have upheld allegedly fraudulent elections to confirm Museveni's electoral victory,

[67] See Tom Gerald Daly and Dinesha Samararatne (eds), *Democratic Consolidation and Constitutional Endurance in Asia and Africa: Comparing Uneven Pathways* (OUP 2024).

[68] See e.g. Tarunabh Khaitan, 'Directive Principles and the Expressive Accommodation of Ideological Dissenters' (2018) 16 *International Journal of Constitutional Law* 389; Jeff King, *Judging Social Rights* (CUP 2012) chapter 10.

yet in their reasoning also acknowledged electoral malpractice and the compromise of citizens' political rights. The court had let the authoritarian prevail while endorsing liberal constitutional norms in their judgment.[69] Some readers may be reminded of the *Marbury* decision, where a proregime outcome coincided with reasoning that was supportive of judicial power. Additionally, a court does not have to adopt the same language and tone throughout its judgment. Countless combinations exist, but the general lesson here is that the techniques can and should be combined to create multidimensional and complex social effects that fit the strategic aims of constrained judges.

6.3.6 *Sensitivity to Audiences*

The last point to be discussed is one that has been emphasized throughout this chapter and the previous one: Judges need to be sensitive to their audiences if these strategies are to be deployed effectively. The social authority of a court rests primarily on their audiences' regard for them.[70] Many of the strategies outlined in this chapter should be deployed in ways that account for the characteristics and interests of the relevant audiences. Populistic rhetoric, for instance, would not fit systems that are more accustomed to a legalistic language, despite the theoretical payoffs explored earlier. The importance of audience sensitivity is not limited to language, either: Strategic citations and other reasoning techniques can be catered to different kinds of audiences as well.

Audience sensitivity involves not only knowing the background and culture of relevant audiences, but also understanding and exploiting their preferences and priorities. The Pakistani courts, for example, have been able to assert themselves successfully outside the prerogatives of the military.[71] Similarly, the Hong Kong courts showed consistent deference in cases that concerned the interests of local and Chinese authorities, such as over national sovereignty and electoral reform, but developed their powers and human rights jurisprudence outside those areas.[72] A similar pattern is found in Uganda, as liberal constitutional developments there

[69] See Jude Murison, 'Judicial Politics: Election Petitions and Electoral Fraud in Uganda' (2013) 7 *Journal of Eastern African Studies* 492.

[70] See Lawrence Baum, *Judges and Their Audiences: A Perspective on Judicial Behavior* (Princeton University Press 2009); Nuno Garoupa and Tom Ginsburg, *Judicial Reputation: A Comparative Theory* (University of Chicago Press 2015).

[71] Kureshi (n 21).

[72] Yam (n 21) 153.

coincided with "consistent defer[ence]" by the courts over issues that may have fundamentally undermined Museveni's power.[73] These courts have been able to discriminate between questions that impinge upon the core interests of the authoritarian – which are typically out of bounds, given the political risks involved – and those where the political stakes are lower. Their use of judicial strategies reflects their savviness and sensitivity. In addition, audiences' preferences may change over time. As the incumbent regime becomes more connected to the West or internationalized, for instance, certain domestic audiences may become more tolerant of liberal-constitutional norms. This creates new opportunities for a democratically committed court to build alliances and acquire leverage. The effective deployment of judicial strategies requires judges to discern their audiences' motivations and remain alert to how ongoing political changes might affect the preferences of their audiences.

6.4 Conclusion

This chapter considered how judges in hybrid regimes can give effect to their democratic roles sustainably. It proposed the two-step Sustainable Democratic Adjudication framework that integrates judicial strategy with principled adjudication. The framework is designed to guide judges in hybrid regimes who play a role in imposing meaningful constitutional constraints on authoritarian power. To better understand how judges can accommodate prudential concerns during the adjudicative process, this chapter outlined a wide range of judicial strategies, described their social effects, and specified the conditions under which the strategies may be salient.

It bears repeating that the goal of strategizing is not simply institutional preservation, but to enable judges to more fully embody their constitutional role. While constitutional democratic norms take priority over institutional preservation, a court must be institutionally resilient in order to advance those norms effectively. Difficulties arise when trade-offs have to be made between these two sets of values. The framework captures these complexities and offers guidance on how to navigate them. It thereby provides a structure for the strategic assessments that judges in

[73] Joseph M. Isanga, 'African Courts and Separation of Powers: A Comparative Study of Judicial Review in Uganda & South' (2009) 2 *Northwestern Interdisciplinary Law Review* 69.

hybrid regimes must make and ameliorates the uncertainty involved in judicial strategizing.

To fully understand the full range of options available to judges and their potential to fulfill their democracy-enhancing roles, we must not ignore their *social* capacity. In the next chapter, we move away from the adjudicative context and explore what democratically committed judges can do outside the courtroom to strengthen their institution. While the non-adjudicative techniques to be proposed might sit uncomfortably with conventional conceptions of the judicial role, we will discuss how judges can take advantage of the social tools they have to establish and maintain relationships with external actors, as well as to fend off attacks.

7

"Mingling in the World"

7.1 Introduction

While a court is principally defined by its adjudicative role, we must not forget that judges not only operate within the courtroom, but also engage with their audiences when they are not deciding cases. They may create allies and defuse enemies to strengthen the court. This chapter focuses on what judges can do to protect the judiciary and make their judgments more effective using off-bench tools and by relying on their social networks. These tools further highlight the socially constructed nature of judicial power in a hybrid regime.[1] As Alexei Trochev and Rachel Ellett argue, "law is neither completely autonomous from hybrid regimes nor completely autonomous from informal power networks."[2] When the constitutional protection of judicial powers is not as robust as it is in mature democracies, judges in a hybrid regime may have to rely on their social networks and consider nonjudicial techniques to help reinforce their institutional position.[3]

The chapter discusses four sets of tools. The first is relation-building. No matter how dedicated a court is, it is unlikely to succeed without societal allies. Before expanding on how judges can develop friendly relations with other institutions, we first need to identify institutions that are capable of protecting the court and the ways in which they can support a court. In Section 7.2, we will look at eight potential allies of a committed court: (1) Lawyers, (2) legal academics, (3) the media, (4) civil servants, (5) international organizations, (6) businesses, (7) the

[1] Alexei Trochev and Rachel Ellett, 'Judges and Their Allies: Rethinking Judicial Autonomy Through the Prism of Off-bench Resistance' (2014) 2 *Journal of Law and Courts* 67.

[2] *ibid* 84.

[3] *ibid*; Björn Dressel, Raul Sanchez-Urribarri, and Alexander Stroh, 'The Informal Dimension of Judicial Politics: A Relational Perspective' (2017) 13 *Annual Review of Law and Social Science* 413.

general public, and (8) fellow judges. Establishing and maintaining relationships with them not only offers the court greater leverage, but also strengthens the bonds within the democratic constituency.

A more important question comes after identifying potential allies: What can judges do to bring these institutions onto their side? As argued in the previous chapter, judges can act in ways that offer these groups greater legal and constitutional protection, or build connections by citing in the judgments materials that these institutions produced or resonate with. On top of these in-courtroom strategies, Section 7.3 examines how alliances can be forged through two kinds of off-bench engagement: Public relations and judicial diplomacy. Public relations is a diffuse technique used to build, defend, and maintain the general image of a court, while judicial diplomacy is more targeted. We will also look at some occasions where judges can conduct judicial diplomacy to connect with the institutions identified in Section 7.2.

Section 7.4 explores a second set of tools to address hostile parties. While having allies is important, there are times when they are unable to protect the court, and judges will have to directly engage with parties who oppose them or their decisions. It is challenging to bridge the ideological gap between the court and its adversaries, but establishing diplomatic connections with hostile groups may help smooth relations. In dire circumstances, judges should consider privately negotiating with the adversary. Some scholars have identified instances where judges seem to have secretly negotiated with political elites.[4] Drawing on the concept of backchanneling, I theorize the potential dangers and benefits of clandestine engagement with hostile parties.

The third tool to be discussed is protest. When options are limited, judges may have to consider extreme measures, and protesting is one of them. Section 7.5 will focus on judicial protesting for institutional autonomy or the democratic cause. Judicial protesting is more common that many might imagine. It is a quick and effective way for judges to get the attention of the public and the regime. As powerful as judicial protesting can be, it can also place the career and personal safety of protesting judges in jeopardy. Judicial protesting also raises concerns about the ethical rules around judicial conduct, which are also discussed. Protest is related to the fourth tool, mobilization, in which judges encourage other groups within the state to come to their aid. This tool will be discussed in Section 7.6.

[4] Trochev and Ellett (n 1).

As a last resort, a judge can consider resigning. Section 7.7 focuses on the practical impact of judicial resignation in protest. The resignation of committed judges sends a strong message that could potentially mobilize other constituencies and delegitimize the regime. Judicial resignation may, however, be very costly to the democratic constituency because vacancies are unlikely to be filled by like-minded colleagues. The part will discuss ways to structure the dilemma and argue that resigning should only be considered as a last resort. The chapter concludes by examining the legitimacy of these strategies.

7.2 Identifying the Allies

Before elaborating on how judges can use off-bench techniques to build relationships with institutions that can protect a court, this part identifies *who* these potential judicial allies are by disaggregating the democratic constituency into its common constituents, and the support they can offer to a court.

A key lesson from Chapter 5 is that enhancing a court's position in a hybrid regime requires the support of a democratic constituency. I argued that the democratic constituency can act as a buffer between the court and the authoritarian constituency by politically restraining the hybrid regime incumbent and its supporters. Much of the discussion there builds on the electoral logic in a hybrid regime, and hence the democratic constituency was largely equated with a democratically inclined populace. The reality, though, is that the democratic constituency involves a plurality of social groups. A disaggregation of the democratic constituency allows us to see more clearly the distinct contributions of each constituent institution.

It should be emphasized that some institutions discussed later in this chapter might, in reality, oppose the court, making it harder for judges to maneuver. A common example is state-backed media that acts as the authoritarian's mouthpiece. As Terence Halliday, Lucien Karpik, and Malcolm Feeley find, a court's relationship with these actors may be characterized as unengaged, cooperative, oppositional, or detached.[5] Furthermore, those social groups are not always united in their cause. Hence, cross-cutting situations might appear in which alliances form

[5] Terence Halliday, Lucien Karpik, and Malcolm Feeley, 'The Legal Complex in Struggles for Political Liberalism' in Terence C. Halliday, Lucien Karpik, and Malcolm Feeley (eds), *Fighting for Political Freedom: Comparative Studies of the Legal Complex and Political Liberalism* (Hart Publishing 2007) 7–8.

between factions of these social groups, or temporary alliances are forged over specific issues only.[6] Nevertheless, for reasons to be discussed, the institutions identified are *potential* allies that judges should build relationships with.

7.2.1 Lawyers

Drawing on two decades of research into lawyers and judicial politics, Halliday and his colleagues find a "critical interdependence between the bar and bench for the rise of political liberalism in disparate historical contexts."[7] In the periods considered in this study of Hong Kong, Uganda, and Pakistan, lawyers have proven integral to the development of judicial power and have risen to defend their judiciaries where necessary.

The Hong Kong Bar Association is one of the most outspoken defenders of the rule of law and judicial independence in Hong Kong. One of the many examples of the Bar Association actively mobilizing its members in support of the judiciary goes back to 1999, shortly after the handover.[8] The judiciary was fiercely attacked by Mainland China after the landmark constitutional case of *Ng Ka Ling*. In solidarity, the bar organized their first ever silent march. Since then, members of the bar have stood up for the judiciary time and again and educated the public about the importance of judicial independence and rule of law.

Lawyers in Uganda have shown similar willingness to fight for their courts in critical moments. In 2007, after the High Court granted bail to prominent opposition figures, the Ugandan government sent a group of gunmen, known as the Black Mamba, to rearrest the defendants.[9] Doors were broken down, and a lawyer was beaten unconscious when armed personnel stormed the court. A near-identical event occurred in 2005. In both instances, members of the bar, joined by judges in 2007, organized strikes to protest against blatant government interference. The week-long strike in 2007 ultimately ended with Museveni's apology.

The Pakistani bar supported the judiciary in an even more spectacular fashion. In 2007, after Musharraf suspended the constitution and packed

6 *ibid.*

7 *ibid* 4.

8 Mark Landler, 'After 2 Years, Hong Kong Looks More Like China,' *The New York Times*, July 1, 1999.

9 BBC, 'Uganda Lawyers in Protest Strike,' March 12, 2007, available at http://news.bbc.co.uk/2/hi/africa/6441239.stm, last visited November 9, 2021.

the Supreme Court, the lawyers took to the streets and started the Lawyers' Movement. Lawyers refused to take oath under the newly imposed emergency laws, boycotted the regime by refusing to appear at lower courts, and organized hunger strikes.[10] The movement catalyzed a popular mass protest and confrontations became increasingly violent. Crackdowns on activists and lawyers further exposed Musharraf's authoritarian nature. His party was eventually defeated in the ballot box in 2008. Facing impending impeachment, Musharraf went into exile shortly after.

Lawyers are arguably the most natural ally of judges because of their similar backgrounds and their alignment in interests. Lawyers likely appreciate the importance of constitutional values such as rule of law and judicial independence better than other political actors, because lawyers and judges have undergone similar socialization processes in law schools and legal workplaces.[11] Furthermore, actors within the legal ecosystem are interdependent, and lawyers have an interest in protecting the judiciary. Executive attacks against the judiciary, for example, adversely affect the reputation of the entire legal profession, which might then undermine the stability of the legal practice. The fact that judges and lawyers are often in the same boat incentivizes lawyers to call out judicial interference when judges need assistance.

These examples show that lawyers can offer a wide range of cover to the court, including public education, public statements, government boycott, silent marches, and street protests. The kinds of assistance offered by lawyers may seem no different than those provided by, for instance, a pundit or a street protestor. Rather, the special weight that comes with the words and actions of lawyers stems from their *status* as legal professionals. Professions are "traditionally a set of occupations distinguished from others by their high education, complex body of knowledge and skills, their status, and their fiduciary responsibilities."[12] This special status, which is derived from their legal expertise and

[10] See Shoaib Ghias, 'Miscarriage of Chief Justice: Judicial Power and the Legal Complex in Pakistan under Musharraf' (2010) 35 *Law & Social Inquiry* 985.

[11] Mark Verhagen and Julius Yam, 'The Law of Attraction: How Similarity between Judges and Lawyers Helps Win Cases in the Hong Kong Court of Final Appeal' (2021) 65 *International Review of Law and Economics*.

[12] Marta Choroszewicz and Tracey L. Adams, 'Introduction: Themes, Objectives and Theoretical Perspectives' in Marta Choroszewicz and Tracey L. Adams (eds), *Gender, Age and Inequality in the Professions* (Routledge 2019) 4.

proximity to the court, gives lawyers the power to mobilize other constituencies on legal and judicial topics.

7.2.2 *Legal Academics*

Closely related to lawyers are legal academics. What is especially noteworthy about legal academics is their potential ability to shape social norms[13] and lead public opinion. Having academics on the court's side facilitates the educative role of a court and helps incubate legal professionals that share the aspirations of a democratically committed court.

Legal academics are responsible for producing dedicated and principled lawyers and judges. The quality of, the values within, and the professional role conception of the legal profession are largely determined by the education provided by the legal academy.[14] As I mentioned, legal academies are a key site of socialization for lawyers and judges. Law schools are responsible for setting intellectual directions and ideals. Notions about the proper role of lawyers, judges, and courts are internalized in law school. The educational process significantly influences the general legal culture of a jurisdiction, including the character of the lawyers, as well as the competency and attitude of the legal profession. Research has shown how judicial behavior can be affected by judges' educational background, affirming the importance of legal academies in shaping jurisprudential and ideological norms.[15] Academics may also help consolidate the judiciary by educating a new generation of lawyers in ways that reinforce judges' values.

Aside from teaching, legal academics provide an environment conducive to a democratically committed court by shaping public opinion and constitutional democratic norms.[16] In some countries, the government may habitually consult legal scholars, especially on constitutional issues. Public intellectuals may choose to climb down from the ivory tower and

[13] Terence C. Halliday, 'Why the Legal Complex is Integral to Theories of Consequential Courts' in Diana Kapiszewski, Gordon Silverstein, and Robert A. Kagan (eds), *Consequential Courts: Judicial Roles in Global Perspective* (CUP 2013) 339–40.

[14] See Lisa Hilbink, 'The Origins of Positive Judicial Independence' (2012) 64 *World Politics* 587.

[15] See e.g. Verhagen and Yam (n 11).

[16] As William Twining and his colleagues write, "this mobility [of legal scholars] may be one of the most important channels of influence of law schools on practical legal affairs." William Twining and others, 'The Role of Academics in the Legal System' in Mark Tushnet and Peter Cane (eds), *The Oxford Handbook of Legal Studies* (OUP 2005) 921.

directly engage with a broader audience. Because of their expertise, legal scholars enjoy a social authority similar to that of lawyers, which also gives them the ability to mobilize the public on legal and judicial topics. They may act as intermediaries between laypersons and lawyers, explaining decisions to the public. As pundits, they can also lend legitimacy to constitutional legal developments, while discrediting "bad" laws through their critiques. While academic texts may have a limited audience, some judges do read them and find them helpful, even if they do not always cite them.[17] Hence, academics can also enlighten judges and supply them with ideas when those judges face political or jurisprudential challenges.

7.2.3 The Media

Previously, I suggested that some of the strategic effects produced by the court travel through and depend on sophisticated intermediaries. Much of what the public knows about the court is learnt via the media. As an intermediary, the media interprets the judgment, selects relevant aspects, and broadcasts them to the public. Each step of the process significantly influences the public's perception of the court and its actions. The media may interpret a decision in accordance with judges' intentions, but misinterpretation (accidental or deliberate) can result in misinformation. Media reports filter reality. Framing, or the exercise of deciding what to include or exclude and magnify or downplay, determines the relative salience of the subjects and issues. The reach of the judgments and the transparency of the court are also controlled by the media. Decisions are not always picked up by the media; even if a decision is reported, the reporting style can affect public awareness of courtroom actions.

The media is an indispensable ally of the court, as it helps a court build or defend its image. Shoaib Ghias, for example, argues that the expansion of judicial powers in Pakistan during the 2000s was largely attributable to the judiciary's increased and favorable media coverage.[18] While it varies, the media is often semi-free in a hybrid regime, as opposed to in a pure authoritarian regime where there is little hope for democratization.[19] It is plausible for the media to become an ally of a hybrid regime court.

[17] See e.g. Michel Bastarache, 'The Role of Academics and Legal Theory in Judicial Decision-making' (1999) 37 *Alberta Law Review* 739.

[18] Ghias (n 10).

[19] Katrin Voltmer, Kjetil Selvik, and Jacob Høigilt, 'Hybrid Media and Hybrid Politics: Contesting Informational Uncertainty in Lebanon and Tunisia' (2021) 26 *The International Journal of Press/Politics* 842.

Through its portrayal of the judges and their decisions, the media influences public attitudes toward the court and the court's relationship with other actors. Legitimacy-building involves not only the court of law, but also the court of public opinion. A court needs the media's help to counter and compete against anticourt rhetoric in the public sphere.

Furthermore, the public's ability to monitor the court and regime depends on how informed the public is.[20] Even if the public is ideologically aligned with the court, it cannot sanction the authoritarian if unaware of executive interference and/or the court's decisions. The level of public awareness has a direct effect on the level of protection offered by other constituencies, and the court needs a supportive media to warn judicial allies of possible transgressions by the authoritarian.

7.2.4 *Civil Servants*

Civil servants who respect the court's independence and expertise can protect the judiciary by imposing political transaction costs on the regime. Before I explain the kinds of benefits derived from the civil service, I first address whether those who work for a hybrid regime government can realistically be allies of a democratically committed court.

I have explained in earlier chapters that hybrid regimes, or authoritarians more generally, are not monolithic entities. They are not free to act in whatever way they want because of the agency cost of monitoring and controlling the administrative bureaucracy. The trade-off between competence and loyalty is a classic governance problem felt acutely by authoritarians.[21] The state needs competent agents to enact all sorts of policies effectively, but a high concentration of talented civil servants increases the risk of internal resistance and revolt. For the sake of survival and stability, some authoritarians sacrifice competence for loyalty. This choice by no means guarantees long-term regime survival and stability, as an incompetent bureaucracy leads to poor governance. To address this problem, some authoritarians may choose to indoctrinate their agents. However, as Eric Ip argues, in a hybrid regime, this kind of top-down

[20] Georg Vanberg, *The Politics of Constitutional Review in Germany* (CUP 2004); Jeffrey Staton, *Judicial Power and Strategic Communication in Mexico* (CUP 2010).

[21] Georgy Egorov and Konstantin Sonin, 'Dictators and Their Viziers: Endogenizing the Loyalty–Competence Trade-off' (2011) 9 *Journal of the European Economic Association* 903; Alexei Zakharov, 'The Loyalty–Competence Trade-off in Dictatorships and Outside Options for Subordinates' (2016) 78 *The Journal of Politics* 457.

strategy to maintain ideological homogeneity is "counterproductive in light of the necessity of keeping up a liberal façade."[22] There is no easy way out of this trade-off in a hybrid regime, so diversity within a hybrid regime executive is expected.

Examples from Hong Kong and Pakistan illustrate the challenges a hybrid regime faces in keeping its agencies in line and how certain less-than-loyal factions or institutions within the government can help the court tremendously. As Carol Jones suggests, the idea for a more representative and rule-of-law-based government during colonial Hong Kong came from civil servants.[23] After China resumed sovereignty over Hong Kong, the ideological dissonance between the bureaucracy and the ruling elites became increasingly obvious as Hong Kong took an authoritarian turn. Thousands of civil servants, for instance, joined the anti-extradition bill protest in 2019 and refused to pledge loyalty to the government in 2021.[24] Retired civil servants have become staunch supporters of the court, openly defending judicial independence and the practice of judicial review on numerous occasions.[25]

In Pakistan, the relationship between the bureaucracy, democratic institutions, and the military has historically never been straightforward. Once a powerful and autonomous institution, the bureaucracy was severely weakened after a constitutional reform in 1973 and the subsequent stacking of the bureaucracy with military personnel, especially during Musharraf's rule.[26] Recognizing the potential of the bureaucracy, the Chaudhry court, Asher Qazi argues, "actively attempted to build

[22] Eric C. Ip, *Hybrid Constitutionalism: The Politics of Constitutional Review in the Chinese Special Administrative Regions* (CUP 2019) 47.

[23] Carol Jones, '"Dissolving the People": Capitalism, Law and Democracy in Hong Kong' in Halliday, Karpik, and Feeley (n 5).

[24] *The* New York Times, 'Hong Kong's Civil Servants Protest Their Own Government,' August 2, 2019, available at www.nytimes.com/2019/08/02/world/asia/hong-kong-civil-servants-protest.html, last visited November 9, 2021; Christy Leung, 'About 200 Hong Kong Civil Servants Face Dismissal for Refusing to Pledge Allegiance to City and Mini-Constitution,' SCMP, March 9, 2021), available at www.scmp.com/news/hong-kong/politics/article/3124609/about-200-hong-kong-civil-servants-face-dismissal-refusing, last visited November 9, 2021.

[25] Koel Chu, 'CY's Criticism of Judicial Review Could Damage the Rule of Law – Former Civil Service Sec.,' *Hong Kong Free Press*, January 15, 2016, available at https://hongkongfp.com/2016/01/15/cys-criticism-of-judicial-review-could-damage-the-rule-of-law-former-civil-service-sec/, last visited November 9, 2021. After the passage of the National Security Law in 2020, civil servants are now required to pledge allegiance to the HKSAR or face dismissal.

[26] Andrew Wilder, 'The Politics of Civil Service Reform in Pakistan' (2009) 63 *Journal of International Affairs* 19.

a strong relationship with the civil service" by offering civil servants greater protection and autonomy.[27] The court made matters relating to civil service justiciable, and drastically reduced the government's political control and discretion over the appointment and removal of civil servants. His study finds that the court was largely successful in "capturing" the civil service as an increase in compliance rate was observed.[28]

Fully capturing the executive is hard, but siding with certain factions or executive institutions can prove helpful. Authoritarians and their agents are unlikely to have uniform preferences in a hybrid regime. Ideological and interest-based divisions between the ruling elite and the administrative bureaucracy can be exploited by the court to fracture the regime and create more space for judicial maneuvering. The active support of the civil service can improve the efficacy of the court and delegitimize attacks from the executive. The agents responsible for executing the authoritarian's orders may, for instance, delay policies that are unfavorable to the court, prevent these policies from being realized through internal resistance, weaken them through intentionally poor implementation, provide informational advantages to the judges by whistleblowing, or simply cripple the administration by going on strike.

7.2.5 International Organizations

International organization, as used here, is a large and heterogeneous category; it can include associations of states (such as the United Nations), transnational organizations exercising government-like functions (such as the World Bank), and private or nongovernmental research and advisory agencies operating on a global scale, such as the Economist Intelligence Unit and Freedom House.

International organizations are useful allies to have, especially in jurisdictions that depend on foreign and international recognition.[29] They directly support domestic judiciaries by investing in judicial capacity. Over the past few decades, rule of law has been a multi-billion-dollar investment project worldwide. Regardless of the motives of these programs, domestic judiciaries of recipient countries directly benefit

[27] Asher Qazi, 'A Government of Judges: A Story of the Pakistani Supreme Court's Strategic Expansion' (JSD dissertation, University of Chicago, 2018) 129.

[28] *ibid* 156.

[29] Pakistan, and to a larger extent Uganda, are economies that have benefited tremendously from foreign and international aid, and Hong Kong's prestigious status as an international financial center is built around the esteem held by foreign investors and states.

from these initiatives. Aside from training local judges and reforming judicial laws, some of these programs, with the help of activists, have led to ideational changes among the bench and more rights-protective judicial decision-making patterns.[30]

International organizations also protect these courts by threatening to sanction hybrid regimes that attack judicial independence. Judicial independence and rule of law are conditions of many development assistance programs. Donors regularly monitor the recipient state, and issue warnings if the conditions are not met. These measures are sometimes in tension with state sovereignty. Nevertheless, they create pressure points to the advantage of domestic judiciaries.

Similarly, international organizations can control the authoritarian impulses of hybrid regimes through periodic appraisals. Rule-of-law and judicial independence rankings are seen as indicators of economic competitiveness and good governance. Hong Kong and Singapore frequently rely on these indices to promote their polities. Attacking the court can trigger a ripple effect when the economy depends on the reputation of the judicial system.

Some international organizations play a watchdog role. International organizations such as Amnesty International, Human Rights Watch, the Economist Intelligence Unit, and Freedom House periodically publish updates and reports on constitutional and legal developments around the world, flagging court-curbing attacks. Through naming and shaming, these international organizations may mobilize local and international constituencies to support the court.

Last, international organizations can legitimate the actions of a democratically committed court. Some of them are in charge of promoting liberal democratic norms and best-practice guidelines regarding judicial independence on the international stage. These instruments offer justifications that a domestic court can use to ground its liberal rulings, as hybrid regimes claiming to be democracies may feel obliged to adopt and follow these norms.

7.2.6 *Business Community*

In jurisdictions that are keen to promote economic growth or maintain economic competitiveness, establishing friendly ties with the business

[30] Ezequiel González-Ocantos, *Shifting Legal Visions: Judicial Change and Human Rights Trials in Latin America* (CUP 2016).

community is a potential asset for judges. Investors' confidence in the judiciary and legal system as a whole is crucial to the health of an economy, and could be undermined by any suggestion that judicial independence is under threat. To reap the economic benefits of an independent judiciary, the regime must convince investors that their assets will be protected from opportunistic behavior, especially by those in power.[31] By making court-curbing actions economically costly, a business community with diplomatic ties to sitting judges indirectly constrains executive power over the judiciary.

7.2.7 *The General Public*

Theories of the social legitimacy of courts suggest that the general public can protect the court through the threat of voting enemies of the court out of office. While these theories rest on the electoral logic of democracies, they are, to an extent, relevant to semi-authoritarian or hybrid regimes, where electoral competitiveness is weak but still exists.[32] The public may also support the court by protesting (or threatening to protest), which could potentially destabilize the incumbent. A court-supporting public acts as a crucial buffer between judges and political actors looking to weaken the judiciary's authority.

7.2.8 *Fellow Judges and Overseas Colleagues*

Throughout this book, I have assumed that it is possible for democratically committed judges to exist in a hybrid regime. This contrasts with many works on courts in authoritarian regimes, which tend to depict judges as loyal to the regime or even cowardly. The reality, of course, is that judges are not a monolithic group either. Judges in every polity differ in their personal views, with some more committed to democracy than others. Borrowing González-Ocantos' typology, there are three kinds of judges in a hybrid regime: Committed judges, indifferent judges, and recalcitrant judges.[33] Committed judges are those who have already internalized constitutional democratic norms. Recalcitrant judges are "unpersuadable," that is, will never be receptive to constitutional

[31] See Tamir Moustafa, *The Struggle for Constitutional Power: Law, Politics, and Economic Development in Egypt* (CUP 2007) 44.

[32] Brad Epperly, *The Political Foundations of Judicial Independence in Dictatorship and Democracy* (OUP 2019).

[33] *ibid* 8.

democratic ideals. Indifferent judges are those who show no signs of sympathy toward constitutional democratic norms, but could possibly be transformed.

The pool of democratically committed judges can be expanded by converting indifferent judges into committed ones. While data on how judges interact behind closed doors are often incomplete, judges do interact and influence each other. They deliberate and decide how to write a judgment together.[34] A phenomenon known as "panel effect" describes how the combination of judges on a judicial panel can create significantly different voting patterns.[35] Social interactions between judges create meaningful behavioral or even ideational change, and committed judges could conceivably persuade their indifferent colleagues.

Recalcitrant judges are more challenging. Seeking to capture the judiciary, authoritarian regimes sometimes intentionally stack the bench with recalcitrant judges.[36] Ideational transformation, by definition, is almost impossible for recalcitrant judges. Removing them is hard as the power to appoint judges lies with the regime. Civil society may organize campaigns to push recalcitrant judges into resigning,[37] but this is not a strategy available to an individual judge. Since recalcitrant judges are likely a given in hybrid regimes, committed judges should find ways to work with them amicably. Even if they may never become allies, recalcitrant judges can be important sources of information as they are part of the authoritarian network, enabling committed judges to stay informed of possible risks.

Aside from domestic judges, judges in foreign jurisdictions and international courts can sometimes offer symbolic, practical, and moral support to domestic colleagues. The symbolic support offered by overseas peers is similar in function to citing comparative law. Receiving the validation of reputable judges elsewhere lends legitimacy to the actions of the committed judges. The endorsement of reputable judicial figures overseas increases the political costs of executive interference. Foreign and international judges can also understand the challenges faced by the constrained domestic judges, as every constitutional judge faces political

34 See Lee Epstein and Jack Knight, *The Choices Justices Make* (Sage 1997).

35 See Cass R. Sunstein, David Schkade, and Lisa Michelle Ellman, 'Ideological Voting on Federal Courts of Appeals: A Preliminary Investigation' (2004) 90 *Virginia Law Review* 301.

36 Authoritarians may intentionally keep some committed judges for legitimacy purposes.

37 González-Ocantos (n 30) 8.

challenges to some extent. Domestic judges may learn about the jurisprudential and strategic techniques necessary to survive and develop the judiciary. In addition to offering their practical experience and legal ideas, overseas colleagues may give understated moral support to besieged judges. A chief justice of the Zimbabwean Supreme Court recounts how letters and faxes received from colleagues around the world when the court was threatened and attacked by the Mugabe regime reminded him that "I am not alone."[38]

7.3 Relation-building

The institutions discussed earlier in this chapter may not always be allies of the court, but theories and comparative experiences have shown that they can create conditions favorable to the protection of judicial autonomy and enable the democratic roles of a hybrid regime court. A more important question is: Are there ways for courts to bring these institutions onto the courts' side?

The strength of the courts' bonds with other actors depends partly on the sitting judges' preexisting social networks. Before becoming full-time judges, judges in many jurisdictions were lawyers, prosecutors, and academics. These judges not only bring their expertise to the bench, but also expand the social network of the judiciary. Elite lawyers, for example, would be more willing to extend their help to the judiciary if the judges were once part of their networks. Similarly, academics would naturally be more inclined to speak out for judges who are ex-colleagues. This is perhaps a good reason to diversify the bench. Having judges of different career and educational backgrounds not only lowers the risk of biases arising from groupthink,[39] but also creates a more well-connected judiciary.[40]

As we saw in the previous chapter, judges can develop connections with other institutions in the adjudicative context. The hope is to build on the "politics of reciprocity"[41] to create mutually supportive relationships with their allies. Providing greater constitutional protection to judicial allies not only strengthens their constitutional position, but also

[38] Anne-Marie Slaughter, *A New World Order* (Princeton University Press 2009) 99.

[39] Verhagen and Yam (n 11); N. W. Barber, 'Two Meditations on the Thoughts of Many Minds' (2010) 88 *Texas Law Review* 807.

[40] Career-judge systems may be disadvantaged in this regard as their judges may lack exposure beyond the judiciary.

[41] Ghias (n 10) 989.

demonstrates the court's willingness to stand up for its allies. Language and citations can also be deployed strategically to create favorable attitudes toward the judiciary. Adopting a liberal narrative and citing foreign rights-protective judgments, for instance, may impart a more progressive image of judges among certain social circles. Judges may also engage in a "dialogue" with foreign and international courts through the decisions and citations.[42] Some judges have admitted that they intentionally cite a certain jurisdiction's judgment in order to establish friendly relationships with their overseas peers.[43]

Going beyond the adjudicative context, this part adds to the list by exploring two kinds of nonjudicial techniques for relation-building – public relations and judicial diplomacy.

7.3.1 Public Relations

Public relations is a diffuse method for a court to manage its public image and build good will. According to public relations theorists, the typical way courts disseminate information falls under the "public information model."[44] The model is characterized by its one-way mode of communication. A court transmits information to the public through, for example, the publication of the judgment and press releases, without expecting a response or a dialogue. Intermediaries interpret and disseminate the information provided by the court, but judges ultimately decide what information to communicate with their audiences.

Traditionally, courts dealt with the media and the public through the "judicial ethos of silence in the public sphere."[45] The classical public relations strategy for courts is nonengagement. Many courts did not even have an established communication practice.[46] Some judges believe that

[42] See e.g. Slaughter (n 38) 65–103; Michael Kirby, 'Transnational Judicial Dialogue, Internationalisation of Law and Australian Judges' (2008) 9 *Melbourne Journal of International Law* 171.

[43] David Law, 'Judicial Comparativism and Judicial Diplomacy' (2015) *University of Pennsylvania Law Review* 927, 1005–6.

[44] Bryna Bogoch and Anat Peleg, 'Silence Is No Longer Golden: Media, Public Relations and the Judiciary in Israel' (2014) 4 *Oñati Socio-Legal Series* 819; Philipp Meyer, 'Judicial Public Relations: Determinants of Press Release Publication by Constitutional Courts' (2020) 40 *Politics* 477.

[45] Bogoch and Peleg *ibid* 822.

[46] See Leslie Moran, 'Judicial Institutional Change and Court Communication Innovations: The Case of the UK Supreme Court' in Richard Davis and David Taras (eds), *Justices and Journalists: The Global Perspective* (CUP 2017) 257; Gunnar Grendstad, William R. Shaffer, and Eric N. Waltenburg, 'Norway: Managed Openness and Transparency' in

arguing with critics "lowers the judge into the arena of public opinion and all who scrabble there."[47] Aside from publishing their judgments, judges typically refrained from talking to the public and journalists. As David Taras observes, "High Court judges in most countries seem to share many of the same fears in dealing with journalists."[48] Judiciaries would rather let their decisions speak for themselves.

Under a new journalistic landscape, however, "silence is no longer golden."[49] Traditional media is increasingly replaced by digital media. Information is becoming more fragmented and traveling faster. Unfiltered and unmediated content can more easily enter public spaces. Communication is now mostly interactive. New platforms have allowed people around the world with common interests to connect and exchange ideas. The divide between producers and consumers of content has also blurred. Publishing information is no longer the exclusive prerogative of journalists.

These shifts have impacted judiciaries across the world in profound ways. The ease with which information can be accessed has led to increased coverage of constitutional judgments and cases with political overtones across the borders.[50] These cases tend to have great media value because they have a broader and/or deeper social impact. However, the democratization of the journalistic landscape has also resulted in a higher level of reporting inaccuracies on court-related topics, as those who write on these topics may have no legal expertise.[51] To undermine resistance, authoritarian regimes may even use disinformation and internet trolls to deliberately subvert public discourse.[52] The classical nonengagement strategy does not address these problems at all. If anything, this ostrich mentality invites misinformation and manipulation. At the very

Richard Davis and David Taras (eds), *Justices and Journalists: The Global Perspective* (CUP 2017) 245.

[47] The Honourable Madam Justice Beverley McLachlin NPJ, 'Judges and the Public: Ivory Tower Recluses or Engaged Actors?', High Court of Hong Kong, December 12, 2019, 12, available at www.hkcfa.hk/filemanager/speech/en/upload/2248/20191212%20McLachlin%20NPJ%20-%20Address%20to%20Judiciary%20(final%20for%20uploading).pdf, last visited November 9, 2021.

[48] David Taras, 'Introduction: Judges and Journalists and the Spaces in Between' in Davis and Taras (n 46).

[49] Bogoch and Peleg (n 44).

[50] Moran (n 46).

[51] See Rachel Spencer, 'Communication beyond the Judgments: The Australian High Court, Speaking for Itself, but Not Tweeting' in Davis and Taras (n 46).

[52] Seva Gunitsky, 'Corrupting the Cyber-commons: Social Media as a Tool of Autocratic Stability' (2015) 13 *Perspectives on Politics* 42.

least, most modern judges would agree that factual clarification is sometimes necessary to fend off baseless political attacks.[53]

Judges must respond to these new challenges, and many courts are making efforts to adapt. As Richard Davis notes, "justices have begun to realize that judicial communication serves the interests of the courts since the messages about the institutions and their specific actions may be more accurate and thorough if accommodations are made to serve press interests."[54] Studies on a court's public relations are drawn mainly from courts in democracies, but their insights can still be useful to hybrid regime courts that enjoy sufficient administrative and financial autonomy to implement public relations strategies.[55]

Most obviously, courts issue press releases and press summaries to communicate their judgments more effectively. This provides an opportunity for courts to present information in ways that align with the judges' intention and interests, and help the media and lay audiences translate legal jargon and better understand the contents of the judgments. The hope is to "encourag[e] timely and accurate reporting."[56] In addition to official government websites, many constitutional courts have established dedicated websites. Apart from introducing their composition, structure, and values, these websites may also include lay-friendly content, such as virtual tours explaining the art and architecture of their courthouses.[57] Because the COVID-19 pandemic made judicial outreach activities impossible, a group of Polish judges created websites for public educational events.[58] Social media has made it possible to provide real-time updates and clarifications on court-related subjects. To increase the court's exposure and relevance, some courts live-stream judicial proceedings through their official social media accounts, especially in cases of public importance. The UK Supreme Court, for instance,

53 McLachlin (n 47) 17.

54 Richard Davis, 'Conclusion' in Davis and Taras (n 46).

55 See e.g. Davis and Taras (n 46).

56 Moran (n 46) 267.

57 See e.g. New Jersey Courts, Supreme Court Virtual Museum, available at https://web.archive.org/web/20220819200608/https://www.njcourts.gov/courts/supreme/vm/scvirtual.html; Supreme Court of Canada, Art Gallery, September 4, 2008, available at https://web.archive.org/web/20250114180021/www.scc-csc.ca/about-apropos/art/index-eng.aspx; UK Supreme Court, Artworks and 360 Degree Virtual Tour, available at https://web.archive.org/web/20240603051631/www.supremecourt.uk/visiting/new-artwork.html.

58 Claudia-Y Matthes, 'Judges as Activists: How Polish Judges Mobilise to Defend the Rule of Law' (2022) 38 *East European Politics* 468, 480.

has a dedicated webpage, which streams its proceedings live,[59] as well as its own YouTube channel, which posts seminars it previously organized and archives footage of the cases it heard.[60] By making proceedings public, courts in hybrid regimes not only educate the masses about the legal process, but also protect their decisions, reducing the time political actors have to interfere with the outcome of cases. This move limits the scope of misrepresentation, as well as subjects the government's actions in court to greater public scrutiny.

Judges are experts in the court of law, but are not necessarily talented at public communication. Or, as a Polish judge notes, "we are not trained to talk to the public . . . we were told the only way to express your idea is the written verdict."[61] Delegating to experts in public communication allows for more effective promotion of the courts' views to the public, and some courts have also experimented with branding strategies more commonly found in the private sector to maximize their influence. The New Jersey state judiciary has published a children's playbook to reach younger audiences.[62] On top of creating cartoons, the Korean Constitutional Court recruited a celebrity athlete as its goodwill ambassador.[63] Courts in Uganda,[64] Hong Kong,[65] Slovenia,[66] and Nebraska[67] and

[59] UK Supreme Court, Watch Supreme Court Live, available at www.supremecourt.uk/live/court-01.html.

[60] Its most popular clip has 86,000 views as of January 10, 2026. UK Supreme Court, 'UK Supreme Court,' YouTube, available at www.youtube.com/user/UKSupremeCourt/videos?view=0&sort=p&flow=grid.

[61] Matthes (n 58) 478.

[62] New Jersey Courts, 'Student Resources', available at www.njcourts.gov/public/kids/assets/activity_book.pdf?c=new, last visited July 19, 2022.

[63] David Law, 'Judicial Comparativism and Judicial Diplomacy' (2015) 163 *University of Pennsylvania Law Review* 927, 976.

[64] Uganda Judiciary Head Office, 'Judiciary Gets Brand Identity' (2017) 8 *The Judiciary Insider*, available at http://judiciary.go.ug/files/publications/issue%208%20for%20print.pdf, last visited January 10, 2026; Lady Justice Lydia Mugambe Ssali, 'Launch of Brand Identity', available at http://judiciary.go.ug/files/downloads/Launch%20of%20Brand%20Identity%20Presentation_Judiciary%20[Compatibility%20Mode].pdf, last visited January 10, 2026.

[65] Stepworks, 'Judiciary Unveils Brand to Signify Institutional Independence,' 2022, available at https://stepworks.co/en/hk-branding-agency-portfolio/judiciary-of-the-hong-kong-special-administrative-region-of-the-peoples-republic-of-china-brand-development/, last visited January 10, 2026.

[66] Renderspace, 'Making a More Citizen-Centered Judicial System,' 2019, available at https://renderspace.si/en/work/supreme-court-of-slovenia/.

[67] Unanimous, 'New Nebraska Supreme Court Web Design Launched,' May 24, 2017, available at web.archive.org/web/20221003182008/ https://www.beunanimous.com/unanimous-blog/new-nebraska-supreme-court-web-design-launched, last visited 19 July 2022.

Michigan[68] in the United States hired marketing agencies to, inter alia, redesign their logos and websites, conduct market research to better understand how the judiciaries were perceived, and develop promotional materials to advance the institutions' agendas. The Brazilian Supreme Court has its own "in-house media operations – including televised coverage of plenary sessions and a wide range of educational programming on TV Justiça, daily programming on Radio Justiça, and a strong social media presence, specifically on YouTube and Twitter."[69] In addition, judges can rely on judicial press officers for "damage control" after issuing an unpopular decision.[70] These press officers are often lawyers who have worked in the marketing sector or retired judges.[71] They possess the legal knowledge to properly explain rulings, as well as the media training to handle the press and the public. Public relations experts have also helped review and develop communication guidelines within the court, since, as mentioned, many courts do not have established communications practices aside from general judicial ethics rules.

There is no hard-and-fast rule when it comes to the public relations strategies for courts, aside from the fact that nonengagement or silence *alone* is outdated and incapable of dealing with the complexities arising from modern judicial politics. The Brazilian Supreme Court, for example, is regarded as "the most transparent high, constitutional court" in the Americas.[72] Some evidence shows that media exposure is positively correlated with confidence in the Brazilian court.[73] Nevertheless, this strategy may not work elsewhere. Too much transparency can bring problems. The Brazilian approach invites closer public scrutiny, which can potentially lead to media overexposure. This risks turning judges into celebrities and creating a more politicized impression of the court. Contrast this with the experience of the Norwegian Supreme Court. The Norwegian communicative approach is characterized by

[68] Diamond eVentures, 'Recent Works,' 2022, available at web.archive.org/web/20220926095139/ https://www.diamondeventures.com/recent-work/, last visited July 19, 2022.

[69] Matthew Ingram, 'Uncommon Transparency: The Supreme Court, Media Relations, and Public Opinion in Brazil' in Davis and Taras (n 46) 77.

[70] Alexei Trochev, *Judging Russia: The Role of the Constitutional Court in Russian Politics 1990–2006* (CUP 2008) 253.

[71] France, for example, employs retired judges as "press judges" who are responsible for explaining important decisions. Bogoch and Peleg (n 44) 823.

[72] Ingram (n 69).

[73] *ibid* 74.

"managed openness," as Gunnar Grendstad and his colleagues describe it.[74] The Norwegian Supreme Court is consistently ranked as one of the most trusted courts in Europe. Yet, unlike some of its overseas colleagues, these judges lead more reclusive public lives and prefer a more guarded approach to public communication. While the two examples illustrate almost diametrically opposing public relations strategies, they plausibly have legitimating effects for the respective courts. Effective image-building depends on judges' ability to adjust to social conditions while pursuing their communicative agendas.

In short, what kind of communication strategy is called for depends on a few factors: The journalistic landscape, the resources available to the court, and, most importantly, the kind of image that the court wants to advance. That being said, there are three important lessons for hybrid regime courts that may be generally applicable.

First, judges should always be selective when it comes to what information to communicate. Jeffrey Staton's monograph builds on public support theories of judicial legitimacy to make this point.[75] Using Mexican constitutional judges as a case study, Staton argues how judges can manage public opinion of the court through the information the court communicates to the public and the media. He acknowledges that the power to influence media coverage and public perception is, perhaps, limited, but is nonetheless important, as it provides another way for judges to manipulate the boundaries of their power.[76] A key assumption behind public support theories of judicial legitimacy is public awareness of court actions. The public is incapable of supporting the court if it cannot access information about the court.

Extending this logic, Staton rightly points out that judges can adjust the transparency of their actions to strategically influence the public's perception of the court. He observes how the Mexican Supreme Court selectively promotes decisions in their press releases to media outlets. The emphasis here is selectiveness.[77] For instance, decisions that might be considered biased could be downplayed if judges want to impart an image of impartiality, whereas underscoring the court's assertiveness against the government may help depict a principled court. A study found that the German Constitutional Court tends to be reluctant to mention decisions in press releases when the decisions involve dissenting

[74] Grendstad, Shaffer, and Waltenburg (n 46).
[75] Staton (n 20).
[76] *ibid* 16.
[77] *ibid* 124.

opinions,[78] perhaps because the court wants to maintain a picture of judicial unity. These arguments are not limited to press releases. What sort of information judges or the court decide to communicate on social media websites, during public interviews, and so on all shape public perception of the court.

The second lesson is about the potential benefits of institutionalizing public relations,[79] such as investing in public communications, establishing communications practices, and developing a court's public relations arm. What I have in mind here are not simply the logistical and technical aspects of information dissemination, which are tasks already performed by regular administrative staff within the judiciary. Instead, I am referring to "formal and informal mechanisms for developing the relationship between courts, the media and the public."[80] This is a proactive and specialized role that requires *both* legal and public relations expertise. The judiciary's institutionalization of public relations is a logical response to an "increasingly critical ... media."[81] For example, according to Druscilla Scribner, the Argentinian judiciary's legitimacy crisis, which spanned decades, led to the decision to invest in communication and media strategies.[82] Similarly, Trochev finds that, facing mounting criticism, the Russian Constitutional Court "launched a massive PR campaign to mark the 10-year anniversary of the Court."[83] There seems to be a general agreement among scholars and judges that these initiatives, if properly executed, tend to bring about positive results.[84]

Also, experts may help review and develop communication guidelines within the court. As I mentioned, many courts do not have an established communications practice, aside from the general judicial ethical rules. As Jane Johnston eloquently puts it, "the world *around* the courts has radically changed, while changes *within* courts' structures have been far more subtle."[85] Internal guidelines over how to deal with the outside world need to be revamped. Common themes that need to be addressed

[78] Meyer (n 44).
[79] Davis (n 54) 288–9; Jane Johnston, 'Three Phases of Courts' Publicity: Reconfiguring Bentham's Open Justice in the Twenty-first Century' (2018) 14 *International Journal of Law in Context* 525.
[80] Johnston *ibid* 530.
[81] *ibid.*
[82] Druscilla Scribner, 'Judicial Communication: (Re)Constructing Legitimacy in Argentina' in Davis and Taras (n 46).
[83] Trochev (n 70).
[84] See Johnston (n 79) 530; Davis (n 54) 288–9; Bogoch and Peleg (n 44).
[85] Johnston (n 79) 534.

include: When public interviews by judges are allowed, reporting guidelines for the press, procedures for judges when engaging with the press, processes to involve judges in media inquiries, even if they are not directly answering questions, and protocols to deal with media attacks. Establishing a more sophisticated system of managing public relations would allow the judiciary to swiftly and effectively adapt to shifting circumstances.

Finally, when designing public relations strategies, it is important to frame them in accordance with the public's expectations. Generally speaking, the social expectations of a court are fundamentally different to those of political institutions. The judiciary is commonly associated with values such as transparency, professionalism, accountability, and openness. Judicial public relations strategies should accordingly be framed around these values, even though the kind of communication advocated earlier is, in fact, purposeful and strategic. Similarly, the court needs to adapt to the contextual characteristics of the community as well. As the Brazilian and Norwegian examples show, the "right" degree of transparency depends on prevailing conceptions of law and politics within a given society. In hybrid regimes with a more legalistic sociolegal culture, such as Hong Kong and Singapore, creating a relatable judicial image might lower the prestige of a court by demystifying its social status. Different societies may have different understandings of legitimate judicial authority, and effective image-building depends on the court's ability to adjust to its social conditions while pursuing its communicative agendas.

7.3.2 Judicial Diplomacy

Judicial diplomacy also involves strategic communication, but judicial diplomacy is a more targeted form of communication involving a high degree of intentionality.[86] While public relations is one-way, judicial

[86] The concept of judicial diplomacy as used here is inspired by the international relations concept of public diplomacy. As Giles Scott-Smith points out, a key feature that distinguished public diplomacy from other channels of diplomacy is "the intention to direct specific ideas at specific targets for specific political goals." Giles Scott-Smith, 'Mapping the Undefinable: Some Thoughts on the Relevance of Exchange Programs within International Relations Theory' (2008) 616 *The Annals of the American Academy of Political and Social Science* 173, 186. Traditionally, the concept of public diplomacy excludes communications with nonstate actors. With the increased involvement of nonstate actors in global policymaking, many are now drifting away from a state-centric understanding of the term, and defining public diplomacy by the capabilities of

diplomacy is more interactive, requiring judges to interface with other actors outside the courtroom. And while public relations is about shaping the attitudes of the general public, judicial diplomacy functions to establish and build relationships with specific audiences. Another characteristic of judicial diplomacy is that the interactions are seen as representative of the judiciary, hence there are practical implications for the institution. Whether the judge actually has the authority to represent the judiciary is irrelevant here; what matters is if the audiences believe that the diplomatic activities represent the judiciary.[87]

My account of judicial diplomacy does not envisage judges acting as diplomats or ambassadors of the state. Nevertheless, the activities that judges pursue in non-adjudicative contexts do resemble the practices of a diplomat. Judicial diplomatic activities include negotiations, advocacy, exchanges, promotion, representation, and consultation.

The literature on judicial diplomacy is in its infancy. Existing works largely focus on the judicial networks formed between national courts of different regions,[88] and how transnational and international judges interface with domestic actors to assert their authority.[89] The traditional usage of the term diplomacy is limited to interstate activities. By analogy, since the subject of diplomacy under judicial diplomacy is the court as opposed to the state, internal-versus-external is defined against the *court* instead of the *state*. Accordingly, there is no reason why we should limit the term judicial diplomacy to engagements with actors in foreign jurisdictions or international actors, as appears to be the case in the current literature. National courts have used similar diplomatic means to interface with international and foreign courts, as well as domestic constituencies such as government officials, the legal profession, civil society, international organizations, academia, and so on.

the actors, formally recognizing the possibility for nonstate actors to engage in diplomatic actions. See Kadir Jun Ayhan, 'The Boundaries of Public Diplomacy and Nonstate Actors: A Taxonomy of Perspectives' (2019) 20 *International Studies Perspectives* 63.

87 Andrew Rehfeld, 'Towards a General Theory of Political Representation' (2006) 68 *The Journal of Politics* 1.

88 See e.g. Klodian Rado, 'The Judicial Diplomacy of the Supreme Court of Canada and Its Impact: An Empirical Overview' (2020) 58 *Alberta Law Review* 1, 1; Gregory Davies, 'The Rise of Judicial Diplomacy in the UK: Aims and Challenges' (2020) 40 *Legal Studies* 1, 77.

89 See e.g. Ezequiel González-Ocantos, 'Communicative Entrepreneurs: The Case of the Inter-American Court of Human Rights' Dialogue with National Judges' (2018) 62 *International Studies Quarterly* 737; Theresa Squatrito, 'Judicial Diplomacy: International Courts and Legitimation' (2021) 47 *Review of International Studies* 64; Allan Tatham, '"Off the Bench But Not Off Duty": The Judicial Diplomacy of the Court of Justice' (2017) 22 *European Foreign Affairs Review* 303.

The institutions explored in Section 7.2 are those that a court should prioritize building alliances with. Judicial diplomacy should be directed toward those actors in order to win their trust and support. Judicial diplomacy can enable a hybrid regime court's relation-building agenda in three ways. First, judicial diplomacy can be used to promote the court. As discussed previously, it is important for the court to combat disinformation and misinformation. This is especially the case in a hybrid regime, where the government may limit the support of a defiant judiciary through propaganda. Judicial diplomacy involves tailor-made solutions for different kinds of audiences who are ignorant of or indifferent about the court and its role. By meeting with these actors, judges can inform them of the different aspects of the judiciary and clarify any misconceptions. Aside from being informative, the court can also use this as an opportunity to deliver value-laden narratives to promote the substantive goals of the court.[90]

Second, hybrid regime courts may conduct judicial diplomacy to mobilize support from relevant constituencies. The judiciary might, for example, need the legal profession to stand up for them, or the active support of international organizations to draw attention to threats to judicial independence. Judicial diplomacy of this sort may require persuasion and negotiation, or even happen behind closed doors. Before enlisting the active support of its audiences, it is important to establish common goals and form a good mutual understanding to start with. I will return to the topic of mobilization in Section 7.6.

Third, judicial diplomacy can be deployed to change normative structures. This involves judges convincing or "educating" their audiences about what the law or constitution ought to be, and socializing its audiences into conforming with the standards set by the committed judges. At times, this approach might seem confrontational in a hybrid regime where the authoritarian is also engaged in an ideological battle with the democratic constituency. Socialization techniques need not always be highly scripted, as committed judges can also work with their audiences to come up with new normative standards. This is a softer technique that speaks to a more collaborative relationship between the judges and their audiences.[91]

Judges may occasionally reach out directly to other actors. However, separation of powers principles and judicial ethic rules may limit the

[90] Squatrito *ibid.*
[91] González-Ocantos (n 89).

scope of diplomatic practices, forcing judges to conduct judicial diplomacy in secret. That need not always be the case, as there are plenty of socially legitimate opportunities for judges to connect with the institutions identified in the previous part. The rest of this part sets out common formal occasions where judges can engage with some of the institutions discussed in Section 7.2.[92]

7.3.2.1 Judicial Networks

There are many transnational and international judicial networks in the world that judges can join, such as the Association of Asian Constitutional Courts, the Union of Arab Constitutional Courts and Councils, the Africa Judges and Jurists Forum, the Conference of European Constitutional Courts, the Ibero-American Conference of Constitutional Justice, the International Association of Women Judges, and the International Commission of Jurists. Informal networks involving multilateral collaborative relationships between different transnational and domestic courts also exist. Judicial networks allow judges of different jurisdictions to convene and discuss judicially related topics such as legal developments and case management. On top of providing networking opportunities, these meetings might also facilitate norm diffusion. The Supreme Court of Singapore, together with judges from a number of common-law jurisdictions, has promulgated the Judicial Insolvency Network Guidelines. It is not only a useful guide for judges and other stakeholders handling complex bankruptcy issues in Asia and beyond,[93] but also an instrument to improve the social standing of the Singaporean judiciary domestically and internationally. Hybrid regime courts can also be on the receiving end of the norm-diffusion process and gain valuable legal insights that help them navigate challenging circumstances. Latin American courts, for example, have also worked closely with the Inter-American Court of Human Rights to develop their human rights jurisprudence.[94]

[92] There may also be informal occasions for judges to socialize with other actors, such as private gatherings and dinners at private clubs or people's houses. These are also opportunities for judges to create informal links and can be similarly effective, but they are very hard to document.

[93] Emily Lee and Eric C. Ip, 'Judicial Diplomacy in the Asia-Pacific: Theory and Evidence from the Singapore-initiated Transnational Judicial Insolvency Network' (2020) 20 *Journal of Corporate Law Studies* 389.

[94] González-Ocantos (n 30).

7.3.2.2 Foreign Visits

The judicial networks discussed earlier are multilateral in nature. Many judiciaries also have bilateral engagements with one another, setting up exchange programs and sending judges to visit their overseas counterparts. Canadian judges, for example, visit the apex courts of many countries, ranging from the United States and the United Kingdom to Israel and Germany.[95] Similarly, the UK Supreme Court meets with common-law courts such as the Canadian Supreme Court and the South African Constitutional Court.[96] The Hong Kong chief justice also regularly invites overseas senior judges to sit on the bench and give talks. These foreign visits overlap in function with the judicial networks discussed in previous paragraphs. Foreign visits, however, tend to be more intensive experiences, as visiting judges will have prolonged exposure to one court. These are opportunities to consolidate relations with foreign judiciaries and build deeper ties.

7.3.2.3 Academic Conferences and Writings

From time to time, judges are invited to participate in academic workshops and conferences. Perhaps the most famous one in this category is Yale's Global Constitutionalism Seminar, where constitutional judges from around the world are flown in to meet with academics and debate important constitutional topics.[97] Local conferences of a smaller scale also exist. In these intimate academic settings, judges get to meet colleagues and academics relevant to their areas. Constitutional judges may also advance their understanding of the constitution and law under the auspices of "intellectual exchange," learn about doctrinal tools from other jurisdictions, and acquire fresh perspectives on their judicial role. Conference proceedings may sometimes turn into academic publications, allowing the judges' views to reach a wider audience.

7.3.2.4 Professional Seminars

Similar in format to conferences are seminars organized by the legal profession. Obvious differences are that the topics here are more likely to concern legal practice, and the audiences involved are lawyers and other actors in the legal field, such as prosecutors and lawmakers. Judges

[95] Rado (n 88) 6.
[96] Davies (n 88) 80 note 24.
[97] Yale Law School, 'Global Constitutionalism Seminar,' available at https://law.yale.edu/centers-workshops/gruber-program-global-justice-and-womens-rights/global-constitutionalism-seminar, last visited November 9, 2021.

might receive helpful feedback about the judiciary's performance in the exchanges and gain a better understanding of the profession's view of the court and its concerns. Judges might also be asked to train the legal profession, giving judges the chance to devise new behavioral standards for the field.

7.3.2.5 Policy Committees

Occasionally, judges may be invited to sit on domestic or international policy committees. These are rare occasions to exchange ideas with politicians and policymakers. For example, judges are sometimes asked to be a member of a law reform working group. By working together, judges may foster friendly but professional relations with government officials. These collaborations might promote mutual support and improve intrabranch relations. The same logic applies to international policy committees. The United Nations Office on Drugs and Crime, for example, organizes the Global Judicial Integrity Network, with the aim of "assist[ing] judiciaries across the globe in strengthening judicial integrity and preventing corruption in the justice sector."[98] Judges from different jurisdictions are part of the network. The network collaborates with other transnational and regional organizations and offers virtual and in-person seminars and conferences to develop best-practice guidelines, allowing participating judges the opportunity to connect with policymakers and representatives of international organizations.

7.3.2.6 Local Exchanges

Politicians regularly meet with their constituencies and engage in public consultations. Similar opportunities sometimes arise for judges. For example, they might be asked to give a speech at the university's graduation ceremony, offer some remarks at the closing of a legal year, or speak about a legal topic at a charity event organized by an NGO. Functionally similar to policy consultations, exchanges with local communities allow judges to collect views about the preferences and perceptions of different domestic audiences. When the occasion is a public one, how judges present themselves will directly affect public attitudes toward the court.

[98] For the official website of the Global Judicial Integrity network, see www.unodc.org/ji/.

7.4 Engaging Hostile Parties

The focus so far has been on developing relationships with institutions that can provide cover to the court. Despite the court's best efforts, however, there will be groups that are hostile toward the judiciary because of ideological differences and prior rulings. Furthermore, judicial allies do not always effectively defend the court, especially in situations where the expected benefits of pushing through a court-damaging policy outweighs the costs. This leaves judges with no choice but to engage with hostile parties themselves.

7.4.1 Judicial Diplomacy and Hostile Relations

The idea of engaging those who oppose the court – generally or on specific issues – may seem dangerous at first, as it may create the impression of a politicized or pressurized court. The whole idea of judicial diplomacy, as argued so far, is to foster better relations with other institutions. It should not be forgotten that the institutions identified earlier are only *potential* allies, and some of their members may actually be antagonistic. The fact that some of these audiences may be hostile offers a strong reason for engagement as well. Some diplomatic theorists argue that continuous dialogue between adversaries is conducive to peace-building.[99] By analogy, maintaining some level of communication between the court and its opponents is generally desirable. The same benefits mentioned previously with regard to judicial diplomacy can be adopted here too. It is important to be aware of the preferences and views of all relevant constituencies, even those that are ideologically distant from the court. The information gained helps courts strategize and better understand the motivations of those who oppose or are dissimilar to them. A further step would be to convert these groups through norm-promoting judicial diplomatic activities. Recalcitrant groups are unlikely to shift their ideology anytime soon, but over time, and through dialogue and exposure to the "right" standards and norms, some hostile groups might one day become allies.

The greater the ideological gap between the court and its audiences, the harder it will be for judges to develop friendly relationships with others. Hence, judicial diplomacy directed toward an authoritarian constituency

99 See Geoffrey Wiseman, 'Engaging the Enemy: An Essential Norm for Sustainable US Diplomacy' in Costas M. Constantinou and James Der Derian (eds), *Sustainable Diplomacies* (Palgrave Macmillan 2010).

is likely to have limited immediate effect. Nevertheless, establishing diplomatic relations with hostile groups is still a worthy investment considering the possible payoffs. The fear that judicial diplomacy of this sort might weaken the image of the court is mitigated by the fact that there are legitimate forms of public engagement, as discussed previously. For example, if invited, committed judges should participate in and speak at professional and academic conferences organized by the government and proregime think-tanks. The content and tone of judges' speeches will, of course, have to be adjusted accordingly, but these occasions may nevertheless be useful for the judges to connect with the regime and gain information about the preferences of its members.

When serious challenges to core democratic principles loom on the horizon, judges may consider a more hawkish form of diplomacy by sending a judicial flare that warns hostile parties of the unconstitutionality of an impeding policy or bill and the likelihood of judicially striking it down if the government tries to push through it. Part of the flare's preventive function derives from its ability to create public pressure. These flares can take different forms, including extrajudicial remarks made on a public occasion and an open letter to the government. Lord Woolf, for example, famously delivered a lecture at the University of Cambridge criticizing the British government's plan to remove judicial powers over asylum review cases. His language was described by the press as "militant," and provocative soundbites of his speech sparked public debates.[100] In a mature democracy, where there is mutual respect between the branches of government, judges can afford to be more fearless when speaking in public. However, such a confrontational approach is inevitably riskier in a hybrid regime, and judges need to be sure that the issue at stake is worth taking a stand against the authoritarian, given the possibility of backlash against the individual judges *and* the judiciary.

7.4.2 *Backchanneling*

More controversial is the idea of making a deal with the devil: Backchanneling. Sometimes known as the "black markets" of

[100] Woolf for instance noted, "I am not over-dramatising the position if I indicate that, if this clause were to become law, it would be so inconsistent with the spirit of mutual respect between the different arms of government that it could be the catalyst for a campaign for a written constitution." See The Guardian, 'Woolf Leads Judges' Attack on Ministers,' March 4, 2004.

negotiations,[101] backchanneling is a concept borrowed from international relations. It describes secret bargains that operate alongside or at times override other channels of communication. In politics, backchanneling is commonly used between adversarial parties in conflict resolution processes and labor disputes.[102]

I have been using the metaphor of a tacit bargain to describe the relationship between a semi-autonomous court and a hybrid regime. A court enjoys the space it is given at the price of self-restraint in matters that the authoritarian cares most about, and the authoritarian in return obtains legitimacy gains and other associated benefits. This bargain will be unstable and the relationship will start to break down when either side begins to relentlessly push for more. Negotiations may then have to become explicit.

Judges do regularly engage in some form of bargaining with the government in court over certain issues pertaining to a case. Judges might, for example, persuade the government to drop certain points because they do not sound convincing, and the government, through its legal representatives, might explain how much it is willing to concede. This is a legitimate and semi-open form of negotiation between the authoritarian and the judiciary, with lawyers acting as the conduit.

In contrast, backchannel negotiation is more controversial because it is secretive, lacks any form of public scrutiny, and the negotiation terms are completely dictated by the negotiating parties. While secret negotiations involving judges are very hard to detect, we know that they probably exist. Ellett and Trochev find traces of evidence to support the claim.[103] For example, judges in East Africa would approach political elites to "smooth the way forward" in anticipation of a difficult judgment.[104] Similarly, in Uganda, officials reportedly visited a judge's chambers before a presidential election, and the court that the judge headed had previously released the leading opposition leader on bail.[105] The examples they give are all from authoritarian regimes. This is expected because, as previously mentioned, there is a real need for weakly

[101] Anthony Wanis-St. John, 'Back-channel Negotiation: International Bargaining in the Shadows' (2006) 22 *Negotiation Journal* 119, 120.

[102] See Dean Pruitt, 'Back-channel Communication in the Settlement of Conflict' (2008) 13 *International Negotiation* 37.

[103] Trochev and Ellett (n 1).

[104] *ibid* 72.

[105] *ibid* 73.

protected judges to find unorthodox means to maintain their institutional position.

The contents of backchannel negotiations are unknown to the public, making it nearly impossible to assess the implications of these negotiations. Since the methodological problem cannot presently be overcome, I look for insights from international relations, where the concept of backchanneling originates.

As noted, backchanneling is a very common form of diplomacy intended for conflicting groups to reach settlements. The advantages of backchanneling are derived from secrecy. Taking negotiations underground frees negotiating parties from the pressure and manipulation of the public and third parties. Public scrutiny incentivizes negotiators to adopt hardline positions, especially when tensions are high. This audience effect hinders settlement processes.[106] There is no need to perform for an audience or grandstand when backchanneling, because there is no audience to begin with.[107] Backchanneling as a result allows for a "more inventive negotiation context."[108] Compared to the public and more ritualized channels of communication, parties engaging in secret negotiations have greater space to explore compromise options without fearing how the public might react. Backchanneling can occur alongside public or frontchannel negotiations, and negotiators can adjust public expectations before reaching an agreement through backchanneling. Frontchannel negotiations and public responses may also affect how backchannel negotiations are conducted. Feedback mechanisms exist between the frontchannel and backchannel.

These insights from international relations are relevant to courts in hybrid regimes. Many forms of public communication are not available to a court, and judges need to be very careful about how they present themselves and speak in public. Even when there is an impending threat to the judiciary, judges may be handicapped in responding to the situation because ethical rules forbid ostensibly political involvement, or because it is deemed socially unacceptable for courts to take a public stand. The alternative techniques previously mentioned may be inconclusive,

[106] Anthony Wanis-St. John, 'An Assessment of Back Channel Diplomacy: Negotiations between the Palestinians and Israelis', Program on Negotiation at Harvard Law School, available at www.american.edu/sis/faculty/upload/wanis-back-channel-working-paper.pdf, last visited January 10, 2026.

[107] Niall Ó Dochartaigh, 'Together in the Middle: Back-channel Negotiation in the Irish Peace Process' (2011) 48 *Journal of Peace Research* 6, 767, 774.

[108] Wanis-St. John (n 101) 7.

exhausted, or have already proven to be ineffective. Backchanneling provides another avenue to defuse the threat while preserving the image of judicial independence. Judges can more honestly express themselves and bargain with hostile parties without the need for public posturing.

Backchanneling, however, raises normative and pragmatic challenges. How can a court claim to be autonomous when it is engaging in clandestine deals with the authoritarian? Removing the negotiation process from public view further weakens public accountability over the government, which goes against the very objective of the constitutional democratic project. Backchanneling, if exposed, also severely undermines the democratic constituency's image of the court and weakens its bonds with its allies. One might also argue that the idea of backchanneling is self-defeating. Judges would presumably have to give up something to reach an agreement, and that something would usually be antiregime decisions. To use the words of Cecilia Sosa, ex-president of the Venezuelan Supreme Court, "a court that committed suicide to avoid being assassinated has the same result – it is dead."[109] Surrendering to prevent an attack sounds as futile as being attacked by the adversary. Being in a stronger bargaining position, the authoritarian will take advantage of the secret nature of negotiations to bully the court into carrying out its preferences. There are also trust problems, such as the possibility of the regime not following through on its promise, because there is no third party to enforce the agreement.

These critiques are hard to refute. Indeed, sometimes it may be in the court's favor to confront the regime publicly, especially when the public is sympathetic to the court and willing to stand up for it. This will be explored shortly. Nevertheless, backchanneling is built on mutual trust and reciprocity. Both sides – the authoritarian and the court – care about their image and can expose each other. While there is little formal protection offered to judges during backchannel negotiations and their bargaining power is not necessarily equal to the regime's, judges can sometimes count on the self-interest of the adversary to sustain an agreement.

Backchanneling is unquestionably dangerous for judges, but it is an option that they should consider when other adjudicative and diplomatic means have been tried and failed. In desperate times, backchanneling might offer a way forward. Backchanneling appears to undermine the

[109] Freedom House, *Freedom in the World 1999 – Venezuela* (1999), available at www.refworld.org/docid/5278c6c214.html, last visited November 9, 2021.

idea of judicial independence as it invites undue interference, but it is perhaps justifiable when undue interference is inevitable anyway. Backchanneling may allow judges to exercise some control over and minimize the severity of this influence. As counterintuitive as it may sound, without better options, backchanneling seeks to preserve judicial independence as much as possible, both in appearance and in substance. Backchanneling can also be used to induce the regime into doing something *for* the court. Increasing the capacity of the judiciary or implementing a judicial decision, for example, requires the active support of the regime. It may be worthwhile in these instances to "trade" with the authoritarian in return for its support. Judges will have to manage negotiations very carefully, ensuring that they are not conceding so much ground that the space for playing a democratic role in hybrid regime politics is virtually eliminated. In such cases, backchanneling becomes no different from "telephone law," when judges are routinely forced to do whatever they are told. If a bottom line is crossed, judges should consider further escalation, including more dramatic forms of response. These are discussed in the following sections.

7.5 Collective Protest

There may be times when judges have to make their point loud and clear. Protest is another form of diplomacy that involves the collective expression of disapproval or objection. Most protests are reactive, meaning they are in response to and seeking to change what is happening in society.[110] The power of protests lies in their ability to mobilize the mass public, attract attention, influence public opinion, and potentially destabilize the regime.

Protests around the world are increasingly common and widespread.[111] What is especially interesting for our purposes is that judges are sometimes joining, or even initiating, these protests. The themes of these protests vary: They range from court-centered topics, such as judicial pay rises and judicial reform, to more macropolitical issues such as anticorruption and

[110] María Inclán and Paul D. Almeida, 'Ritual Demonstrations versus Reactive Protests: Participation across Mobilizing Contexts in Mexico City' (2017) 59 *Latin American Politics and Society* 47, 49–50.

[111] The Economist, 'Political Protests Have Become More Widespread and More Frequent,' March 10, 2020, available at www.economist.com/graphic-detail/2020/03/10/political-protests-have-become-more-widespread-and-more-frequent, last visited November 9, 2021.

democratization. Some of these protests may be more confrontational, involving strikes or even violence, while others are tamer, such as sit-ins and silent marches. The impact of these protests may not always be tangible, and at times amount to no more than an expression of disapproval. Still, on occasion they might mobilize other constituencies, leading to more dramatic changes such as political reform or regime change.

The Ugandan boycott and protest against the Black Mambas' siege of the court and Pakistan's Lawyers' Movement, mentioned previously, are two examples of judges taking an active role in nationwide protest movements. Asking his colleagues and allies outside the courtroom to take action, an outspoken Ugandan judge publicly stated that, "the [Museveni] government has not developed a culture of killing vocal judges so judges should use this opportunity to resist anything that smells like dictatorship and abuse of human rights."[112] Several protests during Mubarak's regime that demanded judicial independence and opposed election fraud involved Egyptian reformist judges and the politically active judicial organization the Judges Club.[113] In 2012, judges in Egypt again went on strike to protest a decree that effectively immunized the president from judicial challenge.[114] Magistrates in France organized a boycott against Nicolas Sarkozy in 2011 and accused the president of meddling with the judicial system to gain political capital.[115] Around a thousand judges and prosecutors staged a silent protest in Romania in 2017 opposing a proposed change in the criminal code that would allegedly undermine the investigative power of prosecutors and afford potential victims fewer protections.[116] In 2020, judges and lawyers of the European Union took to the streets in solidarity with Polish judges and to protest the Polish government's

112 As quoted in Rachel Ellett, *Pathways to Judicial Power in Transitional States: Perspectives from African Courts* (Routledge 2013) 193.

113 Michael Slackman and Mona El-Naggar, 'Police Beat Crowds Backing Egypt's Judges' *The New York Times*, May 12, 2006, available at www.nytimes.com/2006/05/12/world/middleeast/12egypt.html, last visited November 9, 2021.

114 Sarah El Deeb, 'Egypt Judges Strike to Protest President's Decrees,' Associated Press, November 29, 2012, available at https://apnews.com/b7c91e7fc0b24f0c88f2c3878507cb4a, last visited November 9, 2021.

115 The Guardian, 'Sarkozy under Pressure as French Judges Take to the Streets,' February 10, 2011, available at www.theguardian.com/world/2011/feb/10/sarkozy-french-judges-protest, last visited November 9, 2021.

116 The Seattle Times, 'Fresh Protest in Romania over Legal System Changes,' December 19, 2017, available at www.seattletimes.com/nation-world/fresh-protest-in-romania-over-legal-system-changes/, last visited September 12, 2024.

attempt to introduce a judicial disciplinary chamber to curb judicial powers.[117] The list goes on.[118]

More and more judges may be protesting, but the idea of protest might sit uncomfortably with the conventional understanding of the judicial role. The exact rules governing judges' participation in street protests and workplace strikes varies jurisdiction by jurisdiction, but most jurisdictions have standards limiting judges' involvement in ostensibly "political" events. For instance, a rule in Pakistan stipulates: "Functioning as he does in full view of the public, a Judge gets thereby all the publicity that is good for him. He should not seek more. In particular, he should not engage in any public controversy, least of all on a political question, notwithstanding that it involves a question of law."[119]

Similarly worded restrictions are found in other hybrid regimes such as Uganda[120] and Hong Kong,[121] as well as democracies. Judges in the EU are advised to "exercise their freedom of expression in a manner compatible with the dignity of their office" and "refrain from public statements or remarks that may undermine the authority of the Court or give rise to reasonable doubt as to their impartiality."[122] Following widespread protests against racial injustice in the United States, judicial ethical committees around the country issued guidelines to judges, warning them that participating in politically charged public events could stain the courts' image of impartiality or create an appearance of impropriety.[123]

These rules impart the same message: Appearances matter. There are concerns about judges being seen to operate outside "judicial" confines.

[117] Reuters, 'Thousands Protest Against Poland's Plan to Discipline Judges,' January 12, 2020, available at www.reuters.com/article/us-poland-judiciary-toga-march-idUSKBN1ZA0PD, last visited November 9, 2021.

[118] See Trochev and Ellett (n 1) 67–8.

[119] Article V of the Code of Conduct to be Observed by Judges of the Supreme Court of Pakistan and of the High Courts of Pakistan (September 2, 2009).

[120] Clause 4 of The Uganda Code of Judicial Conduct (June 20, 2003).

[121] Clause 75 and 76 of the Guide to Judicial Conduct of the Hong Kong Judiciary (October 2004).

[122] Point VI of the Resolution on Judicial Ethics adopted by the Plenary of our European Court of Human Rights on June 23, 2008.

[123] See 'In Response to Recent Events: Judicial Participation in Demonstrations, Protests, Marches, and Rallies,' Judicial Ethics and Discipline: Blog of the Center for Judicial Ethics of the National Center of State Courts, July 28, 2020, available at https://web.archive.org/web/20230605223927/https://ncscjudicialethicsblog.org/2020/07/28/in-response-to-recent-events-judicial-participation-in-demonstrations-protests-marches-and-rallies/, last visited November 9, 2021.

To what extent a matter is "too political" for a judge to be publicly involved in is open to debate. Regardless, protesting risks tarnishing the court's reputation by politicizing judges. It makes judges look weak and vulnerable, and this may adversely impact the public's confidence in the court. Judicial protesting may also provide ammunition for critics to weed out defiant judges. Conduct rules will be cited by hostile parties in alleging professional misconduct. Furthermore, the development of a protest is beyond the control of judges. Judges involved in protests that turn out to be unlawful or violent may be arrested and charged for serious crimes. The uncertainty that comes with protesting poses safety and career concerns for individual judges as well.

Protesting is risky for the judiciary and for judges. There are safer ways to express judges' views – through, for example, judgments, public interviews, and more diplomatic means. Why, then, should judges protest at all, given this is fraught with danger?

Desperate times call for desperate measures. When the court is facing an imminent attack, long-term image-building techniques such as public relations cannot address pressing problems. Alternative means such as judicial diplomacy or backchanneling might have also failed. Judges, especially in authoritarian contexts, may be deprived of powerful allies to negotiate on their behalf. In these instances, judges are essentially forced to go public to fend off attacks. Organizing a protest enables rapid response to an event of great immediacy and appeals to the court-supporting mass public. In support of the EU-wide protest supporting the Polish judges, Kees Sterk, a Dutch judge and president of the European Network of Councils for the Judiciary, sums up this point perfectly: "Judges are reaching out to citizens, saying 'defend us, so that we can defend you' ... In countries where judicial independence is respected, then of course judges should not get involved in politics. But when judicial independence is being destroyed, you cannot expect them to allow themselves to be led like lambs to the slaughter."[124]

On top of protesting to protect their own autonomy, judges may find it necessary to take a public stand when a hybrid regime faces a constitutional crisis, such as when rule of law and democratic norms are fundamentally at stake. Judges cannot always resort to protesting when they disagree with a policy; for ethical and institutional reasons,

[124] Christian Davies, 'Judges Join Silent Rally to Defend Polish Justice,' *The Guardian*, January 12, 2020, available at www.theguardian.com/world/2020/jan/12/poland-march-judges-europe-protest-lawyers, last visited November 9, 2021.

they must keep a professional distance from politicians and protestors. However, when features that define the democratic half of a hybrid regime are under existential threat, committed judges may feel compelled to do everything in their power to prevent authoritarian backsliding. Because judges rarely participate in public events, the hope is that they are seen as symbols of justice, and their participation during critical moments in a major protest movement will end the crisis.

7.6 Mobilization

Just as politicians mobilize voters and supporters, judges can mobilize their constituencies using non-adjudicative strategies. Mobilization and judging do not seem to go together. However, judges are sometimes left with no choice but to become activists and assemble their allies in order to defend their interests.

To successfully mobilize certain constituencies or the general public against enemies of the court, judges need to overcome the problem of collective action. Broadly speaking, there are two approaches to judicial mobilization. One is *indirect*, whereby judges incite mobilization through signaling. In the Pakistani example relayed earlier in this chapter, judicial protests and resignations triggered large-scale protests, which eventually removed Musharraf from power. Judges may also *directly* mobilize their constituencies. They may, for example, hold public or private meetings with lawyers and political actors calling for their active support, or even organize protest movements themselves.

Polish judges' resistance to court-curbing measures in recent years illustrates the process behind and complications of mobilization strategies. Since 2015, populist forces in Poland have gradually tried to subvert judicial powers in order to remove constitutional checks and consolidate executive powers. One of the many responses of the defiant judges was to rely on existing professional judicial networks within Poland, namely, Iustitia and Themis, to mobilize a range of sociopolitical actors to stop, or at least delay, authoritarian encroachment.[125] Judges belonging to these organizations publicly and privately lobbied legislative and judicial institutions of the European Union to highlight constitutional violations by the Polish government.[126] Some judges used social

[125] Matthes (n 58).
[126] *ibid* at 8–11.

media to counter smearing campaigns with the aim of altering public discourse.[127] They also worked closely with lawyer groups and civil society organizations to extend their influence.[128] Their strategic efforts led tens of thousands of people in Poland and across Europe – including many judges and lawyers – to demonstrate against judicial interference in Poland.[129]

Mobilization in today's world has unpredictable results and often proves fruitless.[130] Widespread coordination is required to resolve the collective action problem inherent in mobilization strategies. Several factors may contribute to effective mobilization. First, well-connected judges have an advantage. Judges in Poland were able to coordinate with allies domestically and on a European level because their membership in professional judicial networks gave them the platform to organize and instigate mobilization. Second, the social standing of judges directly impacts their ability to activate the public. Chaudhry, for instance, achieved celebrity-like status in Pakistan well before the Lawyer's Movement. As a prominent Pakistani journalist describes, the Chaudhry Supreme Court was then regarded as "the last station on the line, the only forum capable of providing relief."[131] To a large extent, the Lawyer's Movement was triggered by his direct appeal to the masses following his suspension. Finally, some level of judicial backchanneling may be necessary to mitigate the costs of mobilization strategies. Because of its confrontational nature, mobilization is always a risky endeavor for participating judges, who may be subjected to disciplinary consequences, removed from power, or even personally endangered. Judges who go public also risk politicizing themselves and the judiciary. To minimize the side-effects of mobilization, some judges, as in the case of Poland, have lobbied in secret, letting their allies serve as the face of the mobilization movement.

7.7 Resignation

Judicial resignation is the most radical option in the list and, for reasons I explain in this section, should be considered only as a last resort. I am

[127] *ibid* at 12.
[128] *ibid.*
[129] Davies (n 124).
[130] See Helen Margetts and others, *Political Turbulence: How Social Media Shape Collective Action* (Princeton University Press 2015).
[131] As cited in Ghias (n 10) 993.

not interested in judicial resignation for age or health reasons. Rather, judicial resignation here refers to judges who voluntarily resign in protest of the regime or for a political cause.

In authoritarian regimes, quite a number of judges have resigned in protest. Laurie Ackerman resigned during apartheid South Africa and described the decision as "an exclusively personal matter of conscience."[132] He subsequently accepted a university chair in human rights law, stating he "believe[s] that the effective protection of human rights in this country is the most important issue facing lawyers in the short, medium and long term."[133] In German-occupied Norway during World War II, Norwegian Supreme Court judges resigned to "sen[d] a clear message to the Norwegian population about the illegitimacy of the civil rule established by the Germans."[134] Pakistani judges resigned as a response to Musharraf's removal of Chief Justice Chaudhry.[135] Ever since Beijing's clampdown on Hong Kong in 2020, nine nonpermanent overseas judges have resigned from the Hong Kong Court of Final Appeal, six of whom cited concerns about the political environment.[136] Foreign and local judges in Fiji have also resigned

[132] David Dyzenhaus, *Judging the Judges, Judging Ourselves: Truth, Reconciliation and the Apartheid Legal Order* (Hart Publishing 1998) 79–80.

[133] *ibid* 79.

[134] Hans Petter Graver, 'Why Adolf Hitler Spared the Judges: Judicial Opposition Against the Nazi State' (2018) 19 *German Law Journal* 845, 851–2.

[135] The Seattle Times, '5 Pakistani Judges Resign to Protest Removal of Chief Justice,' March 19, 2007, available at www.seattletimes.com/nation-world/5-pakistani-judges-resign-to-protest-removal-of-chief-justice/, last visited November 9, 2021.

[136] They are former Chief Justice of New South Wales Mr James Spigelman: www.abc.net.au/news/2020-09-18/judge-quits-over-hong-kong-national-security-law/12679318; former President of the UK Supreme Court Baroness Hale: https://hongkongfp.com/2021/06/04/senior-british-judge-to-quit-top-hong-kong-court-media/; President of the UK Supreme Court Lord Reed and UK Supreme Court Justice Lord Hodge: www.supremecourt.uk/news/role-of-uk-supreme-court-judges-on-the-hong-kong-court-of-final-appeal-update; former Chief Justice of Australia Mr Anthony Gleeson: www.thestandard.com.hk/breaking-news/section/4/214263/Veteran-Australian-judge-Murray-Gleeson-retires-from-HK%E2%80%99s-top-court,-cites-age-as-reason; former UK Supreme Court Justice Lord Collins: https://hongkongfp.com/2024/06/06/breaking-two-uk-judges-quit-hong-kongs-top-court-as-lord-collins-cites-political-situation/; former UK Supreme Court Justice Lord Sumption: www.ft.com/content/60c825be-b70a-4152-895f-f6127974570a; former Chief Justice of Canada Beverley McLachlin: www.cbc.ca/news/politics/beverly-mclachlin-to-step-down-hong-kong-court-1.7230103; and former President of the UK Supreme Court Lord Phillips: https://hongkongfp.com/2024/09/30/uks-nicholas-phillips-steps-down-as-hong-kong-top-court-judge-cites-personal-reasons-for-not-extending/ (all URLs in this footnote last visited January 10, 2026).

after military coups in 1987 and 2000.[137] More strikingly, Nicaraguan Supreme Court Judge Rafael Solís Cerda resigned in 2019 with an open letter to the president, writing, "I fought against a dictatorship and I never believed that history would repeat itself on account of those who also fought against that same dictatorship."[138] The same letter also accused the Ortega government of transforming the country into a "state of terror."

A judge usually resigns when he or she believes that the judicial oath can no longer be upheld. When assuming office, judges take an oath that they will administer justice. This oath defines duties relating to the judicial office. The extent to which the oath binds the moral conscience of a judge is very much a personal question. Some judges might treat oath-taking as a ceremony with no moral significance, but it is likely that many judges would feel morally bound by the oath. The contents of the oath and the political reality judges face may create a cognitive dissonance for those working in "wicked" or oppressive regimes, as judges might feel incapable of continuing their duties. Or, as Raymond Wacks puts it, "[a judge] is unable to reconcile his function as repository of justice with statutes which mock that very role."[139]

The oath provides the grounds and justification for resignation, but of greater interest here is the practical impact of judicial resignation. Resigning can be a way for judges to publicly condemn objectionable laws and an oppressive system. The message sent by resigning is significant because of what judges represent. Judges who have acted in accordance with the principles of justice are seen as a living embodiment of the rule of law. Stepping down would effectively be a vote of no confidence in the government. Judicial resignation is particularly damaging to a hybrid regime's reputation, because a hybrid regime relies on semi-autonomous judges to uphold an impression of judicial independence and democracy. Resigning can spark transformative change by piercing through the "democratic" veneer engineered by the hybrid regime. The

[137] Tupou Draunidalo, 'The Rule of Law and Judicial Independence Amidst the Coups and Attempted Coups in Fiji since 1987' in Jon Fraenkel, Stewart Firth, and Brij V. Lal (eds), *The 2006 Military Takeover in Fiji: A Coup to End All Coups?* (ANU 2009) 311–12.

[138] ABC News, 'Nicaraguan Supreme Court Justice Resigns in Protest,' January 11, 2019, available at https://web.archive.org/web/20210308041534/https://abcnews.go.com/International/wireStory/nicaraguan-supreme-court-justice-resigns-protest-60300659, last visited November 9, 2021.

[139] Raymond Wacks, 'Judges and Injustice' (1984) 101 *South African Law Journal* 2, 266, 268.

hope is that resigning in protest delegitimizes a hybrid regime *and* inspires other judges and constituencies to resist, thereby destabilizing the regime.

The signaling effects produced by resigning can vary depending on how judges resign. The more reputable or senior a judge is, the more symbolic weight his or her resignation will carry. Making the reasons for resignation public, as in the Nicaraguan case, would guarantee headlines. A silent resignation may create less controversy, but still generate suspicion. The number of judges resigning is also telling. Resigning *en masse* is a very powerful statement and unequivocally shows that the resigning judges' concerns are widely shared.[140] The timing of a resignation also affects whether it can actually drive tangible political change. John Dugard argued that, "there is little doubt that . . . resignations would have had considerable effect" if the South African judges during the apartheid period had resigned much earlier.[141] Similarly, resigning when a hybrid regime becomes fully authoritarian would probably be futile, as by then the regime has given up on pretending to be a democracy.

Like most options discussed here, committed judges contemplating resignation face a trade-off: The resulting vacancy will most likely be filled by a loyalist, which could potentially accelerate the consolidation of authoritarian power. In addition, even if favorable political conditions reappear, the right kind of judges will not be present to identify and/or take advantage of those opportunities. In the worst-case scenario, resignation weakens the democratic network within a hybrid regime for nothing in return.

From a utilitarian perspective, whether to resign or not is a very difficult issue. This topic was hotly debated during apartheid South Africa. At the time it was argued that judges, for moral reasons, should not continue in their judicial office, as that would be lending legitimacy to a wicked regime.[142] Similar debates are ongoing in Hong Kong after the passing of the national security law.[143] The potential gain of resigning is rather "speculative"[144] and is done under highly uncertain conditions. Whether

[140] John Dugard, 'Should Judges Resign: A Reply to Professor Wacks' (1984) 101 *South African Law Journal* 2, 286, 292.

[141] *ibid.*

[142] Wacks (n 139); see also *ibid*; Dyzenhaus (n 132).

[143] SCMP, 'National Security Law: No Hong Kong Judges Should Resign, Justice Kemal Bokhary Says, Amid Pressure on Foreign Jurists to Quit,' March 21, 2021, available at www.scmp.com/news/hong-kong/law-and-crime/article/3126359/no-plan resign-justice-kemal-bokhary-says-amid, last visited November 9, 2021.

[144] Dugard (n 140) 206.

judicial resignation can actually damage the regime's legitimacy hinges on how political events unfold at the time. Almost all the resignations mentioned previously fell short of instigating transformative change. Given how costly resignation may be to the democratic constituency and its speculative gains, the expected returns of doing so tend to be low. If anything, likely effects tend to be symbolic only.

When thinking about the impact of resigning, we should also consider what happens to judges after resignation. Some judges might simply decide to go into exile or retreat into the private sector,[145] abdicating their moral and professional responsibility altogether. Others, like Ackerman, may switch to another position, such as becoming a pundit, engaging in international advocacy, or advising allies within the democratic network, and continue their efforts to fight against authoritarianism.

A retired judge may still be able to contribute to the cause in other social roles, but the key question is whether he or she could have contributed more in *or* outside of his or her capacity as a judge, bearing in mind that his or her successor would likely be a recalcitrant or indifferent judge. This involves an even more complex question about whether "the scope for judicial maneuver and creativity in support of human rights" still meaningfully exists if he or she decides to keep the position.[146] Indeed, much jurisprudential discussion about this topic is centered around the nature of judicial discretion. Those in favor of resignation believe that judges are "plainly at the mercy of the legislature" and/or the regime,[147] while others are more optimistic about the interpretative room of constitutional judges. There is no easy answer here, as it depends on one's view of the nature of the law and deeper personal convictions. Judges themselves are in the best position to answer these questions, as they are the people directly experiencing political interference.

While judicial resignation should not be ruled out as a technique, historical examples suggest that it is generally more meaningful to stay on the bench because there are unique opportunities that come with the adjudicative role. Even defiant judges under Hitler's Germany secretly found ways to combat discriminatory and unjust laws, sometimes saving the lives and improving the detention conditions of Jews.[148] Documents released by WikiLeaks revealed that, in 1999, all five judges of the Hong Kong Court of Final Appeal did consider resigning when Mainland China issued its first

145 Some jurisdictions bar judges from practicing as lawyers ever again.
146 Dugard (n 140) 205.
147 Wacks (n 139) 193.
148 Graver (n 134).

ever constitutional interpretation that effectively overruled the local court's decision. The idea was ultimately dropped as, according to the report, "'the justices feared they would be replaced by less independent or competent jurists."[149] Their decision not to resign has paid off, as the first decade posthandover witnessed many judgments protecting human rights. It may seem futile to a helpless judge to remain in office, but, all things considered, staying on the bench as a general strategy is more likely to maximize the capabilities of a committed judge.

7.8 When Can Non-adjudicative Strategies Be Legitimately Deployed?

Having examined what non-adjudicative strategies are and their potential to institutionally strengthen courts, this final section shifts focus to a normative inquiry, exploring the extent to which judges *should* embrace non-adjudicative strategies.

The comparative examples surveyed so far in this chapter can be interpreted as attempts at institution-building by judges. However, "institution-building" can be motivated by the wrong reasons, which may then be perceived by others as an illegitimate attempt by judges to expand their powers. Some judges may pursue institution-building for personal gain, using non-adjudicative strategies to enhance their personal prestige and influence. Others may utilize these strategies to advance their own political agendas. In such instances, non-adjudicative strategies can be especially controversial due to their nature. Being outside the bounds of the adjudicative process, they are not subject to the constraints of legal methodologies. This lack of constraint raises concerns about whether non-adjudicative strategies will be properly employed to uphold the fundamental values that underpin the judicial system and the constitution. Critics may even argue that non-adjudicative strategies enable judges to directly intervene in policy-making, making it easier for judges to infringe on the remit of the democratically elected or political branches of government.

Uncovering the "real" reasons why judges deploy non-adjudicative strategies is beyond the scope of this chapter, but the fact that such strategies can be used for illegitimate purposes suggests a real need to

149 SCMP, 'All City's Top Judges "Considered Quitting",' September 8, 2011, available at www.scmp.com/article/978391/all-citys-top-judges-considered-quitting, last visited November 9, 2021.

study when non-adjudicative strategies are justified. For the purpose of normative evaluation, it is inappropriate to draw categorical conclusions from the *form* of non-adjudicative strategy used. The mere fact that a strategy is radical and involves substantial departure from the judicial role does not necessarily mean that judges should never consider it. Any case-specific assessment requires contextual analysis that pays close attention to local factors, such as social expectations of the judiciary, formal and informal norms relating to the boundaries of the judicial role, as well as judicial political dynamics. Acknowledging that social, political, and legal contexts play a huge part in shaping how non-adjudicative strategies should be used, this section elaborates on some of the standards that can be used to ascertain the boundaries of legitimate uses of non-adjudicative strategies.

I argue that non-adjudicative strategies are *legitimate* when they are *used to improve judges' long-term ability to do justice, including to perform the democratic roles outlined in* Chapter 4, and, given the costs and benefits of adopting these measures, are likely, on balance, to achieve such an effect. This account includes non-adjudicative strategies deployed to improve the public and salient audiences' confidence in the judiciary, developing judges' capacity to withstand a hostile environment, and, in exceptional circumstances, defending themselves against undue external interference.[150] Radical non-adjudicative strategies may sometimes be acceptable, especially under the latter scenario. This account naturally excludes the deployment of strategies for purely self-serving reasons, such as merely for advancing a particular judges' career or political agenda.

As reiterated throughout this chapter, judges' ability to do justice primarily depends on the public and key audiences' regard for them. These actors must have confidence that judges will settle cases impartially; else, there is no good reason for people to obey their decisions or the law, or use the courts at all. It is therefore unsurprising that the judiciary has been described as having a "preoccupation with appearance."[151] Non-adjudicative strategies equip the judiciary with the tools to maintain an impression that bolsters the public's confidence in the court. The claim here, I emphasize, is not that judges should care

[150] The use of non-adjudicative strategies to improve a court's long-term ability to do justice may be, all things considered, unjustified when such a need is outweighed by other more important goals.

[151] Leslie J. Moran, 'Judicial Bodies as Sexual Bodies: A Tale of Two Portraits' (2008) 29 *Australian Feminist Law Journal* 91, 94.

about their social status per se, but that judges' social capital enables them to more effectively realize their role to do justice. This helps explain why public relations activities, such as speaking in public lectures to clarify any misconceptions about the law, branding strategies to increase the transparency of the judiciary, and outreach programs to educate communities about the legal process should be considered justifiable non-adjudicative strategies. Judicial diplomacy with external audiences, such as the local and international bar and rule-of-law organizations, can be explained by the need to maintain public confidence as well, albeit more indirectly. Informing the public of the general importance of constitutional concepts such as judicial independence and the rule of law depends in large part on these mediating actors' actively engaging with relevant communities. In turn, an informed citizenry is more likely to support and retain confidence in judges who are doing their jobs properly. What these strategies have in common is that they involve judges actively trying to gain recognition from external audiences as independent and professional actors who are integral to the administration of justice.

Just as great marketing cannot save a bad product, the legitimating effects of non-adjudicative strategies will be limited if the image judges seek to portray is wildly inconsistent with their actual behavior. In other words, non-adjudicative strategies will likely be ineffective if the problem confronting the judiciary lies deep within the performances of judges themselves. Reflecting on the reasons contributing to these legitimacy crises is crucial to devising the right solutions.

Sometimes, the problem may be that the judges have yet to adapt to a new media environment. As Jane Johnston notices, "the world around the courts has radically changed, while changes within courts' structures have been far more subtle."[152] Non-adjudicative strategies are likely to be an appropriate remedy if ineffective communication and poor relations management lead to public misunderstanding of the judiciary and the constitution. For instance, Druscilla Scribner explains how, beginning in 2006, the Argentinian judiciary adjusted its communication strategies in order to address the changing media landscape there.[153] Most of the Argentinian population had internet access, and digital media coverage of judicial topics began to take off. In response, the Argentinian judiciary

[152] Jane Johnston, 'Three Phases of Courts' Publicity: Reconfiguring Bentham's Open Justice in the Twenty-First Century' (2018) 14 *International Journal of Law in Context* 525, 534.

[153] Druscilla Scribner, 'Judicial Communication: (Re)Constructing Legitimacy in Argentina' in Davis and Taras (n 46) 14.

created the Center of Judicial Information. The Center was staffed by seasoned journalists and acted as the judiciary's news agency.[154] The judiciary also adopted an "open government" approach[155] by digitizing information about the court and actively promoting their decisions and proceedings online, in order to make it more informative and accessible to the public.

If, however, judges are perceived as corrupt or partisan because of how cases are actually decided, it is highly questionable whether non-adjudicative strategies can be of any significant help. What is instead needed is judicial reform and a transformation in how judges approach cases. In these instances, expanding the space for non-adjudicative activities by judges, as some judges are advocating for,[156] may even be counterproductive, as judges seen to be actively engaging with the outside world may further undermine public confidence and entrench their politicized image.

Non-adjudicative strategies are legitimate when used to boost the public's confidence in the judiciary, although, as we have seen, there are limits as to what these strategies can achieve. Non-adjudicative strategies can also enhance judges' ability to deliver justice by improving their capacity to withstand hostile environments. For example, judges' strong ties with international actors will increase the political cost of executive attacks against the judiciary, especially for states that rely on the affirmation of foreign and international entities. Judges may use their relationships with intermediary actors as leverage against their adversaries. Allying with audiences who can support judges when they need assistance boosts the judiciary's immunity: The more judges are surrounded by politically powerful allies, the more likely that they will be able to deliver justice despite challenging circumstances.

We can also understand some of the judicial diplomatic strategies and backchanneling techniques discussed in this chapter as ways of building the judiciary's resilience and fortifying them against future attacks. In the case of Hong Kong, judicial leaders' attempt to forge a more harmonic

[154] *ibid* 25.

[155] *ibid* 22.

[156] See e.g. Raymond J. McKoski, 'The Political Activities of Judges: Historical, Constitutional, and Self-Preservation Perspectives' (2019) 80 *University of Pittsburgh Law Review* 245, Part I; Owen Bowcott, 'Judges Must Engage in Politics to Preserve Rule of Law – Lord Chief Justice' *The Guardian*, September 17, 2015, available at www.theguardian.com/law/2015/sep/17/judges-engage-politics-preserve-rule-law-lord-chief-justice, last visited January 12, 2026.

relationship with the national authorities and other branches of government may be aimed at reducing the likelihood and severity of political interference by state officials. Exchanges between judges and political representatives may help promote mutual understanding of each other's role within the constitution. Hong Kong judges' ability to withstand a hostile environment seems to have yielded some benefits, as they have utilized the limited space available to continue advancing human rights jurisprudence outside the prerogatives of the Chinese authorities. A notable example is how Hong Kong courts are still handing down relatively progressive rulings on LGBTQ issues, which are deemed non-politically sensitive, with no apparent backlash from the mainland authorities.[157] Even in the face of new authoritarian realities, the courts have persisted in capitalizing on this limited space to push for meaningful social change, which would not have been possible if they maintained a confrontational attitude in politically high-stakes issues and ended up having their constitutional review function crippled, as once threatened by China's top legislative body.[158]

There may, however, be occasions when non-adjudicative strategies fail to preempt an attack. In these situations, judges who seek to give effect to the values that define their role may have good reasons to consider using some of the more radical techniques, such as judicial protest and resignation, to more directly respond to the danger. Of course, radical strategies can be highly risky, as judges may breach judicial conduct rules and the law, attract political backlash, and even endanger themselves. Hence, the strategy judges choose must be proportionate to the size of the threat they face. It would likely be considered unreasonable and excessive if judges took to the streets simply because of negative publicity, for instance. In other words, the fact that judges are under pressure does not automatically justify deploying strategies that are inconsistent with what is normally expected of judges by society.

157 See e.g. Jessie Pang, 'Hong Kong Court Rules That Gay Couples Get Equal Housing Rights,' Reuters, October 17, 2023, available at www.reuters.com/world/asia-pacific/hong-kong-court-rules-that-gay-couples-get-equal-housing-rights-2023-10-17/, last visited January 10, 2026; Jessie Pang, 'Hong Kong's Top Court Urges Alternative Legal Framework for Same-sex Couples,' Reuters, September 5, 2023, available at www.reuters.com/world/asia-pacific/hong-kongs-top-court-urges-alternative-legal-framework-same-sex-couples-2023-09-05/, last visited January 10, 2026.

158 Julius Yam, 'Hong Kong's Anti-mask Law: A Legal Victory with a Disturbing Twist,' IACL-AIDC Blog, December 3, 2019, available at https://blog-iacl-aidc.org/2019-posts/2019/12/3/hong-kongs-anti-mask-law-a-legal-victory-with-a-disturbing-twist, last visited January 10, 2026.

Assuming that non-adjudicative strategies can be used for self-defense purposes under exceptional situations, determining what *counts* as an exceptional situation is a contested question with far-reaching implications.[159] The moral legitimacy of these self-defense strategies rests largely on selecting the right time to deploy them, but judges need some guidelines to help them identify the right moment with sufficient precision. Otherwise, "broad appeals to exceptionalism," as Daly warns, "could see judges merely mirroring the 'darkly alluring' Schmittian perspective on exceptional executive powers."[160]

What counts as "exceptional" depends on jurisdiction and context, but one scenario that potentially satisfies the exceptional requirement is when there is an immediate crisis that threatens the very existence of the judiciary or even the constitution. Judicial independence is often said to be crucial to the judicial advancement of justice. However, judges cannot be said to be exercising their powers independently if they fear political reprisals. Even if they can and do exercise their powers independently, the values of judicial independence, and, accordingly, the rule of law, will still ring hollow if their decisions fail to be implemented by political actors. In extreme cases, such as when judges are likely to be subjected to physical violence, they are justified in withholding their powers. In short, an independent judiciary can only meaningfully exist when others in society are also committed to rule-of-law values. Maintaining judicial independence is impossible if the basic norms of the constitution are being eroded by other sociopolitical actors.[161] These norms include obeying the letter of the law, exercising political restraint, showing mutual respect, and being able to tolerate reasonable disagreements.[162]

When the necessary conditions for judges to exercise their powers effectively are absent or likely to disappear in the near future, there may be good reason to consider using non-adjudicative strategies for self-protection, even if the strategies themselves may be considered dangerous. This perhaps also explains why there is a greater imperative for judges operating in authoritarian contexts to consider using non-adjudicative strategies in self-defense, because they are much more

[159] See the discussion in Section 6.2.3.

[160] Tom Daly, *Extra-Judicial Protest in Defence of Democracy: Towards a Normative Theory* (draft), 27.

[161] See Scott Stephenson, 'Constitutional Conventions and the Judiciary' (2021) 41 *Oxford Journal of Legal Studies* 750, 762–4.

[162] See Steven Levitsky and Daniel Ziblatt, *How Democracy Dies* (Broadway Books 2018).

susceptible to pushback and backlashes than those in democracies. Courts in democracies are generally most concerned with their decisions being reversed or ignored, or, in extreme cases, judicial reform that might undermine judicial powers. In authoritarian regimes, these kinds of attacks, alongside other kinds of constitutional violation, are the norm, and not many judges have been able to sustainably challenge the incumbent regime without suffering repercussions. In some authoritarian regimes, there is even a culture of physical violence against judges. A notable and gruesome instance is how, in 1972, then-President of Uganda Idi Amin abducted Chief Justice Benedicto Kiwanuka from his judicial chambers, then reportedly tortured and murdered him afterwards.[163] Political retaliation against judges who defy authoritarian regimes can be life-threatening. And, ironically, political actors who supposedly are constitutionally bound to protect the judiciary, such as the executive, are often the perpetrators of attacks against judges.

Even adjudicative strategies may sometimes be incapable of dealing with authoritarian challenges, since most adjudicative strategies assume that other sociopolitical actors have some degree of respect for the rule of law. This is often missing in authoritarian regimes. Strategic vagueness is meaningless, for instance, if judicial decisions are treated as mere rhetoric. Alternatively, there are times when judges may run out of adjudicative strategies, as we saw that some have argued in the case of Hong Kong.

When judges are unable to count on other constitutional actors for protection, and when other methods have been tried and proven futile, they may have no choice but to rely on their own social networks and consider non-adjudicative techniques to fend off attacks. In such instances, scholarly observers have generally been sympathetic to and supportive of judges. Alexei Trochev and Rachel Ellett's study of hybrid regime judges concludes by noting that, "while at first glance they appear to be antithetical to the traditional norms of judicial independence, off-bench resistance strategies may well represent the only way to protect judicial autonomy against blatant attacks."[164] Judicial protests and attempts to mobilize the public against the executives in Poland and Pakistan, for instance, have likewise been celebrated as valiant, and regarded by some as successful in curbing authoritarian encroachment.[165]

[163] Ellett (n 112) 49.

[164] Trochev and Ellett (n 1) 85.

[165] Matthes (n 58); Sahar Shafqat, 'Civil Society and the Lawyers' Movement of Pakistan' (2018) 43 *Law & Social Inquiry* 889.

These views are further legitimized by the recent case of *Żurek v. Poland*.[166] Judges in Poland have been punished by the authorities for speaking out and acting against those in power. One such instance was brought to the European Court of Human Rights, which recently found that the Polish government's attempts to "intimidate" and "silence" the applicant judge violated his freedom of expression. While the ECHR acknowledges that there are limits to the applicant's freedom of speech, what is perhaps remarkable is how the court recognized not just a right, but also the applicant's (and other judges') "*duty*" to "speak out in defence of the rule of law and judicial independence when those fundamental values come under threat."[167] In reaching this conclusion, the court relied on submissions made by groups allied to the liberal faction of the Polish judiciary, including the aforementioned European Network of Councils for thc Judiciary,[168] as well as on international instruments issued or adopted by European judicial organizations.[169] From a sociolegal perspective, this example not only reinforces the importance of judicial allies, but also illustrates how non-adjudicative strategies can impact jurisprudential developments that are favorable to judges themselves. For our purposes, the case shows that the self-defense logic is gaining legal ground as well.[170]

When the judiciary or the constitution is existentially threatened, judges may have no choice but to deploy non-adjudicative strategies. But even in these situations, there might still be tremendous disagreement within society or even among judges over what amounts to an existential threat. For instance, as suggested, based on the conflicting responses we saw from the judicial leaders of Hong Kong and their liberal-minded colleagues, there are clearly empirical disagreements between the two sets of judges about whether Hong Kong courts are currently facing an existential crisis. Furthermore, the guiding concepts underlying this line of logic, such as judicial independence and rule of law, are value-laden notions

166 App. no. 39650/18, June 16, 2022.

167 *ibid* 55.

168 *ibid* 31–2.

169 *ibid* 26–8.

170 See also Martin Sunnqvist, 'A Judge Must Not Be Influenced by Fear. Must a Judge Be Brave? The Duty of Judges to Defend Judicial Independence and the Rule of Law' (2025) 15 *Oñati Socio-Legal Series: Judges Under Stress: Institutions, Ideology and Resistance* 2, 648–61, where the author uses the *Żurek* case to argue that judges are required to be "courageous enough to speak to protect independence, impartiality and the rule of law at large."

with "soft-edged" boundaries.[171] The exercise of identifying the exceptional moment that justifies self-defense strategies is even more challenging when the threat emanates from the insidious hollowing-out of constitutional norms, as opposed to sharp, one-off assaults against the constitution or the judiciary.[172] In light of these issues, and, given the profound risks attached to radical departures from the judicial role, judges should always exercise extra caution when using radical non-adjudicative strategies for self-preservation, and only consider them when there is a lack of better alternatives.

7.9 Conclusion

The off-bench tools discussed in the chapter are in stark contrast with what might be called the "classic" view of the judicial role. As former Chief Justice of Canada Beverley McLachlin describes, "Judges are different, set apart, aloof from the world. They live in ivory towers, remote from the bustle and controversy of the real world far below. They do not go to community meetings. They do not talk to the press. When people criticize them, they do not respond, bearing their frustration in silence."[173] The classic view, however, is incapable of dealing with the challenges and complexities of today's world *and* the authoritarian realities faced by a hybrid regime court. As McLachlin also notes, judges today are "climbing down from their ivory tower and mingling in the world."[174] This should not be a surprise: It is a natural response to the new environment confronting today's courts.

The goal of this chapter has been to show that hybrid regime judges may find the off-bench tools helpful or even necessary to maximize their chances of survival and sustainably play their democratic roles. The relational focus of the discussion highlights the influence of judicial–political networks on judicial power.[175] Some of the tools may at first appear to be in tension with familiar conceptions of the judicial role and

[171] Thomas Poole, 'Constitutional Exceptionalism and the Common Law' (2009) 7 *International Journal of Constitutional Law* 247, 268.

[172] Tom Gerald Daly, 'Democratic Decay: Conceptualising an Emerging Research Field' (2019) 11 *Hague Journal on the Rule of Law* 9; Anna Lührmann and Staffan I. Lindberg, 'A Third Wave of Autocratization Is Here: What Is New About It?' (2019) 26 *Democratization* 7, 1095.

[173] McLachlin (n 47) 1.

[174] *ibid* 2.

[175] Dressel, Sanchez-Urribarri, and Stroh (n 3).

concepts such as judicial independence and separation of powers. My defense is they are justifiable under the circumstances, as constitutional protection of the judiciary is weak in a hybrid regime. The examples discussed in this chapter show how the techniques can be applied and framed in ways that strengthen judicial autonomy and appear consistent with judicial values. The institutional position of a hybrid regime court is likely to be weakened further if judges ignore the potential that comes with their social role and fail to utilize the leverage they can create through relationships with other actors and social networks.

8

Conclusion

Of Judicial Choices

The thesis is ultimately about the choices judges *can* and *should* make in hybrid regimes if they seek to push the constitution closer to the democratic end sustainably. These questions are worth asking because many parts of the world are struggling to democratize or experiencing democratic backsliding, *and* that more and more works are showing that somewhat autonomous and powerful courts can exist in this ambiguous regime-type (Chapter 1).

A hybrid regime is a kind of authoritarian regime, but its semi-competitive elections and claim to be a democracy have significant implications on its constitution and create judicial–political patterns worthy of closer examination (Chapter 2). While courts are not substitutes for an effective democratic process, we should not be too pessimistic about the democracy-enhancing potential of courts in hybrid regimes either. This book adopts "a more realistic model of law and of the judicial process" and recognizes the dynamic role that courts can play in hybrid regimes.[1] Courts are not merely on the receiving end of regime-politics; they are also in a position to make meaningful democratic contributions (Chapter 3). They play a role in refereeing the rules of the political game, shoring up democratic norms, protecting the rights of and providing participatory opportunities to the politically disenfranchised, mitigating the problems arising from an unfair electoral system, and strengthening the democratic culture of a hybrid regime (Chapter 4). Putting into practice these democracy-enhancing roles will win the support of the part of the population that subscribes to democratic norms – the democratic constituency – but it will also risk antagonizing the incumbent and its allies – the authoritarian constituency. The dilemma is that both constituencies are crucial to the maintenance and development of judicial power in a hybrid regime but tell conflicting stories of judicial legitimacy (Chapter 5).

[1] Robert M. Cover, *Justice Accused: Antislavery and the Judicial Process* (YUP 1975) 6.

To address the practical challenges created by the legitimacy paradox, this book has drawn on interdisciplinary and comparative insights to illuminate a range of options available to committed judges in hybrid regimes to address the goal of sustainable democracy advancement under constraining political spaces. A theoretical framework that seeks to integrate democracy-enhancing adjudicative approaches with judicial strategy was proposed in Chapter 6. It shows that judges are not limited to the simplistic options of applying the law formalistically, lying about the law, or resigning. The reality is much more complex: They should consider when it would be permissible to factor in prudential considerations and tinker with different aspects relating to judicial decision-making to create nuanced strategic effects that address those concerns. Judges may also take advantage of its sociopolitical role to generate political leverage and enhance its institutional position. More specifically, in addition to their adjudicative responsibilities, they may also need to build allies and defuse enemies. The techniques proposed in Chapter 7, the application of which is illustrated in the Appendix, further highlight the socially constructed nature of judicial power in a hybrid regime.

The efficacy of the theories and tools provided in this book ultimately depend on the choices judges make. They might look like legal choices but have significant implications on the democratic health of the constitutional order. They are in substance value choices but rarely in absolute terms (such as maximum fulfilment of democracy versus a total regression to authoritarianism); rather, judges must constantly choose between "incremental furtherance" and "marginal vitiation" of competing values.[2] The choices are complicated by a layer of strategic consideration. Like an "evolving hands of cards," as Aziz Huq puts it, the "tactical options" available to a court would vary depending on how the judicial–political relationship unfolds over time.[3] Since this is a matter of choice, a judge's personality and personal motivations would also influence the extent to which a constitutional court can live up to the democratic roles proposed. Not every judge is convinced by the ideal of democracy, and there may be other judicial beliefs and motivations at play, such as career advancement concerns and jurisprudential thoughts. The risk-tolerance level of each individual judge may also differ.

[2] *ibid* 198.

[3] Aziz Z. Huq, 'Democratic Erosion and the Courts: Comparative Perspectives' (2018) 93 *New York University Law Review Online* 21, 27.

This book is aware of and reflective of the intricate interplay between moral values, regime politics, and constitutional law. The ideas presented may not resonate with all judges, while some may need a bit more persuading. For judges who are democratically committed, the book has attempted to show how the theories and tools offered can help them build institutional resilience *and* contribute to democratic values. The suggestions by no means guarantee these goals, as there is a limit as to what judges have control over in authoritarian environments. Nevertheless, constitutional courts are often heavily involved in the shaping of constitutional norms and structures. The choices judges make can influence the path of constitutional development, sometimes in subtle and unexpected ways. By pushing beyond the boundaries set by conventional conceptions of the judicial role, the book hopes to have instilled optimism in politically challenging environments and demonstrated how judges who are committed to the democratic cause can improve the chances of survival and success of constitutional courts.

APPENDIX

Applying the Framework – Socializing a Way Out of Hong Kong's National Security Law?

Chapter 7 drew on contemporary examples to better understand the kinds and strategic functions of non-adjudicative practices. To illustrate how this helps us analyze how non-adjudicative strategies are deployed in reality, this Appendix will examine the case of Hong Kong judges' use of non-adjudicative strategies in response to the city's turn to authoritarianism. Furthermore, tentative lessons that may potentially expand the scope of our discussion on this topic will be drawn toward the end of this Appendix.

The Challenge: New Authoritarian Reality Confronting Hong Kong Courts

The environment in which Hong Kong courts operate has fundamentally shifted since the enactment of the Hong Kong National Security Law (NSL) in the aftermath of the 2019 protests. What started out as a peaceful demonstration against a bill that would have allowed Hong Kong people to be extradited to mainland China for trial morphed into the largest pro-democracy movement in post-handover Hong Kong. The Chinese Communist Party interpreted the protests as attempts to subvert state power, and felt that there was a security gap that ought to be plugged.[1] One response was to pass the NSL in 2020. The law was drafted behind closed doors by the Mainland Chinese authorities with no public consultation in Hong Kong.[2]

1 RFI, 'Carrie Lam: The Enactment of the National Security Law by the Central Government Is Inevitable; Opposition Can Only Be Dealt with in Accordance with the Law,' May 26, 2020, available at www.rfi.fr/tw/港澳台/20200526-林鄭-若反對港版國安法立法只能依法處理-避談未來承諾 [Chinese], last visited January 10, 2026.

2 Ng Cheuk-On, 'Hong Kong National Security Law: Bar Association Writes to the NPC Urging Public Consultation Hoping the Draft Law Would Be Publicized,' HK01, June 3, 2020, available at www.hk01.com/%E6%94%BF%E6%83%85/481178/%E6%B8%AF%E7%89%88%E5%9C%8B%E5%AE%89%E6%B3%95-%E5%A4%A7%E5%BE%8B%E5%B8%AB%E5%85%AC%E6%9C%83%E5%8E%BB%E4%BF%A1%E4%BA%BA%E5%A4%A7%E4%BF%83%E5%85%AC%E7%9C%BE%E8%AB%AE%E8%A9%A2-%E5%86%80%E5%85%AC%E9%96%8B%E6%B3%95%E5%BE%8B%E8%8D%89%E6%93%AC%E6%96%87%E6%9C%AC [Chinese], last visited January 10, 2026.

A senior Chinese official in charge of overseeing Hong Kong and Macau affairs described the NSL as part of a broader policy to "combat anti-China forces."[3] National security crimes are vaguely defined, interpretation of the NSL is vested with Beijing, and security enforcement agencies are granted wide-ranging powers to enforce the NSL.[4] As Surabhi Chopra and Eva Pils observe, the NSL "has drastically thinned out the range of civil society actors advocating for civil and political rights, separation of powers and democratisation, as well as the range of opinions that can be comfortably aired."[5]

These political changes have had profound effects on the judiciary's institutional health. Before 2020, Hong Kong courts were largely successful in navigating the political circumstances of post-handover Hong Kong. Widely considered as strategic and savvy, Hong Kong judges deferred on issues that touched the prerogatives of the Chinese authorities while asserting themselves forcefully outside those areas.[6] The judiciary served as a meaningful check on undemocratically elected political representatives, and, as Eric Ip writes, is "the only political organ that has ever succeeded in continually resisting Beijing in the constitutional history of the People's Republic of China."[7] The Hong Kong authorities almost always complied with judicial decisions, and the public generally held the judiciary in high regard.[8]

The passage of the NSL, together with the overhaul of Hong Kong's electoral system to effectively eliminate meaningful political opposition,[9] marked

3 Liaison Office of the Central People's Government in the Hong Kong S.A.R., 'Xia Baolong: Taking the Spirit of President Xi Jinping's Important Speech as a Guide, Striving to Write a New Chapter in the Practice of "One Country, Two Systems",' July 18, 2022, available at https://web.archive.org/web/20220728004656/www.hmo.gov.cn/xwzx/zwyw/202207/t20220718_23582.html [Chinese], last visited January 10, 2026.

4 See Surabhi Chopra and Eva Pils, 'The Hong Kong National Security Law and the Struggle over Rule of Law and Democracy in Hong Kong' (2022) 50 *Federal Law Review* 292; Johannes Man-mun Chan, 'National Security Law in Hong Kong: One Year On' (2022) 30 *Academia Sinica Law Journal* 39.

5 Chopra and Pils *ibid* 307. See also Cora Chan, 'From Legal Pluralism to Dual State: Evolution of the Relationship between the Chinese and Hong Kong Legal Orders' (2022) 16 *The Law & Ethics of Human Rights* 99.

6 See e.g. Po Jen Yap, 'Twenty Years of the Basic Law: Continuity and Changes in the Geoffrey Ma Court' (2019) 49 *Hong Kong Law Journal* 209; Julius Yam, 'Approaching the Legitimacy Paradox in Hong Kong: Lessons for Hybrid Regime Courts' (2021) 46 *Law & Social Inquiry* 153; Eric C. Ip, 'Constitutional Competition between the Hong Kong Court of Final Appeal and the Chinese National People's Congress Standing Committee: A Game Theory Perspective' (2014) 39 *Law & Social Inquiry* 824.

7 Ip *ibid* 825.

8 Yam (n 6) 160–1.

9 Reuters, 'Hong Kong Passes Sweeping Pro-China Election Rules, Reduces Public's Voting Power,' May 27, 2021, available at www.reuters.com/world/asia-pacific/patriots-rule-hong-kong-sweeping-pro-beijing-electoral-rules-passed-2021-05-27/, last visited January 10, 2026.

Hong Kong's sharp turn toward pure authoritarianism. These dramatic changes created unprecedented challenges for the judiciary. Public trust and confidence in the judiciary suffered a major blow, scoring record-low ratings in polls and surveys since 2019.[10] In addition to losing in the court of public opinion, some Hong Kong judges have also been questioned by the authorities over their "loyalty." Pro-Beijing elites and government officials have suggested reforming the judiciary, including by only allowing "patriotic" judges to stay in office.[11]

If we assume judges behave strategically and have an interest in preserving judicial authority, then it is likely that the goals of the Hong Kong judges have changed given the new political landscape: While judges of previous eras may have harbored ambitions to meaningfully advance liberal constitutional norms, after the enactment of the NSL, institutional survival, that is, the preservation of the judiciary's power and integrity, is now perhaps their top priority. Extremely deferential judicial decision-making patterns are emerging when it comes to NSL cases.[12] The apex court in Hong Kong, the Court of Final Appeal, has also effectively confirmed the reversal of presumption of bail for NSL cases, departing from its previous commitment to protecting people's rights and procedural fairness.[13]

Judicial Responses: Out of the Cocoon and Into the World

Particularly relevant is the social side of judicial strategizing that is currently happening in Hong Kong. On top of adjudicative strategies, Hong Kong judges are noticeably reliant on non-adjudicative strategies to address the institutional risks they face. The current chief justice, Andrew Cheung, has on several public occasions made statements to assure the local and international communities of the judiciary's independence and its commitment to the rule of law.[14] The judiciary also started to live-broadcast some of its proceedings in

[10] Yam (n 6) 181–2.

[11] Tony Cheung and Lilian Cheng, 'Beijing Calls for Judicial Reform in Hong Kong, Declaring Patriotism Is "A Legal Requirement Now",' SCMP, November 17, 2020, available at www.scmp.com/news/hong-kong/politics/article/3110123/top-beijing-official-tells-hong-kong-legal-summit-time-has, last visited January 10, 2026; Ta Kung Pao, 'Zhang Xiaoming: Judicial System Must Keep Pace with the Times and Constantly Reform,' November 18, 2020, available at https://web.archive.org/web/20201202040210/www.takungpao.com.hk/news/232109/2020/1118/521709.html [Chinese], last visited January 10, 2026. See also Jerome A. Cohen, 'The Intensifying Pressures to Further "Reform" Hong Kong's Courts,' *The Diplomat*, November 23, 2020, available at https://thediplomat.com/2020/11/the-intensifying-pressures-to-further-reform-hong-kongs-courts/, last visited January 10, 2026.

[12] Chan (n 4).

[13] *ibid.*

[14] See e.g. James Pomfret and Greg Torode, 'Hong Kong's Top Judge Defends City's Rule of Law in Face of International Concern,' Reuters, January 24, 2022, available at www

2024, with the hope to, as per Cheung CJ, "increase transparency and bolster confidence in the legal system."[15] To use the language of the proposed double typology, in response to growing skepticism over whether the judiciary can remain independent, Cheung CJ has attempted to rely on public relations strategies for legitimation purposes and to improve the judiciary's social standing.

The chief justice had also sought to use public relations strategies to establish more amicable ties with the national authorities, effectively engaging in alliance-building. For instance, during the celebratory speech of the twenty-fifth anniversary of the establishment of the Hong Kong SAR, President Xi Jinping described Hong Kong as having "independent judicial power," which, in the Chinese language, is a concept that is distinct from "judicial independence."[16] Independent judicial power refers to the idea that judges should be free from undue interference when exercising their adjudicative powers, whereas judicial independence can be interpreted as implying the curtailment of political powers. Judicial independence, along with separation of powers, were constitutional principles entrenched in Hong Kong's jurisprudence in the two decades following the handover.[17] In recent years, however,

.reuters.com/world/asia-pacific/hong-kongs-top-judge-defends-citys-rule-law-face-international-concern-2022-01-24/, last visited January 10, 2026; James Griffiths, 'Hong Kong's New Chief Justice Has Vowed to Uphold the City's Judicial Independence. Can He?' CNN, January 13, 2021, available at https://edition.cnn.com/2021/01/12/asia/hong-kong-judiciary-china-intl-hnk, last visited January 10, 2026; Ming Pao, 'Andrew Cheung Welcomes Xi Jinping's Affirmation of the SAR's "Independent Judicial Power",' July 1, 2022, available at news.mingpao.com/ins/%E6%B8%AF%E8%81%9E/article/20220701/ s00001/1656682877904/%E5%BC%B5%E8%88%89%E8%83%BD-%E6%AD%A1%E8%BF%8E%E7%BF%92%E8%BF%91%E5%B9%B3%E8%82%AF%E5%AE%9A%E7%89%B9%E5%8D%80%E6%93%81%E6%9C%89%E3%80%8C%E7%8D%A8%E7%AB%8B%E7%9A%84%E5%8F%B8%E6%B3%95%E6%AC%8A%E3%80%8D [Chinese]; Chu Yau-lai, 'Andrew Cheung Reiterates That Judicial Power Is Free from Interference; Raising Unnecessary Challenges Purely Out of Dissatisfaction with the Ruling Harms the Rule of Law,' HK01, May 29, 2021, available at www.hk01.com/社會新聞/631319/張舉能重申司法權不受干預-純因不滿裁決提不必要質疑-有損法治 [Chinese], last visited January 10, 2026.

[15] Jess Ma, 'Hong Kong Courts to Live Stream Some Proceedings to Boost Transparency, Confidence in Justice System,' SCMP, November 21, 2023, available at www.scmp.com/news/hong-kong/law-and-crime/article/3242360/hong-kong-courts-live-stream-some-proceedings-boost-transparency-confidence-justice-system, last visited January 10, 2026.

[16] *Ming Pao*, July 1, 2022 (n 14). It is worth mentioning that the Basic Law, the de facto constitution of Hong Kong, uses the term "independent judicial power" instead of "judicial independence." Judges previously treated the two terms as synonymous, though "judicial independence" was used far more in past speeches and judgments. See Articles 2 and 19 of the Basic Law of the Hong Kong Special Administrative Region.

[17] See Johannes Man-mun Chan, 'The Judiciary' in Johannes Man-mun Chan and C. L. Lim (eds), *Law of the Hong Kong Constitution* (Sweet & Maxwell Asia 2021) 365–7; P. Y. Lo and Albert H. Y. Chen, 'The Judicial Perspective of Separation of Powers in the

Chinese authorities have openly rejected them, labeling them as "western ideals."[18] In 2017, the president of China's Supreme People's Court told its officials to "bare your swords towards false western ideals like judicial independence."[19] In response to Xi's statement, Cheung CJ adopted the term "independent judicial power" in his extrajudicial response.[20] By affirming Xi's remarks, this could be interpreted as an effort by the chief justice to demonstrate the judiciary's alignment with the state.

Meanwhile, Cheung CJ, together with other leaders of the judiciary, would also visit Beijing and meet with their counterparts as well as representatives of other law-related political bodies in Mainland China.[21] These trips were portrayed as professional knowledge exchanges, but were also seen by the media as part of a broader strategy by the Hong Kong government to foster greater "integration" into Mainland China's development.[22] Or in other words, the visits were a form of judicial diplomacy to fortify the judges' alliance-building efforts.

While the judicial leaders are busy finding ways to navigate through rough seas, some liberal-minded judges have pursued another set of non-adjudicative strategies. Several Hong Kong judges conducted anonymous interviews with the foreign press. In these interviews, which could be interpreted as a form of judicial backchanneling, those judges expressed their reservations and disappointment with constitutional legal developments in Hong Kong.[23] In an

Hong Kong Special Administrative Region of the People's Republic of China' (2018) 5 *Journal of International and Comparative Law* 337.

[18] Charlotte Gao, 'Xi: China Must Never Adopt Constitutionalism, Separation of Powers, or Judicial Independence,' *The Diplomat*, February 19, 2019, available at https://thediplomat.com/2019/02/xi-china-must-never-adopt-constitutionalism-separation-of-powers-or-judicial-independence/, last visited January 10, 2026; Patrick Wintour, 'Hong Kong Judicial Independence Under Systematic Attack, Legal Figures Warn,' *The Guardian*, May 26, 2022, available at www.theguardian.com/world/2022/may/26/hong-kong-judicial-independence-overseas-judges, last visited January 10, 2026.

[19] Lucy Hornby, 'China's Top Judge Denounces Judicial Independence,' *Financial Times*, January 17, 2017, available at www.ft.com/content/60dddd46-dc74-11e6-9d7c-be108f1c1dce, last visited January 10, 2026.

[20] *Ming Pao*, July 1, 2022 (n 14).

[21] Danny Mok, 'Hong Kong's Top Judge Andrew Cheung Leaves for 4-Day Beijing Trip, Expected to Meet New Head of Country's Highest Court,' SCMP, May 21, 2023, available at www.scmp.com/news/hong-kong/law-and-crime/article/3221328/hong-kongs-top-judge-andrew-cheung-leaves-city-4-day-beijing-trip-expected-meet-new-head-chinas, last visited January 10, 2026.

[22] Kahon Chan, 'Hong Kong's Top Officials to Take More Day Trips to Greater Bay Area to Promote Integration, John Lee Says Before Visit to Guangzhou and Shenzhen,' SCMP, May 23, 2023, available at www.scmp.com/news/hong-kong/hong-kong-economy/article/3221499/hong-kongs-top-officials-take-more-day-trips-greater-bay-area-promote-integration-john-lee-says, last visited January 10, 2026.

[23] Greg Torode and James Pomfret, 'Special Report: Hong Kong Judges Battle Beijing Over Rule of Law as Pandemic Chills Protests,' Reuters, April 14, 2020, available at www.reuters.com

interview with VICE World News in 2021, a judge described a high-profile NSL verdict as "unfair," criticizing its reliance on a "questionable" understanding of the law and the trial's lack of a jury.[24] Comparing the NSL to a heart disease, the same judge commented, "if the [NSL] continues to develop, it will lead to cardiac arrest."[25] In another interview with Reuters in 2020, published shortly before the passage of the NSL, a judge expressed their concerns, noting, "we're worried that [the Chinese authorities] are losing patience, and will find ways of tightening the screws," forewarning what the future lies ahead for Hong Kong's constitutional order.[26] By speaking off the record, these judges may have aimed to draw the attention of the international community and potentially mobilize crucial stakeholders, such as the legal community and those with vested interests in Hong Kong's constitutional development, to put pressure on both the local and national authorities.

Some foreign judges also decided to remove themselves from the Hong Kong judiciary in protest against authoritarian encroachment. The Court of Final Appeal has an established practice of having overseas judges on the bench, typically from common-law apex courts such as Australia, New Zealand, and the UK, jurisdictions that once was described by the city's post-handover inaugural chief justice as having "the closest affinity" to Hong Kong.[27] This arrangement is a contributing factor that has facilitated Hong Kong judges' inclusion in a transnational network of common-law judges, as evidenced by frequent and regular judicial exchanges between Hong Kong and common-law jurisdictions.[28] According to a senior judge in Hong Kong, foreign judges exist to "provide a valuable external affirmation of the health of the rule of law in Hong Kong and the independence both of the Court and the Hong Kong Judiciary."[29]

/article/hongkong-politics-judiciary-idUSL3N2C21IB, last visited January 10, 2026; Holmes Chan, 'Inside the Surreal Trial of the "Most Benevolent Terrorist in the World",' VICE World News, September 20, 2021, available at www.vice.com/en/article/93y47p/hong-kong-national-security-trial-tong-ying-kit, last visited January 10, 2026.

24 Chan *ibid.*

25 *ibid.*

26 Torode and Pomfret (n 23). The judge further remarked, "we know from our interactions with senior mainland judges that they just don't get Hong Kong at all," which might be another reason why the judicial leaders of Hong Kong felt a need after the enactment of the NSL to engage in judicial diplomacy with the mainland authorities.

27 Andrew Kwok Nang Li, 'The Chief Justice Andrew Li's Address at His Farewell Sitting on 16 July 2010,' July 16, 2010, 9, available at https://gia.info.gov.hk/general/201007/16/P201007160173_0173_67253.pdf, last visited January 10, 2026.

28 David Law, 'Judicial Comparativism and Judicial Diplomacy' (2015) 163 *University of Pennsylvania Law Review* 927, 996–7.

29 Justice Joseph Fok, 'Judges from Other Common Law Jurisdictions in the Hong Kong Court of Final Appeal,' paper presented at IBA Annual Conference, Seoul, September 24, 2019, para 25, available at www.hkcfa.hk/filemanager/speech/en/upload/2237/IBA%

Two foreign judges from the UK, Lord Reed and Lord Hodge, have, however, recently resigned.[30] Lord Reed's resignation statement reads: "I have concluded, in agreement with the [UK] government, that the judges of the Supreme Court cannot continue to sit in Hong Kong without appearing to endorse an administration which has departed from values of political freedom, and freedom of expression."[31] Baroness Hale of the UK cited "personal reasons" for refusing to renew her appointment in 2021, and Australian judge Spigelman left the court in 2020, allegedly due to "the content of the national security laws."[32] These resignations have been interpreted by commentators as evidence of the decline of Hong Kong's judicial independence.[33] Considering that the judiciary plays a significant role in upholding the city's status as an international financial center, these instances of self-removal signal to businesses who plan to invest, foreign governments with stakes in the city's affairs, and the Hong Kong government about the city's future economic competitiveness.

Are the Non-adjudicative Strategies Successful?

This leaves us with the question of whether the two strands of strategies – the radical approach adopted by the liberal-minded judges and the conciliatory approach taken by judicial leaders – prove effective in achieving the presumed objective of institutional survival. Although it may be premature to draw definitive conclusions since Cheung's tenure as chief justice only started in 2021, a preliminary assessment can be offered based on observations so far.

Regarding the techniques pursued by the liberal judges, there is no question that their remarks and resignations have successfully captured the attention of the international community, thereby delegitimizing authorities in Hong Kong, at least from the perspective of the liberal segment of the international community. We are also witnessing frequent and persistent calls by activists in Hong Kong and elsewhere urging the remaining foreign judges to follow suit and step down.[34] Interestingly, the local and national authorities

20Seoul%20-%20Global%20Justice%20and%20Globetrotting%20Judges.pdf, last visited January 10, 2026.

30 Haroon Siddique and Helen Davidson, 'UK Judges Withdraw from Hong Kong's Court of Final Appeal,' *The Guardian*, March 30, 2022, available at www.theguardian.com/world/2022/mar/30/uk-judges-withdraw-from-hong-kong-court-of-final-appeal, last visited January 10, 2026.

31 *ibid.*

32 *ibid.*

33 See Timothy McLaughlin, 'The Final Blow to Hong Kong,' *The Atlantic*, April 7, 2022, available at www.theatlantic.com/international/archive/2022/04/hong-kong-uk-judges-resignation-democracy-risk/629494/, last visited January 10, 2026.

34 See e.g. Jonathan Ames, 'UK Judges in Hong Kong "Should Quit" over Bounties for Dissidents,' *The Times*, July 4, 2023, available at www.thetimes.com/uk/law/article/uk-

have refrained from responding to the comments made by the anonymous interviewees. The Hong Kong government has even attributed the departure of those foreign judges to "the external political pressure" put on those resigning judges instead of blaming the judges themselves.[35] Thus far, these strategies have not produced any noticeable repercussions on the judiciary, and the practice of having foreign judges on the bench remains intact.

On the other hand, the political pressure generated by these radical strategies has not translated into tangible outcomes to the benefit of the city's judiciary either. NSL and the hawkish stance of the local and national authorities persist, and there are no indications of plans to change course. Additionally, the approach by those liberal judges carries risks. One such risk is the potential reinforcement of Beijing's suspicion toward the local judiciary, potentially paving the way for future reforms. Furthermore, concerning the resignations of foreign judges, although this has not yet transpired, there have been calls from legislators to replace them with non-Western foreign judges, such as those from Singapore and Malaysia,[36] allegedly because these judges have a "greater sensitivity to Asian values and the traditional family system" and so "their judgments might be better aligned with [Hong Kong's] core values."[37]

What about the strategies employed by the judicial leaders? Their legitimation strategies may have helped regain the trust of the general public. Polls and surveys indicate that the public's perception of the judiciary's fairness and impartiality has been slowly recovering in recent years, although it has not yet reached the pre-NSL levels.[38] More importantly, there is evidence to suggest that attempts at alliance-building have helped bolster the confidence of Mainland officials in the judiciary. After the judicial leaders' visit to Beijing,

judges-in-hong-kong-should-quit-over-bounties-for-dissidents-w6tccd6pr, last visited January 10, 2026; Benedict Rogers, '2022 Was the Year Hong Kong's Rule of Law Died,' *The Diplomat*, January 3, 2023, available at https://thediplomat.com/2023/01/2022-was-the-year-hong-kongs-rule-of-law-died/, last visited January 10, 2026.

35 Chris Lau, 'National Security Law: Hong Kong, Beijing Condemn British Judicial Body's Withdrawal of Judges from City's Top Court,' SCMP, March 30, 2023, available at www.scmp.com/news/hong-kong/politics/article/3172402/british-judicial-body-withdraw-judges-hong-kongs-top-court, last visited January 10, 2026.

36 Tony Cheung, 'National Security Law: Hong Kong Should Appoint Judges from Singapore, Malaysia to Limit City's Reliance on Western Jurists, Lawmakers Say,' SCMP, June 7, 2023, available at www.scmp.com/news/hong-kong/politics/article/3136381/national-security-law-hong-kong-should-appoint-judges, last visited January 10, 2026.

37 Priscilla Leung, 'Judges' Departure Is Chance to Fine-Tune Appointments,' *China Daily*, April 8, 2022, available at www.chinadailyhk.com/hk/article/266930, last visited January 10, 2026.

38 HKPORI, 'The Rule of Law, Fairness of the Judicial System, Impartiality of the Courts – Combined Charts (6/1997–2/2023),' available at www.pori.hk/research-result/combined, last visited January 10, 2026.

the director of the Hong Kong and Macau Affairs Office, Xia Baolong, "fully affirmed" the Hong Kong judiciary's vital role in safeguarding national security and upholding the rule of law.[39]

The leaders' emphasis on appealing to Beijing similarly comes at a cost, particularly in terms of international credibility. This is exemplified by a recent bill proposed by a group of American lawmakers, which sought to impose sanctions on forty-nine Hong Kong officials for "human rights violations," including seventeen local judges.[40] Cheung CJ, alongside leaders of the lower courts, are also in the list. In the past, political attacks by foreign officials against the Hong Kong government or its officials rarely, if ever, involved members of the judiciary, presumably because the judiciary was generally seen as impartial. However, due to the judiciary's handling of NSL cases and perhaps the leaders' perceived strong preference for Chinese audiences, the old view has eroded among certain segments of the international community, as evidenced by the inclusion of judges in the bill.

Hong Kong's judiciary is currently faced with the reality that Beijing maintains the capability and willingness to override the guarantees outlined in the Basic Law whenever it deems necessary. Earlier this year, the political authorities introduced yet another national security law.[41] The two strategic approaches described create clear tensions that impact the judicial institution in distinct and arguably opposing ways. Comparing them then, which has been more effective? Given these circumstances, and assuming once again that the judiciary's overall objective is to weather the storm, it appears that the conciliatory strategies employed by the judicial leaders prevail and yield greater results. A judiciary that enjoys the trust of the authorities is likely to reduce the likelihood of attempts to curtail or pack the courts. Moreover, Beijing appears impervious to international pressure concerning Hong Kong affairs,

[39] RTHK, 'Xia Baolong Meets with Andrew Cheung, Claims the Central Government Supports the Independent Exercise of Judicial Power,' May 22, 2023, available at https://web.archive.org/web/20230601143614/https://news.rthk.hk/rthk/ch/component/k2/1701670-20230522.htm [Chinese], last visited January 10, 2026.

[40] These judges are designated national security judges who are tasked to handle national security cases. James Lee, 'US Lawmakers Introduce Bill to Sanction Hong Kong Judges and Prosecutors; Gov't Slams "Despicable" Intimidation,' *Hong Kong Free Press*, November 3, 2023, available at https://hongkongfp.com/2023/11/03/us-lawmakers-introduce-bill-to-sanction-hong-kong-judges-and-prosecutors-govt-slams-despicable-intimidation/#:~:text=The%20Hong%20Kong%20Sanctions%20Act,as%20figures%20to%20be%20sanctioned, last visited January 10, 2026.

[41] Lilian Cheng, '"Historic Moment": Hong Kong Passes Domestic National Security Law After Marathon Session, Fast-tracking Legislation Shelved for 2 Decades,' SCMP, March 20, 2024, available at www.scmp.com/news/hong-kong/politics/article/3255999/historic-moment-hong-kong-passes-domestic-national-security-law-after-marathon-session-fast-tracking, last visited January 10, 2026.

and the liberal judges' attempt to gain political leverage has not resulted in discernible improvements for the judiciary or the constitutional order.

Lessons for Studying Non-adjudicative Strategies?

Applying the typology set out in the chapter, we can more clearly see how Hong Kong judges have sought to address the institutional pressures arising from the NSL by tapping into their social capacity, as well as differentiate between the various kinds of non-adjudicative strategies they used. Also, as briefly highlighted, even though the judges surveyed might all share the same motivation of maintaining the judiciary's institutional position, different kinds of strategies with potentially conflicting social effects were pursued. This should not come as a surprise, however. After all, the judiciary is not a monolithic entity. Judges within the same institution may have different preferences and ideologies, or even different interpretations of the empirical reality surrounding them, hence leading to different strategies being pursued. The judges with more liberal inclinations may perceive the NSL as a pivotal moment that could make or break the judiciary; on the other hand, judicial leaders may hold another perspective and still see a potential opportunity for the judiciary to gain some breathing room.

The story of Hong Kong judges' struggle with the NSL may still be unfolding, but what else can this case tell us about the study of non-adjudicative strategies?

First, the case of Hong Kong reinforces the notion that non-adjudicative strategies can play a role in both democracies and authoritarian regimes, although potentially with different mechanisms at work. Some might assume, not without good reason, that non-adjudicative strategies are only relevant or effective in jurisdictions with at least minimal electoral competition. Jeffrey Staton, for instance, has famously argued that judges in Mexico employed non-adjudicative strategies to build and maintain public support to deter attempts by political actors to attack or defy the court; the underlying logic there posits that electorally accountable actors would hesitate to undermine a popular court considering electoral backlashes.[42] However, even in Hong Kong where effective electoral connection no longer exists and political authorities face no electoral repercussions for targeting the judiciary, we can still find judges deploying non-adjudicative strategies. This is because non-adjudicative strategies come in many different forms and serve purposes beyond solely legitimatizing the judiciary in the public's eyes, as suggested previously. Some of these strategies, for example, enable judges to directly communicate with their intended to foster closer connection audiences (such as the Mainland

[42] Jeffery Staton, *Judicial Power and Strategic Communication in Mexico* (CUP 2010) 197–9.

Chinese authorities in the case of Hong Kong), or to activate protection from audiences beyond the general public (such as the liberal-minded judges attempts to rally support from the business, legal, and international communities).

Second, and relatedly, it could even be argued that non-adjudicative strategies hold particular significance in authoritarian settings. In Hong Kong, judges employed non-adjudicative strategies alongside adjudicative ones to address institutional challenges. Nevertheless, critics such as Yan-ho Lai and Thomas E. Kellogg have raised doubts about the continued efficacy of adjudicative strategies that had previously bolstered the judiciary's social legitimacy prior to the city's shift toward authoritarianism in 2019.[43] The reason for this, they argue, is that formal changes in laws have severely restricted the scope of judicial maneuvering, thereby frustrating these adjudicative strategies. In such scenarios, alternative solutions beyond adjudication may be the kind of "mitigation strateg[y]"[44] that judiciaries under authoritarian pressure are desperately seeking. Courts in authoritarian regimes may simply have no choice but learn to play authoritarian politics if they intend to maintain their institutional power. Hence, non-adjudicative strategies may be an especially salient topic in these settings. This, together with the fact that the effective implementation of non-adjudicative strategies does not seem to rely on the existence of competitive elections, underscores the importance for scholars, especially those interested in authoritarian constitutional studies, to broaden their investigation and look into judicial responses beyond the confines of the courtroom.

Third, in Chapter 7, we have discussed in theory some of the strategic functions of the non-adjudicative strategies. However, non-adjudicative strategies may not also produce the judges' desired outcomes. As the analysis on Hong Kong shows, when assessing whether these strategies *actually* make a difference, it is essential to examine them within the specific context, taking into account the strategies' recipients and their reactions. Relatedly, it is crucial to recognize that deploying non-adjudicative strategies often comes with associated costs, some of which have been briefly highlighted in Chapter 7. The same non-adjudicative strategy, when deployed by judges operating within different political contexts, can yield different consequences, as the exact effects a non-adjudicative strategy generates depend on the prevailing political climate, the level of judicial independence, and the dynamics between the judiciary and other sociopolitical actors. Considering these contextual factors is crucial when assessing the real impact, both positive and negative,

[43] Yan-ho Lai and Thomas E. Kellogg, 'Departure from International Human Rights Law and Comparative Best Practice: HKSAR v Tong Ying Kit' (2022) 52 *Hong Kong Law Journal* 466, 484–5.

[44] *ibid* 485.

of non-adjudicative strategies utilized by judges within diverse political environments.

Fourth, the case exemplifies the strategic interplay between adjudicative and non-adjudicative techniques. Adjudicative strategies can complement non-adjudicative strategizing, or lead to blowback, and vice versa. For instance, the Hong Kong courts' conservative adjudicative strategies in relation to NSL cases were arguably enhanced by judicial leaders' efforts to build closer ties with mainland authorities outside the courtroom, but these may have been undermined by the strategies adopted by the liberal-minded judges. Their resignations, together with the anonymous interviews, go against adjudicative and non-adjudicative efforts to assuage local and international constituencies.[45] While beyond the scope of this book, empirical studies will be needed to measure how adjudicative and non-adjudicative strategies interact, which will help inform future discussions on this topic.

[45] See McLaughlin (n 33).

INDEX

academic conferences, 216
Africa Judges & Jurists Forum, 215
Argentina, 211, 235–6
Aristotle, 39
Arrington, Celeste, 125
Association of Asian Constitutional Courts, 215
audience sensitivity, 188
audience-based approach, 143–5
authoritarian regimes, 21
agency in, 198–9, 200
agents in, 198–9, 200
arbitrariness in, 21
bureaucracy in, 198–9, 200
constitutional court in, 53–5, 65
constitutional dynamic and, 47
democracy and, 27
dual state and, 42–3
election in, 32, 47, 92
electoral pressure in, 140–1, 145–6
guardianship and, 39
interest-based politics in, 91
judges in, 164, 203
judicial public communication in, 221
legal mobilization in, 112
political branches in, 90
political legitimacy and, 37
public opinion in, 140–1, 145–6
autocratic legalism, 3, 43
autocratization, 2–3
avoidance, 153

backchanneling, 219–23
Barber, Nick, 21
Bar-Siman-Tov, Ittai, 107, 108
Baum, Lawrence, 143
Beetham, David, 135
Belgium, 107
Bellamy, Richard, 70
Biagi, Francesco, 66
Blauberger, Michael, 181
Brazil, 209, 212
Brennan, Jason, 39
Brumberg, Daniel, 36
Busch, Marc, 181
business community, 201–2
judicial independence and, 201–2
Bussey, Erica, 121

Canada, 216
case administration, 184–6
Chan, Cora, 41
Chang, Wen-Chen, 175
Cheema, Moeen, 124
Cheeseman, Nic, 31
Chilton, Adam, 8
Chopra, Surabhi, 247
Cichowski, Rachel, 109
citations, 178–9
civil servants, 198
Colombia, 107, 108
comparative citation, 179–80
comparative jurisprudence, 179
Conference of European Constitutional Courts, 215
constituency
authoritarian constituency, 148–50, 151–3
democratic constituency, 148–50, 151–3, 193
constitution, 6–8, *See also* constitution of hybrid regime
constitutional court, 9, 15

apex courts, 16
as political institutions, 16
centralized constitutional court, 15
constitutional accountability and, 98–9
constitutional adjudicative powers of, 15
constitutional interpretation of, 101–2
decentralized constitutional court, 15
democracy and, 82–6, 92
democratic roles of, 68–70, 72–3, 92–3
effectiveness of, 7
impartiality of, 17
institutional competency of, 129–31
institutional legitimacy of, 128
judicial discretion of, 101–2, 232
proportionality and, 104–5
judicial interpretation of, 101–2
legitimacy of, 7
perceived legitimacy of, 137, 142, 143–5
roles of, 16–17
rule of law and, 99
standard account of, 15
constitutional courts in
Colombia, 108
Egypt, 57, 74
Europe, 66
Germany, 181, 210
Hungary, 67, 136, 152
Kenya, 136
Poland, 136
Russia, 74, 211
South Africa, 107, 136, 185, 216
South Korea, 175, 208
Taiwan, 175
Turkey, 64, 74
Uganda, 98, 113–14, 121, 136
Ukraine, 74
constitutional dynamic
authoritarian regimes and, 47
democracy and, 47
in hybrid regimes, 46, 47–50, 60, 146–7
constitutionalism
abusive constitutionalism, 3
as source of legitimacy, 70
comparative constitutionalism, 9
court-centric constitutionalism, 3–4
legal constitutionalism, 8
normative constitutionalism, 5
political constitutionalism, 8
popular constitutionalism, 85
court
audience of, 142–5
communication strategies of, 209–10, 211
confidence in, 138–9, 233–4
decision-making patterns of, 154
institutional reform as resistance to, 168
narrative of, 182
negative publicity of, 167
noncompliance to, 167–8
public relations of, 205, 208–10, 211–12, 234
resistance to, 166
violence to, 168
courtocracy, 66–8

Daly, Tom, 86, 238
Davis, Richard, 207
democracy, 18–19, 82, 88–9
as source of legitimacy, 71
authoritarian regimes and, 27
by judiciary, 66–8
citizens and, 30
constitutional dynamic and, 47
constitutional interpretation and, 100–1
election and, 19, 47
electoral pressure in, 140, 145
guardianship and, 39
hybrid regimes and, 34, 41, 61–2
institutional requirement of, 20–2
judicial review and, 86–9
liberal constitutional democracy, 19
liberty and, 19–20
normative account of, 18
political equality and, 19, 88
public opinion in, 140, 145
rule of law and, 20–2
transition to, 13

democratic accountability, 99
democratic backsliding, 2–3
democratic hedging, 69
democratization, 2, 13–14
 constitutional court and, 65–6, 67–70
 new democracy, 65–6, 69
 transitional regimes, 65–6
democratization jurisprudence, 64, *See also* democratization; Optimistic Model of constitutional court
Diamond, Larry, 34
divided politics, 59–61
dock control, 184–5
Dressel, Bjorn, 142
dual agency, 154, *See also* constitutional dynamics; constitutional dynamics in hybrid regimes
Dugard, John, 231
Dworkin, Ronald, 162

East Africa, 220
Egypt, 57, 74, 224
election
 free and fair, 19, 29–31, *See also* democracy and election
 noncompetitive, 30
 political equality and, 30
 semi-competitive, 10, 31–2
election in
 Hong Kong SAR, 11, 31–3, 36, 97, 150
 Malaysia, 32
 Pakistan, 11–12, 31, 32, 36
 Philippines, 31
 The Gambia, 32
 Turkey, 31
 Uganda, 12, 32, 36, 98
Ellett, Rachel, 57, 191, 239
Elster, Jon, 62
Ely, John Hart, 68, 94–6, 101, 115–16
Epperly, Brad, 58
Epstein, Lee, 154
European Network of Councils for the Judiciary, 226, 228, 240
European Union, 179, 224–5

Fiji, 229
Finnis, John, 84
foreign visits, 216
formal legal position, 159–60, 163–4
Fraenkel, Ernst, 42
France, 224
front-channel negotiations, 221
Fuller, Lon, 20

Galanter, Mark, 125–6
Gandhi, Jennifer, 92
Gardbaum, Stephen, 94
Germany, 42, 107, 162, 181, 210, 232
Ghias, Shoaib, 197
Gibson, James, 137
Ginsburg, Tom, 18, 19
Goldsworthy, Jeff, 160
González-Ocantos, Ezequiel, 202
Grendstad, Gunnar, 210
guardianship, 38–9
 elite entrenchment and, 39–40
 in hybrid regime, 40–1

Halliday, Terence, 193
hearing, 185
Hirschl, Ran, 3, 9
HKSAR. *See* Hong Kong SAR
Hong Kong Bar Association, 194
Hong Kong SAR
 access to justice in, 114
 anti-extradition bill protest in, 11, 199
 Basic Law of, 10, 35
 Chief Justice of, 56, 216, 248–50
 civil rights in, 14
 civil servants in, 199
 civil society in, 11
 court in, 13–14, 64, 120–1, 152
 Court of Final Appeal of, 102–3, 248, 251
 election in, 11, 31–3, 36, 97, 150
 foreign judges in, 229, 251–2
 freedom of speech in, 102–3
 independent judicial power of, 249
 judges in, 56, 76, 147, 225, 232–3, 236–7, 240–1, 250–1
 judicial image in, 212

judicial independence in, 57, 201, 249–50
judicial interpretation in, 102–3
judicial legitimacy in, 253–4
judicial mobilization in, 112
judicial protest in, 194
judiciary of, 13, 150, 212, 247
lawyers' protest in, 194
legal mobilization in, 112, 113
legislature of, 150
LGBTQ rights in, 119–21, 237
National Security Law of, 11, 33, 152, 246–7
non-adjudicative strategies in, 248–55
nonpermanent judges in, 229
outward influence of courts in, 124
political opposition in, 11, 60
preroogative power in, 45
protection of rights in, 43
resignation of judges in, 229, 231, 232–3, 251–2
rule of law in, 35, 201
universal suffrage in, 10
Hume, Robert, 177–8
Hungary, 2, 34, 50, 67, 74, 136, 147, 152
Huntington, Samuel, 29
Huq, Aziz, 18, 19, 244
hybrid regimes, 2, 26–8
access to justice in, 113–14
agency in, 56, 198–9, 200
bureaucracy in, 198–9, 200
check and balance in, 43
Constitution in, 6–8, 27, 35, 43
constitutional courts in, 5–6, 7, 17, 46, 62, 132
as referee, 95–7, 100
constitutional dynamics and, 41, 49, 146–7, 153–5
constitutional interpretation and, 100–1
democratic constituency and, 151–2
democratic representation and, 89–90
democratic roles of, 8–9, 74–6, 92–3, 132
extralegal effects and, 122–3
institutional legitimacy of, 127–8
interest-based politics and, 91–2
judicial autonomy of, 6, 63
judicial discretion and, 100
judicial legitimacy of, 141, 146–7
Optimistic Model of, 63–4
Pessimistic Model of, 52–5
political participation and, 110–12
Realistic Model of, 76–8
rule of law and, 93, 99
constitutional dynamics in, 46, 49, 60, 146–7
constitutional ideologies and, 37, 40–1
constitutional legal accountability in, 96
democracy and, 34, 40–1, 61–3
democratic constitutional norms in, 8
democratic institutions in, 36
dual state and, 44, 45
elections in, 27, 31–3, 47–8, 58–9, 97
elites in, 60, 100, 148
guardianship in, 40–1
ideological homogeneity, 60
incumbent bias in, 117–19
incumbent government in, 31, 32, 49–50, 96, 148
judges in, 75–6, 158, 239
judicial autonomy and, 6, 56–7, 60–1, 76
judicial independence and, 6, 36, 62–3
judicial political dynamics in, 55–6
judicial review and, 87
judicial strategies in, 165–6, 170–4
judicial–executive relationship in, 13, 54–6, 124, 200, 239
legal mobilization in, 47–9
liberal democracy and, 35
normative state and, 43–5
opposition in, 47–9, 60
political accountability in, 91
political branches in, 90–1, 108
political legitimacy and, 37
political participation in, 89, 91, 109–10
political pluralism and, 60, 62

hybrid regimes (cont.)
political representation in, 90
prerogative state and, 44–5
proliferation of, 1–3
public opinion in, 141, 198
rule of law and, 35–6
rule of law in, 201
semi-competitive election and, 27, 28–9, 31–3
state agents and, 45–6, 198–9, 200
trifurcated legal order of, 43–4, 45

Ibero-American Conference of Constitutional Justice, 215
incrementalism, 186–7
India, 183, 184
institutional competency, 127–8
of court, 128
of legislature, 128
relative, 131
Inter-American Court of Human Rights, 215
interest of litigants, 161
International Association of Women Judges, 215
International Commission of Jurists, 215
international organizations, 200
judicial independence and, 201
intra-branch relations, 217
Ip, Eric C. 13, 198, 247
Israel, 107, 125
Issacharoff, Samuel, 68–73, 76

Japan, 29, 125
Jenne, Erin, 96, 164
Johnston, Jane, 211, 235
Jones, Carol, 199
judges, 161–2, 164, 202
bilateral engagements of, 216
foreign, 203–4
institution-building by, 233
overseas, 203–4
political acumen of, 161–2
public communication and, 208
social network of, 204–5
violence to, 168
judgment
release of, 186
timing of, 183–4
judicial agency, 162
judicial bargaining, 220
judicial behavior, 53, 143, 196, 203
judicial communication, 123, 125–6, 181–2, 207, 210
selectiveness of, 210
judicial decision, 174–5
deviance to, 167–8
noncompliance to, 167–8
judicial diplomacy, 212–13, 235
hostile relations and, 218–19
public relation and, 213
judicial incrementalism, 187
judicial independence, 4, 53–5, 238, *See also* judicial independence in hybrid regime
business community and, 201–2
de facto, 36
de jure, 36
international organizations and, 201
semi-competitive elections and, 58–9
judicial language, 180
judicial legitimacy, 134, 137, 210
judicial mobilization, 227
judicial mobilization in
Hong Kong SAR, 112
Pakistan, 150, 227, 228, 239
Poland, 227–8, 239–40
Uganda, 113
judicial networks, 215
judicial oath, 230
judicial politics, 162, 169
judicial power, 136
judicial protest, 192, 225–6, 237
judicial protest in
Egypt, 224
European Union, 224–5
France, 224
Hong Kong SAR, 194
Pakistan, 150, 195, 224, 227, 239
Poland, 224, 227–8, 239–40
Romania, 224
Uganda, 194, 224
judicial public relations, 205–6, 208–10, 211–12, 235

judicial reasoning, 176–8
procedural review in, 177–8
specificity in, 182
substantive review in, 177
judicial remedies, 175–6, 186
judicial resignation, 228, 230–1, 237
signaling effects of, 231
judicial review
counter-majoritarian difficulty in, 71–2
counter-majoritarian difficulty of, 82, 86–7
democracy and, 82–6
democratic objections to, 82, 86–90
judicial intervention and, 66–8
legislature and, 85, 106–7, 109
process theory of, 94–6
counter-majoritarian difficulty and, 94
semi-procedural review in, 107, 109
judicialization, 64
judicialization of politics, 4, 123
judiciary
democracy by, 66–8
executive and, 83
juristocracy, 3

Kalb, Johanna, 179
Kavanagh, Aileen, 95
Kenya, 136
Khaitan, Tarun, 153
King, Jeff, 116–19, 130
Klass, Brian, 31
Komesar, Neil, 131
Krygier, Martin, 20

Larsson, Olof, 178
Latin America, 215
lawyers, 194
judicial politics and, 194, 195
Lazarus, Liora, 109
legal academy, 216
legal discontent, 138
legal façade, 3
legal language, 181
legal mobilization, 109, *See also* judicial mobilization
legal mobilization in
Pakistan, 112
legal profession, 195–6, 217
legislature, 83, 128
judicial review and, 85, 106–7
LGBTQ rights, 119–21
Lust-Okar, Ellen, 92

Malaysia, 32
Martinsen, Dorte, 181
Mashaw, Jerry, 88
Mazmanyan, Armen, 64
media, 197–8, 206–7
Mexico, 210, 255
Michigan, 209
Mietzner, Marcus, 66
Moustafa, Tamir, 28, 53, 57
Mudde, Cas, 96, 164
Museveni, Yoweri, 12–13, 32, 98, 125, 147, 187–9, 194, 224
Musharraf, Pervez, 11–12, 14, 32, 34, 150, 194, 199, 227, 229

natural language, 180–1
Nazi Germany, 42, 162, 232
Nebraska, 208
New Jersey, 208
Nicaragua, 230
non-adjudicative strategies, 233–4, 236, 237
non-engagement strategy, 205–7
normative legitimacy, 135
Norway, 209–10, 212, 229

Pakistan
access to justice in, 113
as authoritarian regime, 28
bureaucracy in, 60, 199–200
Chaudhry court in, 56, 64, 97, 113, 150, 199, 228
Constitution of, 35, 113
court in, 56, 64, 97, 113, 150, 183, 188, 200, 228
election in, 11–12, 31, 32, 36
judges in, 50, 56, 76, 184, 225, 229
judicial mobilization in, 150, 227, 228, 239
judicial protest in, 150, 195, 224, 227, 239

Pakistan (cont.)
lawyers' protest in, 150, 195, 224, 227
legal mobilization in, 112
media coverage of judiciary in, 197
military court in, 44
military dictatorships in, 11
military in, 44
Musharraf, Pervez, 11–12, 14, 32, 34, 150, 194, 199, 227, 229
narrative of courts in, 183
outward influence of courts in, 124
political opposition in, 60
protection of rights in, 43
real democracy in, 34
Supreme Court of, 13, 14, 64, 97, 113, 150, 186, 228
the Lawyers' Movement of, 150, 195, 224, 228
parliamentary immunity, 20
Pelc, Krzysztof, 181
People's Republic of China, 2, 13, 28, 38, 147
perceived legitimacy, 135–6, 137–8, 142
Petter Graver, Hans, 162
Philippines, 31
Pildes, Richard, 68
Pils, Eva, 247
Plato, 38
Poland, 2, 50, 136, 207, 224, 227–8, 239–40
political fragmentation, 59–61, *See also* political dynamics and hybrid regime
judicial autonomy and, 60–1
political market, 68
political representation
majority bias in, 116–17
minority discrimination in, 115
substantive representation in, 114
political skepticism, 72
political transaction costs, 56
politics of reciprocity, 204
post-Soviet states, 64
press releases, 207
presumption of constitutionality, 106
priming, 180
professionalism, 139
protest, 223–4
public information model, 205

Qazi, Asher, 199

relational approach, 142
relational networks, 142
relation-building, 204–5, 212
reservoir of good will, 138–9
retired judge, 232
Romania, 224
rule of law, 20–2, 99
competitive elections and, 21
Russia, 2, 34, 74, 113, 211

Sadurski, Wojciech, 85, 123
Saudi Arabia, 28
Schedler, Andreas, 30, 31, 33, 47, 48
Scheppele, Kim Lane, 43, 66–8, 70–3, 74–5
Scribner, Druscilla, 211, 235
secondary materials, 180
Shah, Aqil, 11
Shapiro, Ian, 63
Shapiro, Martin, 134, 153
Simonsen, Natasha, 109
Singapore, 2, 34, 35, 38, 43, 102–3, 215
Slovenia, 208
social legitimacy, 202
social media, 207
Sólyom, László, 66
sophisticated intermediaries, 126, 197
South Africa, 107–8, 136, 162, 185, 229, 231
South Korea, 175, 208
state
dual state, 42–3
institutional guarantees of, 29
normative state, 42–3
prerogative state, 42
Staton, Jeffrey, 168, 210–11
Stone Sweet, Alec, 123
Supreme Court of
Brazil, 209
Canada, 216
India, 183
Mexico, 210

Nicaragua, 230
Norway, 209–10, 229
Pakistan, 13, 14, 64, 97, 113, 150, 186, 228
Singapore, 215
Uganda, 98, 103–4, 121
United Kingdom, 207, 216
United States, 185
Sustainable Democratic Adjudication, 157, 159, 160

Taiwan, 61, 175
Taras, David, 206
Thailand, 147
The Gambia, 32, 149
tolerance interval, 154
trials, 185–6
Trochev, Alexei, 191, 211, 220, 239
Turkey, 28, 31, 64, 74, 113
Tushnet, Mark, 84, 85

Uganda
access to justice in, 113–14
backchanneling in, 220
Chief Justice of, 151
Constitution of, 35, 98
Constitutional Court of, 98, 113–14, 121, 136
court in, 98, 113–14, 147, 151, 179, 187–9, 208
election in, 12, 32, 36, 98
freedom of press in, 103–4
High Courts of, 13
judges in, 14, 50, 76, 225, 239
judicial independence in, 57
judicial mobilization in, 113
judicial protest in, 194, 224
lawyers' protest in, 194, 224
legal mobilization in, 113
military court in, 44
military dictatorship in, 12
military in, 44
Museveni, Yoweri, 12–13, 32, 98, 125, 147, 187–9, 194, 224
no-party democracy of, 12, 34
outward influence of courts in, 125
protection of rights in, 43
Supreme Court of, 98, 103–4, 121
women's rights in, 121–2
UK. *See* United Kingdom
Ukraine, 74, 113
Union of Arab Constitutional Courts & Councils, 215
United Kingdom, 72, 107, 207, 216
United Nations Office on Drugs and Crime, 217
United States of America, 2, 20, 72, 184, 185, 209, 225
US. *See* United States of America
USA. *See* United States of America
use of precedents, 179–80

Vanberg, Georg, 140, 168
Venezuela, 2
Versteeg, Mila, 8
Veto players, 59

Wacks, Raymond, 162
Waldron, Jeremy, 70
watchdog, 130, 201
women's rights, 121–2
World Bank, 64
World Trade Organization, 181
WTO. *See* World Trade Organization

Printed in the United Kingdom by TJ Clays Ltd.